EFFECTIVE FUND RAISING IN HIGHER EDUCATION

Margaret A. Duronio
Bruce A. Loessin

EFFECTIVE FUND RAISING IN HIGHER EDUCATION

Ten Success Stories

Jossey-Bass Publishers
San Francisco • Oxford • 1991

EFFECTIVE FUND RAISING IN HIGHER EDUCATION
Ten Success Stories
by Margaret A. Duronio and Bruce A. Loessin

Copyright © 1991 by: Jossey-Bass Inc., Publishers
350 Sansome Street
San Francisco, California 94104
&
Jossey-Bass Limited
Headington Hill Hall
Oxford OX3 0BW

Library of Congress Cataloging-in-Publication Data

Duronio, Margaret A., date.
  Effective fund raising in higher education : ten success stories /
Margaret A. Duronio, Bruce A. Loessin.
      p.   cm. — (The Jossey-Bass higher and adult education series)
    Includes bibliographical references and index.
    ISBN 1-55542-360-4
    1. Educational fund raising — United States.   2. Universities and
colleges — United States — Finance.   I. Loessin, Bruce A., date.
II. Title.   II. Series.
LB2336.D84   1991
378'.02'0973 — dc20   91-8426
                                                                           CIP

Manufactured in the United States of America

The paper in this book meets the guidelines for
permanence and durability of the Committee on
Production Guidelines for Book Longevity of
the Council on Library Resources.

JACKET DESIGN BY WILLI BAUM

FIRST EDITION

Code 91100

A joint publication in
The Jossey-Bass
Higher and Adult Education Series
and
The Jossey-Bass
Nonprofit Sector Series

Contents

Tables and Figures

Preface

In recent years, institutions of higher education have faced higher costs and lower government financial support. For most institutions, this situation has created a greater need than ever before to increase revenues from private gifts. With more colleges and universities — not to mention other nonprofit organizations — competing for private dollars, fund raising has become more complex and sophisticated, technologically and ethically, and more expensive. Administrators want to know that money invested in fund raising is producing maximum results, and fund raisers are under pressure to account for fund-raising expenditures and performance.

Administrators and fund raisers from different institutions have reached no consensus about how to define fund-raising effectiveness or success. At many institutions, in spite of a general understanding of the vast differences between types of institutions, board members and presidents and others still make totally inappropriate comparisons of their institutions' fund-raising results to those of institutions with considerably greater assets. That fund raising costs money at all is still a contentious point on some campuses, and on all campuses, questions arise about how much to spend on fund raising.

Research to determine what really works in fund raising is still in its infancy. Until recently, most literature in the field was written by practitioners and largely based on their own experiences rather than on research. Although programs for formal training (in some cases, even graduate degrees) and professional development of fund raisers are growing in number, most fund raisers practicing today learned on the job — sometimes without supervisors or other associates as mentors — and from reading and listening to the advice of other practitioners. Liter-

ature based on personal experience and a tradition of learning
by doing has created a rich and continually evolving body of
fund-raising lore, which, infused with fund raisers' own creative
intuitions, has been used for decades to design fund-raising programs, set fund-raising goals, and defend fund-raising budgets.
It is only recently that this lore or conventional wisdom has been
explored through research.

   Effective Fund Raising in Higher Education reports our research into some aspects of the conventional wisdom about fund-
raising success. The research was designed to highlight fund-
raising programs that are effective in their particular institutional contexts. In preparation for the research itself, we col-
lected information about institutional characteristics and fund-
raising results from 550 institutions of higher education. We
used multiple regression procedures to identify institutions in
ten categories (private and public research, doctoral, and comprehensive universities and private and public baccalaureate and
two-year colleges) that were raising more money than our statistics predicted. From a group of 100 such institutions, we selected ten (one of each type) from around the country and visited
their campuses to interview more than 100 people responsible
for fund raising. (More information about the actual research
appears in Chapter One.) The results of our interviews are the
basis for this book.

   Here we explain why and how we carried out the research,
what we found at each institution, and what we learned overall
about the qualitative aspects of effective fund raising. Because
we present fund-raising "how-to's" in the context of the institutions at which we observed them, readers have good information for evaluating which models might fit their own institutions.
The book describes how various approaches to fund raising have
worked (or have not, in some cases) and presents sometimes
conflicting or controversial opinions about issues such as the use
of volunteers in the fund-raising process, the organization of
staff, and the role of planning and goal setting.

   We were surprised by some of what we heard and in-
trigued by all of it. In presenting the case material, we rely heavily on the actual words of those interviewed. As we pored through

more than 1,000 pages of transcripts, we began to see how our interest was held above all by the articulate and personal ways in which people had talked about their institutions, fund raising in general, and their own specific jobs. We thought that a certain flavor, as well as a wealth of information conveyed by their words, would be lost if we tried to tell their stories for them. Although we have, with the interviewees' permission, edited the quotations, we have taken great care to preserve the speakers' intent and meaning.

Readers will note that we have imposed no rigid unifying order in presenting the case study material from the different institutions. Because the institutions and approaches to fund raising differ so widely, each having its own distinctive culture and color, the format we followed for each case study evolved from the material for that institution. Because of the need to condense the 1,000 pages of transcripts, we have not described every interview and have not reported on every aspect of fund raising at each institution. We concentrated instead on what seemed to be the most significant aspects in each case. Outstanding leadership was a factor contributing to fund-raising success at each of the institutions, so most of the material in the case studies focuses directly on how leadership, at either the institutional, the unit, or the program level, enhances fund-raising performance.

The institutions are presented in descending order of complexity, from research universities to two-year colleges. In each instance, the complexity of fund-raising programs mirrors the complexity of the institution. For this reason, the early chapters, discussing institutions with more complex fund-raising programs and larger staffs, are longer than the later chapters.

Some readers may be frustrated to find that outcome data are not yet available for the case studies that describe new programs. Every fund-raising program we studied is in transition, and indeed adaptability may be a critical requirement for fund-raising success in these changing times. Whether the new efforts described in the following pages will meet fund raisers' expectations remains to be seen. Those efforts are, in any case, the product of the creative thinking in some of the most effective fund-raising programs in higher education today.

The optimistic pictures painted in the case studies are not intended to suggest that either we or the persons interviewed thought the institutions or fund-raising departments in question were utopias. As in any complex organization or unit, numerous problems beset them. In several cases, the changes currently under way were designed to correct specific problems. In other cases, changes and new programs were a response to the institution's need to grow. We must also emphasize that we did not undertake in our research to evaluate the impact of fund-raising programs on overall institutional effectiveness. Readers, however, are strongly advised to consider the overall impact of fund-raising efforts in their own institutions.

After presenting the ten cases, we provide an overall summary and analysis of features of effective fund-raising programs, as well as a discussion of how well conventional wisdom about fund-raising success holds up in actual practice. Generally, our research does not so much disprove conventional assumptions as indicate that often more diverse methods will work at a given institution than the accepted conventions of fund raising might indicate.

Intended Audiences

Since each major type of higher education institution is represented, this book will be useful to professionals at many institutions. The book should appeal and be helpful primarily to:

- Newcomers to higher education fund raising who need a general orientation to the field
- Advancement professionals (fund raisers) in start-up fund-raising programs who want to explore the range of possibilities and uncover the institutional resources or other characteristics that signal how successful a specific approach may prove
- Presidents who want to examine other presidents' role in and attitudes toward fund-raising programs
- Senior advancement professionals who are seeking fresh insights to revitalize existing programs

Trustees, students, consultants, and volunteers interested in fund raising in higher education may also find the book helpful, as may those interested in fund raising for other nonprofit organizations.

Overview of the Contents

Chapter One presents an introduction and an overview of recent trends in philanthropy and describes our research on fund-raising effectiveness. Chapters Two through Eleven are actual case studies, consisting of descriptions and analyses of the fund-raising programs at ten different institutions. Chapter Twelve contains both an overall analysis and a summary of insights from the case study chapters. The final chapter, Chapter Thirteen, provides guidelines for assessing and improving fund-raising programs.

Acknowledgments

We are deeply grateful to the presidents and chief development officers who allowed us to study their institutions, something that often involved a considerable investment of staff time. In several cases, it required more than an investment of time — it required courage on the part of the decision makers, who were aware that not everything we would find would be positive. We are especially indebted to the people who were willing to share their less-than-successful efforts along with their successes. We are grateful as well to all the other people we interviewed. Their integrity, skill, knowledge, and commitment were inspiring.

We want to thank the Lilly Endowment for funds to conduct the research on which this book is based, and particularly Charles Johnson of the endowment, who has supported and believed in our work.

Finally, we extend very special thanks to our spouses, Bill Wilson and Sally Loessin, whose support made — and continues to make — all the difference.

July 1991   Margaret A. Duronio
Pittsburgh, Pennsylvania   Bruce A. Loessin

The Authors

Margaret A. Duronio is director of administrative services in the office of the vice president of university relations and development at the University of Pittsburgh. She received her B.A. degree (1969) from Pennsylvania State University in English, her M.S.W. degree (1973) from the University of Pittsburgh, and her Ph.D. degree (1985) from the University of Pittsburgh in higher education. Duronio has directed three national studies on fund-raising effectiveness and has worked as a management development consultant and as a marriage and family therapist.

Bruce A. Loessin is vice president for university relations and development at the University of Pittsburgh. He received his B.A. degree (1965) from the University of Southern California in political science and his M.A. degree (1967) from the University of Wisconsin, also in political science. Loessin has more than twenty years' experience in fund raising, twelve of those at the level of vice president. He was responsible for managing the University of Pittsburgh's recently completed $225 million campaign. In addition to conducting fund-raising and research activities, he serves as chair of the Council for Advancement and Support of Education (CASE) Committee on Research and has lectured in England and the United States on fund-raising effectiveness.

This team of authors has published articles describing their research in *CASE Currents,* the *Review of Higher Education, Planning for Higher Education,* and *New Directions for Institutional Research.*

1

Studying Fund-Raising Effectiveness

The competition for private dollars, both within the field of higher education and throughout the entire nonprofit world, is more vigorous now than ever before. For some institutions, doing well in this competition is no less than a matter of survival. For all institutions, competing successfully for private support provides the means to ensure institutional growth and strength. Additionally, fund-raising success may be the symbol of institutional quality and viability for the 1990s. This success, along with traditional factors (such as number of faculty members holding doctorates, number of books in the library, and average Scholastic Aptitude Test (SAT) scores of entering freshmen), will help to attract additional resources as well as new faculty members and students. Therefore, fund-raising staff face demands for superior performance in securing current funds and building the foundations to ensure a long-term broad base of future private support.

What fund-raising programs will meet these demands? How are limited resources for fund raising best allocated? What are the factors underlying successful fund raising? Do these factors differ across institutions? How do program planners decide between traditional, recent, or even totally new fund-raising approaches? This book, part handbook and part research report, is intended to serve as a resource for fund raisers and administrators by demonstrating how these questions are being answered in ten institutions with documented success in fund raising. The ten institutions and their fund-raising programs are described in Chapters Two through Eleven. The final chapters of the book present an analysis across cases, overall conclusions, and a guide

1

for assessing fund-raising practice in individual institutions. In the rest of this chapter, we summarize recent changes in the fund-raising environment and describe the methodology used in conducting this study of effective fund-raising programs, including how the ten institutions were selected.

The Changing Fund-Raising Environment

Fund raising in the United States is rapidly changing as competition for private gifts soars among all nonprofit organizations. Private citizens, as well as public regulatory agencies, are concerned about the costs and ethics of fund raising.

Scope of the Competition. Fund raising in the United States entered the 1990s as an enterprise generating (in 1989) more than $114 billion (McMillen, 1990b, p. A1), an increase of more than 100 percent over the $49 billion generated in 1980 ("Challenges for the 1990's," 1990, p. 12). Numerous additional indicators of the growth of philanthropic activity during the 1980s indicate that higher education fund raisers face increasing competition from fund raisers in all other areas of the nonprofit world ("Challenges for the 1990's," 1990). The scope of fund raising in all nonprofit areas for the 1990s will continue to increase:

- Cornell, Harvard, and Yale Universities are planning campaigns expected to exceed their goals of raising $1 billion each (McMillen, 1990a, p. A1).
- In 1989, Ohio State University, setting the pace for the 1990s for public institutions, successfully completed the largest campaign ever by a public university. The school raised $429 million, exceeding the original goal of $350 million by $79 million (McMillen, 1990b, p. A27).
- In every other area of the nonprofit sector, major campaigns proliferate, some with astounding goals. For example, Allbright (1990, p. 8) lists campaigns already under way as including

    The United Jewish Appeal and Federation of Jewish
        Philanthropies of New York City campaign for $1.2
        billion

The national Presbyterian church campaign for $150
million

The United States Holocaust Memorial Museum
campaign for $147 million

The Juvenile Diabetes Foundation campaign for $100
million

Colleges and universities received almost $9 billion in pri-
vate gifts in 1989 (McMillen, 1990a, p. A1), an increase of
almost 9 percent over the previous year. On the surface, it appears that education overall continues to fare well in the height-
ened competition for funds. However, a look at how all private
gifts are distributed across all sectors indicates that education
may be losing ground in the competition. Until 1988, gifts to
education consistently represented more than 10 percent of all
gifts to philanthropy, but in that year the percentage dropped
to 9.4 percent (Weber, 1989, p. 9). The percentage dropped
again in 1989 to 9.3 percent (McMillen, 1990b, p. A27). Although it is too soon to conclude that these drops in percentage represent either a significant loss to higher education or an
emerging trend with serious consequences, they do indicate that
fund raisers in higher education need to take seriously the increased competition for private dollars and the fact that higher
education's share of philanthropic gifts is not automatically
assured.

Costs and Public Concerns. Fund raising, remembered by one
author as once "an innocent marriage of artful appeal and traditional school spirit" (Vigeland, 1986, pp. 26–27), has become
a multimillion dollar expenditure for higher education. Fisher
(1989, p. 11) estimates average fund-raising costs at about 8¢
per dollar raised for private institutions and at about 12¢ per
dollar raised for public institutions. Private institutions generally receive about 60 percent of the total voluntary support to
higher education, and public institutions receive about 40 percent (Council for Aid to Education, 1989). On the basis of these
cost estimates and percentages, we believe that all institutions
may have spent as much as $864 million to raise the $9 billion
in voluntary support given to higher education in 1989.

Costs are likely to increase as fund-raising technology rapidly expands to enable fund raisers to reach more donors with personalized appeals. For instance, telemarketing programs, combining carefully crafted telephone and mail appeals to donors segmented by complex demographic variables, have become standard in many institutions. Also, schools and consulting firms have developed sophisticated programs to identify and study new prospects for major and deferred gifts.

Dollars raised, solicitations made, and people and organizations involved in fund raising have all reached staggering numbers. Both the American public and officials of regulatory agencies have taken notice. As a result, fund raisers face greater demands for accountability within their institutions, and all fundraising programs face more public scrutiny as Americans react to the growing requests for donations and express outrage at reported abuses by fund raisers (Millar, 1990). In the "current harsh regulatory climate" for fund raising (Bush, 1990, p. 275), many states are considering legislation to broaden mandatory registration of public charities and increase disclosure of fundraising costs and the actual uses of donated money.

Since overall costs for goods and services to higher education are increasing (McMillen, 1990a) more rapidly than state and federal appropriations (Jaschik, 1990; "President's Proposal . . . ," 1990), leaders in more and more institutions are seeking to make up for these shortfalls through increased efforts to raise funds from private sources. These leaders and fund raisers are playing for high stakes and need to understand the factors that influence fund-raising effectiveness.

Defining Fund-Raising Effectiveness

Little systematic research has been done on fund-raising effectiveness. (For a comprehensive review and insightful analysis of research on fund raising, see Brittingham and Pezzullo, 1990). The primary problem in studying fund raising is defining effectiveness. The amount of money raised by a school has been the most widely used measure of effectiveness, but this measure is inadequate because no norms have been established for comparing dollar amounts. Using money raised as the criterion does not take into consideration the differences between schools in institutional resources for fund raising, including fund-raising costs, and provides no assessment of how a given year's results compare with an institution's potential for raising money. If an institution raises $5 million one year and $6 million the next year, does that 20 percent increase represent success? If two institutions, one a state university in a rural area with 7,000 students and the other a private college in a major city with 600 students, raise $1.5 million each, are these two institutions performing equally well? Using total money raised to define fund-raising effectiveness favors large wealthy institutions that nevertheless may not be reaching their full potential (Dunn, Terkla, and Adam, 1986). This criterion also obscures the success of small institutions.

It is difficult to compare fund-raising costs and budgets across institutions. Accounting and record-keeping systems are not standardized across institutions; direct and indirect fund-raising expenses are listed in many different ways as part of over-all costs for institutional advancement. For example, in some institutions, expenditures that actually contribute to fund-raising results may be included in separate budgets for alumni relations, publications, or public relations and may not be counted as direct fund-raising costs. Furthermore, in many large institutions, individual college and unit budgets usually cover some fund-raising costs. These amounts may be unknown to administrators in the central fund-raising office.

Additional problems in assessing costs include (1) how to assess the value of factors such as the time the president of the institution or volunteers spend in direct fund raising, (2) how to assess actual costs for major gifts that have taken years to come to fruition and deferred gifts that will not come to maturity for years, and (3) how to compare costs across fund-raising programs in various stages of maturity and in institutions with varying amounts of potential in fund raising. (The literature, as summarized by Brittingham and Pezzullo, 1990, for example, and our experiences indicate that new fund-raising programs have higher costs than mature programs and that costs are lower for institutions with greater potential for fund raising than for institutions with less potential.)

Foundation for This Study

Hoping to clarify some of the uncertainties about the potential of higher education institutions for fund raising, we began, in 1986, an analysis of fund-raising results, basic institutional characteristics, fund-raising expenditures, and basic fund-raising methods in 575 institutions. The broad outlines of the early research, those necessary to lay the foundation for the present work, are presented here. (This early research is described more fully in Duronio and Loessin, 1990; Duronio, Loessin, and Borton, 1988; Duronio, Loessin, and Nirschel, 1989).

Ten types of institutions were included in the original analysis: private and public research, doctoral, and comprehensive universities, and private and public baccalaureate and two-year colleges. With one modification, this classification of institutions is the one used by the Council for Aid to Education (CFAE) in its annual reports on fund-raising results, from which we took most of the data for individual institutions (Council for Aid to Education, 1984, 1985, and 1986). We separated CFAE's group of doctoral institutions into two types, distinguishing between major research universities and all other doctoral universities, since an analysis of basic characteristics showed us that differences between these two types of universities in financial resources and money raised are considerable. For instance, the median for gifts to private research universities for the years 1983–1985 (the years for which data were used in this first study) was $39.2 million, and the median for total institutional budget (educational and general expenditures) for this institutional category for the period was $206.5 million. In comparison, the median for gifts to private doctoral universities for this same period was $10.3 million, and the median for institutional budget for this type of university was $96.7 million. We used membership in the Association of American Universities as the criterion to identify major research universities. Only fifty-six institutions are members of this organization. Membership, by invitation only, is based primarily on the total research dollars the institution obtains.

The basic institutional characteristics we studied in our

early research, in addition to type of institution and private or public status, were those most often linked in the literature to fund-raising success. These were: educational/general expenditures, endowment, expenditures per student, cost of tuition, alumni of record (that is, the number of students, usually but not always graduates, that the institution counts as alumni), enrollment, and age of institution. We calculated three-year averages for these characteristics and for voluntary support to help eliminate the effects of any unusual one-year events.

Merely scanning the data confirmed our commonsense knowledge that, overall, the types of institutions that raised the most money also had the most institutional resources. However, when institutions were sorted by type, with private research universities compared only with other private research universities and public two-year colleges only with other public two-year colleges, for example, it became clear that not all institutions with high levels of resources had high fund-raising totals. Conversely, institutions with the lowest resources were not always the ones with the lowest fund-raising totals. For all types of institutions, we found all possible combinations of levels of institutional resources and fund-raising outcomes.

Studying fund raising by comparing basic institutional characteristics and fund-raising results does not fully explain why some institutions raise considerably more money in voluntary support than do other institutions of the same type with roughly equivalent resources. This initial study confirmed our belief that it is not possible to fully understand fund-raising effectiveness by studying quantitative factors alone. The research also indicated that in order to be useful and accurate, research on fund-raising effectiveness must distinguish between types of institutions because the relationships of basic institutional characteristics and fund-raising totals differ across types of institutions. In a second study, the study on which this book is based, we turned from a quantitative study of basic institutional characteristics and fund-raising totals in 575 institutions to the study of qualitative characteristics commonly associated with fund-raising success in just ten institutions.

Methodology for This Study

Defined conceptually, *fund-raising effectiveness* is raising the most money with the least amount of expenditures in a manner that enhances the likelihood that current donors will continue their support and that more new donors will contribute. Although this definition includes references to results, costs, techniques, and donors, it is enormously difficult to turn the definition into a formula that can be used to answer the question, Is our program effective or not?

In contrast to a conceptual definition, an operational definition specifies what is used to measure the concept under consideration. The operational definition of fund-raising effectiveness used in this book is based on the idea that such effectiveness is a measure of how well an institution realizes its full potential in fund raising. Potential is an abstract concept, not well defined or easily measurable, but we know that wealthy, large, prestigious institutions have greater potential for raising money than institutions with more modest enrollments, financial resources, and reputation.

Multiple regression analysis is a statistical procedure that researchers can use to predict what a given institution, with a given set of institutional characteristics, might be expected to raise in voluntary support. Institutions raising an amount close to the predicted amount are probably making good use of their resources and potential for fund raising. Institutions that actually raise an amount greater than predicted may be making exceptionally good use of their resources and potential. Therefore, our operational definition of an effective fund-raising program is one in which actual results exceed predicted results.

Selection of Institutions. After updating information on basic institutional characteristics and fund-raising results using data reported for 1985 through 1987 (Council for Aid to Education, 1986, 1987, and 1988), we sorted institutions from our original group of 575 by type, used multiple regression analysis to predict fund-raising results, and calculated a score for total voluntary support and for gifts from each of four major donor groups—

alumni, nonalumni, corporations, and foundations. This score was obtained by dividing the actual results by the predicted results. Thus the score will be greater than 1 if actual results exceed predicted results or less than 1 if predicted results exceed actual results. For example, if actual results equal $1.8 million and predicted results equal $1.3 million, the score is 1.38. If actual results equal $1.3 million and predicted results equal $1.8 million, the score is .72. From a pool of about 100 institutions with scores above 1.0, we selected ten institutions, one of each type, for further study.

The ten institutions in this study are located in eight different states in the Northeast, the Southeast, the Midwest, the Southwest, and the West Coast. They include institutions in urban and rural settings and, among the private institutions, some with religious affiliations and some without such affiliations. We avoided institutions with reputations for success in fund raising, such as Stanford and the University of Michigan, on the grounds that their high visibility in fund raising now contributes to their continuing fund-raising success and makes them less representative of all institutions of their type.

In some cases, we chose institutions with fund-raising results below the median for institutions of their type but that, nevertheless, had actual fund-raising results that exceeded the statistical prediction (these institutions were doing very well with what they had, even if they did not raise as much money as some other institutions of the same type). The institutions we selected are very diverse in fund-raising results, resources, and institutional personalities, as well as in such factors as maturity of fund-raising programs and fund-raising history. Tables 1.1 and 1.2 show the ranges and medians for institutional characteristics and fund-raising results of these institutions.

Collection of Data. We made site visits of one to four days' duration to each institution to interview people important to successful fund raising and to review materials and documents related to fund raising. We conducted a total of more than 100 interviews with a diverse range of professional staff members, including presidents, chief development officers, academic deans,

Table 1.1. Range and Median for Institutional
Characteristics for Ten Institutions.

Characteristic	Private Institutions (5)	Public Institutions (5)
Educational/General Expenditures	$165,940,000–$2,800,000 (median = $36,669,000)	$348,153,000–$12,452,000 (median = $108,280,000)
Endowment	$243,552,000–$9,761,000 (median = $17,820,000)	$41,100,000–$1,346,000 (median = $1,081,000)
Expenditures per Student	$20,931–$4,590 (median = $6,665)	$12,760–$1,917 (median = $7,091
Cost of Tuition	$12,100–$3,600 (median = $7,500)	$1,900–$840 (median = $1,200)
Alumni of Record	82,500–6,400 (median = 52,600)	125,000–9,800 (median = 56,500)
Enrollment	7,900–500 (median = 5,500)	30,900–6,500 (median = 15,300)
Age of Institution	162–30 years (median = 130)	120–24 years (median = 103)

other administrators with management responsibility in institutional advancement, and professional fund-raising staff members.

To provide a framework for studying each institution's fund-raising program, we developed a list of qualitative characteristics of fund raising from a review of the literature on fund-raising effectiveness (Glennon, 1986; Leslie, 1969; Pickett, 1977; and Willmer, 1981) and on excellence in higher education institutions (Gilley, Fulmer, and Reithlingshoefer, 1986).

Characteristics of Institution

Presidential leadership
Trustees' participation
Institutional commitment to fund raising
    Resource allocation
    Acceptance of the need for fund raising
    Definition and communication of institutional niche
      and image
    Institutional fund-raising priorities and policies

Table 1.2. Range and Median for
Fund-Raising Results for Ten Institutions.

Characteristic	Private Institutions (5)	Public Institutions (5)
Total Voluntary Support	$28,120,000–$809,000 (median = $4,935,000)	$27,905,000–$322,000 (median = $4,700,000)
Alumni Gifts	$8,917,000–$182,000 (median = $1,835,000)	$3,199,100–$6,648 (median = $504,000)
Nonalumni Gifts	$4,506,200–$316,000 (median = $1,366,000)	$13,575,000–$187,000 (median = $2,019,000)
Corporation Gifts	$7,241,000–$144,000 (median = $1,800,000)	$10,588,000–$99,200 (median = $1,243,000)
Foundation Gifts	$8,570,000–$165,000 (median = $519,000)	$3,012,000–$29,100 (median = $860,000)

Characteristics of Fund-Raising Program

Chief development officer's leadership
Successful fund-raising history
Fund-raising history
Entrepreneurial fund raising
Volunteers' roles in fund raising
Emphasis on management of the fund raising function
    Information and communication systems
    Planning, goal setting, and evaluation
    Staff development, training, and evaluation
Staff commitment to institution
Emphasis on constituent relations

The list covers much of the conventional wisdom about fund-raising success. These characteristics are commonly noted in fund-raising literature as related to fund-raising success. Some experienced practitioners believe that one or another characteristic is so important that an institution cannot be successful in fund raising without strength in this characteristic. Some practitioners believe that institutions must have strength in all of these characteristics to be successful in fund raising.

Although none of these characteristics is new in the discussion of fund-raising effectiveness, few researchers have tried to demonstrate that these are the characteristics found in effective programs. In our interviews to collect data, the list served as a guide for discussion only; we did not use formal or standardized methods or instruments to measure the characteristics. Instead, after providing participants with a copy of the list, we asked them to describe their roles, to make observations about the institution's fund-raising success, and to comment on the characteristics on the list as they felt inclined to do so.

Analysis of Data. Data from the site visits were analyzed in two ways: case-by-case and across cases. Although the overall results of our study generally confirm the conventional wisdom of fund raising, the characteristics associated with fund-raising success in these effective institutions are more complex and more varied than conventional wisdom might suggest. No institutions were outstanding in all the characteristics; some institutions were doing very well with strengths in only a few areas. Although all institutions had strengths in one or more of these characteristics, no single pattern emerged for all institutions. The characteristics most consistently found to be strong in these successful programs were related to leadership and institutional commitment to fund raising. Among the characteristics least consistently found to be strong in these institutions were those related to volunteers and trustees.

The case studies that follow emphasize the exceptional aspects of fund-raising programs at each institution. We also present details about some fund-raising efforts that were not entirely successful but that were critical turning points in the respective institutions' fund-raising progress.

2

State of the Art
and by the Book:

A Private Research University

> ALPHA: The latest techniques and technologies are evident in comprehensive programs for all areas of development at Alpha. A major factor influencing the expansion of fund-raising programs is the shift from an almost entirely decentralized development function to the creation of a strong central core.

This private research university, with an enrollment of about 8,000 and annual educational and general expenditures of almost $166 million, is located in a major city. Other descriptive statistics, shown in Table 2.1, indicate that Alpha's resources are modest compared with many other institutions of this type. Educational and general expenditures, endowment, expenditures per student, cost of tuition, and enrollment are all below the median. Alumni of record and age of institution are slightly above the median. All voluntary support outcomes are also below the median for institutions of this type. Nevertheless, Alpha's actual outcomes for total voluntary support, corporation gifts, and foundation gifts are above the predicted amounts, indicating that the school uses its resources well. The organizational chart for development and alumni affairs at Alpha appears in Figure 2.1.

Every aspect of development at this institution has been expanding, auguring well for future overall results and for an upcoming campaign to raise $350 million. At the time of the site visit, staff members were raising advance gifts for the campaign,

13

Table 2.1. Descriptive Statistics (1985–1987 Average) for Alpha University (Private Research).

	Range for Type			Actual	This Institution	
	High	Median	Low		Predicted	Difference
Institutional Characteristics:						
Educational/General Expenditures	$660,469,700	$232,386,500	$30,477,300	$165,939,333	—	—
Endowment	$1,726,792,500	$413,128,437	$29,141,000	$243,552,000	—	—
Expenditures per Student	$72,000	$26,300	$8,000	$20,931	—	—
Cost of Tuition	$12,900	$11,500	$5,100	$10,400	—	—
Alumni of Record	241,900	74,400	16,000	82,518	—	—
Enrollment	32,500	10,200	1,800	7,928	—	—
Age of Institution	350 years	130 years	40 years	162 years	—	—
Fund-Raising Results:						
Total Voluntary Support	$164,274,600	$57,443,800	$3,223,900	$28,119,580	$26,916,683	+1.04
Alumni Gifts	$60,878,200	$11,764,000	$863,200	$8,917,565	$11,134,642	0.80
Nonalumni Gifts	$37,356,100	$10,342,900	$1,025,500	$3,391,357	$4,925,321	0.69
Corporation Gifts	$38,399,100	$12,256,800	$469,500	$7,240,515	$6,064,652	+1.19
Foundation Gifts	$65,151,600	$13,891,800	$624,700	$8,570,143	$7,287,409	+1.18

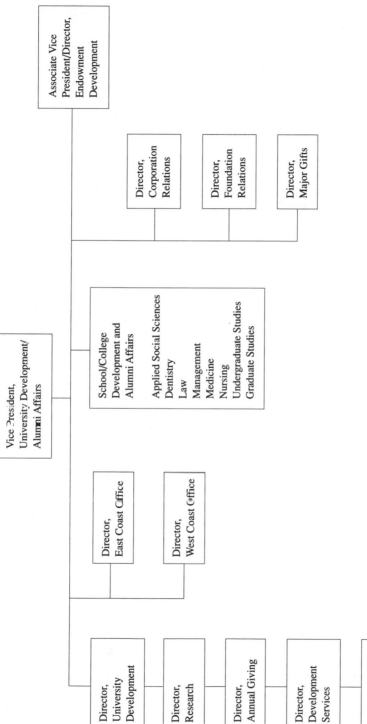

Figure 2.1. Organizational Chart for Alpha University.

Vice President, University Development/ Alumni Affairs

Associate Vice President/Director, Endowment Development

Director, University Development

Director, Research

Director, Annual Giving

Director, Development Services

Director, Alumni Relations

Director, East Coast Office

Director, West Coast Office

School/College Development and Alumni Affairs

Applied Social Sciences
Dentistry
Law
Management
Medicine
Nursing
Undergraduate Studies
Graduate Studies

Director, Corporation Relations

Director, Foundation Relations

Director, Major Gifts

the largest campaign in Alpha's history. The campaign was scheduled to be announced in about six months, and the staff had raised more than $100 million in advance gifts. Although getting the campaign under way was a major effort, it was only part of the extensive changes and new programs of the university, including well-planned programs for major and planned gifts, the annual fund, alumni and parent relations, and foundation and corporate relations. Sophisticated mechanisms for prospect research, rating, and tracking, for management information and planning, and for increasing trustee and volunteer participation and support were also being implemented. One senior staff member described this comprehensive, state-of-the-art approach as a textbook approach to fund raising.

After a long history as a decentralized institution with strong independent colleges and little central control in any area, Alpha is being guided by a new administration toward more centralization. The administration hopes to enhance overall institutional identity and strength while preserving, as much as possible, the autonomy and independence of individual colleges. At least some of the impetus for greater centralization is the result of the need to strengthen universitywide fund-raising efforts, which trustees and administrators believe can best be accomplished through the creation of a strong central development office. Until a few years ago, only four staff members worked in the central development office. At the time of the site visit, more than ninety professional and support personnel worked there. Fund raisers for individual colleges reported only to their deans and operated without central direction. Now, management staff members in the central development office lead the universitywide development effort and college fund raisers report both to their deans and to the vice president for university development and alumni affairs. In addition to various program responsibilities, each central fund-raising manager also has significant responsibility for coordinating activities with the college development staff.

A spirit of renewal and energy, as well as an intense seriousness of purpose, pervades Alpha. One senior development staff member said, "The climate here is very progressive, positive, constructive, upbeat. There is an openness to new ideas, a willingness to try new things, with a lot of emphasis on involving the larger community." Another senior staff member pointed out that a renewed sense of pride exists throughout the university because of some new practices of senior administrators. The administrators have begun to "tell employees that our jobs are meaningful, that what we do is special, and that each one of us can make a difference in how this institution is perceived and in making students' lives easier," the staff member said. "People have really begun to believe it. When you hear old-timers who have been complaining for years say positive things about the institution, you know something important is going on."

History and New Directions

In 1975, Alpha began a $250 million fund-raising campaign, which, the vice president for university development and alumni affairs noted, "was a lot of money in those days." In his words, Alpha may have been "the least likely university in America to announce what turned out to have been the eighth largest campaign in the history of higher education." At that time, he said, Alpha was "caught up in a vigorous internal quarrel, related to almost everyone's preference that Alpha remain a decentralized institution." Nevertheless, with a year's extension on the campaign and a lot of hard work, Alpha raised the $250 million and closed the campaign in 1981.

The vice president indicated that funds were raised by individual colleges, all working in relative isolation from each other, which was the tradition at Alpha. After the campaign, Alpha thanked its volunteers, decreased the number of staff members, closed programs, and cut the fund-raising budget tremendously — a shutdown that the vice president said "is now understood to be suicidal" for long-term fund-raising success. In fiscal 1981, the institution raised $30 million. In fiscal 1982, that figure dropped to $24 million and stayed in that range for five years. The vice president remarked that Alpha "sat out the revolution that was going on in philanthropy to higher education" in the 1980s.

In 1981, this vice president, formerly an academic administrator at Alpha with no experience in development, assumed his position in university development and alumni affairs. The vice president related candidly that it took him some time to realize that "it wasn't the normal pattern to close up shop until it was time for the next campaign." When he realized this, he hired a consultant, who spent a full year analyzing Alpha's fund-raising status and needs.

In late 1986, in an action that marked the beginning of a new stage in Alpha's history, the consultant told university trustees, according to the vice president, "that Alpha had made a big mistake in closing down the shop and that we had to get our alumni relations program started yesterday and turn our whole system on. He also said we had to stop believing that every major gift would come through the annual fund or as a deferred gift and start raising major gifts outright. He said that eventually we needed to have a campaign, but we had much work to do before we started one."

Trustees authorized a substantially increased budget to improve development services; enhance programs for annual gifts, alumni relations, and major gifts; and plan for a comprehensive campaign. Soon thereafter, trustees also authorized a separate seven-year budget for the projected campaign. The vice president emphasized that the current central development function will not be reduced or disbanded when the next campaign ends, noting, "It is abundantly clear that we will campaign forever and that we can never again cut staff and programs when a campaign is over. We have a long way to go, but we sure are having a very different conversation now than ten years ago."

A most important change, the vice president believes, is that Alpha has left behind "the annual fund mentality that drove earlier development efforts" to focus on securing major gifts. He stressed that the annual fund is still important, saying that Alpha is currently spending a lot of money to double the annual fund. The problem, he said, was that previously "Alpha didn't have the institutional self-confidence to talk to our donors about direct gifts of $5 million. It was simply beyond our ability to believe that individuals would give us such a sum. We had focused for years on getting large gifts primarily through deferred mechanisms. When we did get direct major gifts, we never involved donors to help them move up from their first major gifts. We took their $500,000 gift, and then they didn't hear from us. Five years later, if we showed up to ask for another large gift, they were not nearly as interested as they were the first time."

The vice president emphasized that over the long term Alpha must invest time, energy, and money in alumni relations. He said that good alumni relations programs not only help the annual fund but also help turn annual donors into major donors. "We ignored our alumni for so long, assuming that they would continue to care about us, and we paid an enormous price. Now we understand that we have to begin to develop relationships with our alumni when they are age twenty-two rather than waiting until they are sixty-five, when we suddenly say, 'We haven't paid any attention to Smith and Jones, but they are in their sixties now, so we ought to see what they're up to.'"

The vice president pointed out that Alpha constituents are eager to be involved with the university. "Isn't it amazing, the kinds and numbers of people who want to be associated with a first-rate university," he said. "People return my phone calls, not because of me personally, but because I'm from Alpha University. People gain status by being associated with this institution, and somehow we must manage that to the benefit of the institution."

Although he believes in using volunteers in the development process, the vice president noted that the days of using volunteers for every task are over and that in-house staff members must take care of the fund-raising mechanics so that volunteer time is used more effectively. Volunteers, he said, are happier when they are involved in important tasks.

In addition to raising money, expanding programs, coordinating fund raising with college development officers, and preparing for the fund-raising campaign, the vice president and central staff are building infrastructures and fund-raising mechanisms, such as better record-keeping systems, that will survive when individual staff members leave. The vice president said that until recently "if a staff member went on to become the next vice president of Harvard, everything that person knew about Alpha's donors would go out the door with him or her." Alpha had no organized mechanisms to track prospects or to ensure that prospects of staff members who left would be called. Alpha did not debrief staff members or insist on trip reports. "We would spend a year getting a new person up to speed," the vice president said. "If the person who left had been around any period of time, it could take a newcomer five years to be as effective in that position. The structures we are building will eliminate that problem."

President A.

President A., who arrived at Alpha in 1987, is often quoted as having described Alpha as the only university that seemed to be less than the sum of its parts because of the extensive decentralization of colleges and programs. Although the expanded development effort was under way when President A. arrived, his plan to strengthen the university's overall identity provided support for development efforts. The vice president said that at one time "nothing other than the stationery really represented the university," but because of the leadership of President A., "we are beginning to perceive and present ourselves as a university. I don't want to sound like the man is a miracle worker—although he comes as close at this institution as anybody could—but he came in and simply assumed we were a university! People began to act differently and to put aside differences, just because he assumed that some university priorities transcended individual college priorities."

The vice president pointed out that President A. not only is involved in fund raising and is effective as a fund raiser but also that "he just assumed that certain projects and donors would be his to cultivate for university priorities. With his viewpoint, we have grown to be a much bigger institution, with bigger plans and dreams and aspirations than we've ever had before. The whole institution has grown in the way it thinks about itself and how it has set itself up for the future."

Other fund-raising managers also commented on the president's impact. One said, "Prior to the arrival of President A., the university wasn't even a holding company. This institution was connected only by the steam tunnels and the accounting system. This was originally intentional — a variation on the tried-and-true Harvard model — each tub on its own bottom. Individual deans set their own priorities, and we had no universitywide objectives. However, within months after President A. arrived, he set university priorities, not just for the year but for the next decade, and he made them clear to all of us and to the foundation and corporate world."

Another fund-raising manager noted that the president is a popular figure. The feasibility study for the upcoming campaign, she said, indicates that the president is the primary player in the institution's future, that people admire him and want to support him. Pointing out that President A.'s impact at Alpha was both immediate and ongoing, a senior development officer stated, "New presidents usually generate a lot of heat and light, whether in a honeymoon period or an intense clash, and eventually the energy dissipates." But at Alpha, he said, regard for President A. continues to rise. "He makes clear what he believes this institution can and should be, and he has a credibility that is absolutely critical for us now. He seems to be the right person for us." A third manager observed that leadership is the key to successful fund raising. "As I look back on the schools where I've worked before, the leadership was outstanding in all but one. What a difference that makes! I believe very much in the leadership of this university. We all want to help the president make this a great university, and we think we can do it."

Vice President of University
Development and Alumni Affairs

The vice president does not consider himself a development officer but rather a university officer with an assignment in development and alumni affairs, who is having the "most fun I've ever had working." His conception of his primary role as that of a university officer reflects his enthusiasm and the importance he places on supporting the academic mission and providing serious management to the development effort. In describing how fund raising is integrated into academic affairs at Alpha, he said that the relationship between academic planning and fund raising may be tighter at Alpha than at some other places, although, like many other institutions, Alpha used to raise money and then decide how to spend it. "I resist the notion that development should drive the academic planning process," he said, "because that is putting the cart before the horse. Development is the logical extension of the academic planning process. If this university doesn't have academic plans that are interesting and exciting to our external constituents, there is no reason to raise funds. Fund raising should reflect those plans, not drive them."

The vice president believes that staff members who understand the relationship between development and the academic mission of the university are essential to Alpha's fund-raising success. He said, "We don't want hired gunslingers. I am realistic about the job market, but staff members at Alpha must not only raise money but also care about how and why they raise it. I think our development officers should get up every morning and say five times out loud the three top academic priorities for their areas and should believe that every day they are going to find ways to support those priorities."

The vice president and the director of development both teach in academic areas not related to development. Not all development staff members must teach, the vice president said, but everyone in development must be connected to the academic mission of the institution. Another senior staff member indicated that development staff can be connected to the university through their own personal donations. He makes a contribution to Alpha even though this institution is not his alma mater and feels that professionals who have been at Alpha for five years should donate $1,000 to $2,500 a year.

Managing staff members is a major priority for the vice president. He noted that management is difficult in an institution making the transition from decentralization to centralization. "Personnel management takes up a great deal of time. I'm encouraging, coaching, leading, driving, cheerleading. I also find resources and encourage action. I am proud of the fact that we have a seven-year budget in place and the resources for competent staff to do what they need to do. If people aren't producing, we find ways to help them gracefully out of the institution, but I don't believe in beating up on staff: I need to support, guide, cheer for, and encourage them, and they should be able to trust that I will be tough when I must be to get the resources and support they need."

The vice president also said, "After resources and support, the most important thing the staff needs from me is information about our plan — where we're going, why we're doing it, and what exactly is expected of them." Several other managers referred to the participative management style of the vice president and indicated that it has influenced the manner in which they manage staff in their own areas.

Annual Fund

The central annual fund staff includes a director, two professional staff members, and one support staff member. Although Alpha has conducted alumni telethons for fifteen years, the central annual fund office was less than a year old at the time of our site visit. Previously, the small central staff coordinated and provided support for direct mail campaigns and telethons organized by the development officers of individual units, who recruited volunteers and prepared their own solicitation materials. Gifts to the annual fund had not been increasing for several years, and development officers in some colleges or schools were having trouble recruiting enough volunteers. When the annual fund director arrived in 1988, she was charged with doubling the annual fund in five years, a challenge she concluded "would have been impossible to meet without making the drastic program changes needed to reach a much larger segment of the alumni body than the 31 percent we had been reaching."

After six months' evaluation of short- and long-term needs, costs, options, and anticipated results, the director decided to hire a telemarketing firm — an idea she had to work hard to sell within the university. She said, "It was hard for some people here to give up their alumni telethons and accept the idea of paying outsiders to make the calls. Instituting this change took longer than we thought it would, primarily because of how much educating we needed to do along the way." After extensive research, she selected a firm providing an off-site program using well-trained callers as the most cost-effective way to double the annual fund. Because of the long tradition at Alpha of using alumni volunteers as callers, it was very important, according to the director, for paid callers to represent the university as well as alumni had been doing. The director explained that "belief in the soundness of the plan, courage, and the willingness to take risks in educating others" were all necessary. She added, "Courage and vision are important, but you have to absolutely love what you are doing and to love the institution you are serving. You can never be satisfied in development if you love your institution because the institution will always need more."

Staff members' expectations for the new annual fund program, still in the implementation stage at the time of the site visit, are high. The telemarketing firm guaranteed to contact at least 80 percent of Alpha's alumni, including nondonors, lapsed donors, and current donors. Staff members expect that annual fund gifts will increase from $200,000 to $600,000–$800,000 per year, with a significant increase in the number of alumni who make annual gifts. Start-up costs for the complete program, including word processing and mailing costs, are about 30¢ per dollar raised. Costs for the previous volunteer program were about 10¢ per dollar raised (excluding word processing and computer costs). Staff members anticipate that program costs will decrease over a period of years as callers negotiate higher gifts, as the average gift increases, and as the number of participating alumni increases.

Prospects for the new annual fund are contacted by mail prior to receiving a call. The letters they receive, signed by distinguished graduates of their respective colleges, state the case for giving, ask them to consider a gift of $1,000, and explain that they will be contacted by telephone. Each of the 94,000 prospects in the donor data base has been rated by a management consulting firm for ability to give on a scale from 1 (highest) to 26 (lowest). The caller begins a phone solicitation by referring to the letter and then follows a script that explains how gifts will be used.

The assistant director pointed out that because "every prospect has been rated, callers know, for instance, that if they're working with a prospect rated 4, they should try to negotiate for a donation larger than $1,000. If the prospect is rated 26 and responds to the $1,000 ask with a chuckle, the caller moves quickly to suggesting a smaller gift." The telemarketing firm will send reminder letters to all prospects who make phone pledges, reflecting the firm's belief that at least 75 percent of pledges might never become actual gifts without reminders to donors.

The assistant director also explained that staff will systematically evaluate the use of their prospect rating system in annual fund solicitations. A sample of prospects with the highest ratings will receive letters asking for $2,500 gifts, rather than $1,000 gifts. Staff members will analyze results for this sample to see if prospects with similar ratings gave higher gifts when asked for the higher amount. The assistant director described this evaluation as "the first joint effort of a university, consulting firm, and telemarketing firm to test the effectiveness of using this rating system and the mail-phone process."

The annual fund program also recognizes alumni who hold multiple degrees. In the past, alumni with multiple degrees from Alpha were solicited for gifts for the professional schools they attended but not for their undergraduate programs. In the new program, alumni with multiple degrees receive a letter signed by the chairman of the current alumni council that acknowledges their multiple degrees and asks them to consider a significant gift to each school. "In this way," the director noted, "the undergraduate schools — where the needs are terrific — won't be overlooked. We expect this program to enlarge the donor base for undergraduate programs."

The expanded central program for annual gifts also involves personal solicitation of approximately 500 donors who have previously given $1,000 or more and who now will be asked for $5,000 gifts. Schedules for personal solicitations are coordinated with campaign plans to ensure that annual fund asks do not overlap with campaign solicitations and are not overlooked because of these solicitations. In a new approach for Alpha, fifty volunteers who themselves give at the level of $1,000 or above have been trained by central staff members to make personal solicitations and recruit other volunteers. The director noted that although each school has traditionally had an annual fund volunteer coordinator, most alumni volunteers have not been involved in personal solicitations. Development officers with responsibility for the annual fund in various colleges, who, the director noted, "used to spend their time typing their own letters and stuffing envelopes," now are available to support their volunteers in higher-level fund-raising activities. The director believes that development officers can use their time more productively and that staff members and volunteers are more satisfied.

Coordinating central programs with college development officers has been a major task for the director, requiring extensive communication that she has not left to chance. The director convenes regular meetings of development officers responsible for the annual fund in each college. She noted that at first, some were hesitant to share what they were doing or what their problems were, but, as time went on, they began to see that they could learn from each other. Now they work well together. An important by-product of this process was that the coordination of development officers from individual colleges "helped a great deal in getting our mail-phone process authorized because, at the grass-roots level, the annual fund officers were in agreement."

Other Central Fund-Raising Activities

Central staff members coordinate several other fund-raising activities for all university units. These activities include programs to raise foundation gifts, planned gifts, and major gifts; programs to ensure effective relations with alumni and parents; and research and development services.

Foundation Gifts. At the time of our site visit, the office of corporation/foundation relations had recently been reorganized into two separate offices, with a director, assistant director, and one support person for each area. A search was under way to fill the new position of director of corporation relations. The director of foundation relations, in his position for four years, explained that his office oversees and coordinates universitywide foundation relations, including all activities associated with successful solicitations, such as doing research, preparing budgets, or editing proposals, and with effective stewardship, such as writing thank-you letters, writing reminders of reports due, or writing letters to ask for extensions or revisions.

A majority of this director's time is spent in developing and maintaining relationships with foundation officials. He said, "I try to pay attention to our major foundation constituency even if we don't have a current proposal for the foundation. I don't think we should ever have a proposal rejected because we didn't do our homework. I want to be closely enough involved with foundation people to be fairly certain that when we submit a proposal, it will be accepted. I don't want them to be surprised when they receive our proposal, and I don't want to be surprised when we get their response."

The director holds monthly meetings with college development officers and disseminates a newsletter on activities with foundations every six weeks. He thus facilitates communication and coordination of the competition for foundation prospects that flourishes in any large institution, especially one long characterized by highly decentralized and autonomous college units.

President A.'s insistence on coordination provided the initial momentum for more cooperation between units. However, as the director noted, "Now individual development officers see that they're better off letting us all know what they are doing because they can then, in effect, stake a claim and get their interests out in the open."

This senior development manager and his counterparts in other areas of the central office encourage and support the resolution of conflicting interests among development staff members. This manager's approach is "Let's see if we can come to terms with it among ourselves. This is not something we want to put on the provost's desk or take back to the deans. If we want to play a constructive role here, we ought to be able to sort it out. Whose turn is it? What level are you looking at? Let's think over the longer term and work together to parcel out opportunities."

Planned Gifts and Major Gifts. The associate vice president/ director of endowment development is the planned gifts officer. This director is an attorney who has worked in higher education fund raising for thirty years, the last seventeen at Alpha as a specialist in trusts and estates. In 1972, endowment at Alpha was about $65 million; now, in large part because of bequests and maturing life income trusts, endowment is over $420 million. The planned gifts staff includes three professional staff members and one support person. Current programs are geared to alumni who graduated prior to 1950 and who have a history of contributions to the university. The director is also interested in younger alumni who may become good prospects for deferred gifts later on. He said, "If someone starts giving $2,000 a year, I want to make sure that alumnus is on our mailing list. When I talk to this person ten years from now, I can say, 'I hope the literature on estate planning that we've been sending has been useful to you.'"

The director, stating that his staff works closely with the college development staff, said, "We try to promote aggressively the idea that we have specialized knowledge and valuable services to offer. We often see prospects who would rather ask us questions than ask their attorneys or accountants. It doesn't cost money to talk to us, so they read our literature and pick our brains and become more knowledgeable about these matters before they pay to spend time with their attorneys. People appreciate that."

The director of major gifts, in a central office established in 1988, has a staff of two professionals and one support person. At Alpha, a major gift is a gift of six figures. The director of major gifts said, "My mandate is not to poach prospects away from college development officers but to support their work and raise the level of activity in major gifts throughout the university." An important part of his responsibility is to guide the president, trustees, other senior university administrators, and influential volunteers in their solicitations for major gifts.

Alumni and Parent Relations. The alumni relations staff includes
the director, three additional professional staff members, and
two support staff members. Prior to 1987, each college had an
alumni officer, but no central alumni relations office existed.
When the present director assumed her position, only one alumni
chapter was active outside the local area. At the time of our site
visit, eleven regional chapters were active. Additionally, after
conducting a survey to determine the extent of parents' interests,
the new staff started a parents' program, which includes a parents' council and a newsletter.

As have other directors in the central office, this director
has had to work carefully with college alumni officers. She said,
"I was concerned that I would be stepping on their toes, so I
have been careful. I meet with alumni officers monthly. At first,
they were uncomfortable about my holding receptions and forming chapters for alumni from throughout the university. Then
they saw that people were more active and were giving more
money to their colleges as a result of the centrally run alumni
programs, which are more cost effective and attract larger groups."

This director learned about implementing a universitywide alumni program by visiting four other universities that have
excellent alumni programs. "Experienced people in these programs judge their effectiveness by the percentage of alumni in
a given area who attend an event," she said. "Harvard gets about
20 percent attendance, but these other nationally known schools
get about 10 percent attendance, so 10 percent has become my
goal." She plans to monitor monthly reports on annual giving
to see if fund-raising results increase after alumni events in a
given area.

Her vision for the alumni relations program includes the
establishment of a "week-long minicollege for alumni." She believes that the chapters can hold social events but that the central office should provide educational experiences, connecting
alumni with what brought them to Alpha in the first place.

Research and Development Services. The director of research has
a staff of six researchers (up from one part-time and two full-
time researchers in 1987), and an additional staff of seven who
maintain the alumni data base screening project that is used

in conjunction with the prospect ratings provided by the telemarketing firm. The director described the staff's approach to prospect screening: "In forty cities in which we have good concentrations of alumni, we identified alumni who are prominent individuals and past donors of some consequence. We ask these alumni to host two-hour screening sessions, to which we invite donors and prospects with top ratings. They are given alumni's names and asked to rate the potential of each to give. At first, we did not have many people willing to serve as raters. I think it was because we hadn't paid much attention to our alumni in the past. Now we use a more focused and more personal approach to recruit raters, and attendance has improved greatly." With the purchase of new computer software, this office will assume responsibility for maintaining the prospect tracking system for the upcoming campaign.

The director of development services, one of the few veterans on Alpha's central fund-raising staff (at Alpha for over fifteen years), manages a staff of twelve. Her office maintains the development office data base and processes alumni surveys, all gifts, acknowledgments, special reports, and mailing labels.

Analysis of Fund Raising at Alpha

Comprehensive and state-of-the-art, the development effort at Alpha, appropriately described as "a textbook approach" by the director of development, could serve as a general model for new fund-raising programs. Outstanding characteristics in the fund-raising program at Alpha are the leadership of the president and chief development officer, the emphasis on management of the fund-raising function, entrepreneurial fund raising, and institutional commitment to fund raising.

The vice president for university development and alumni affairs had already begun to revitalize development operations at Alpha before the new president arrived to lend his considerable support to the expanded and newly centralized effort. This vice president is particularly interesting because while he is among the most influential fund-raising leaders we encountered in our research, he did not achieve the position of chief development officer by working his way up through the fund-raising ranks. In fact, by his own description, he is not a fund raiser but a university officer assigned to development. He provides leadership through effective management and through his perspective about the correct relationship between fund raising and the academic mission of the university.

The vice president endorses and uses a participative management style, emphasizing input from staff members and effective communication about expectations. As in other institutions, the chief development officer's approach affects management styles of the managers reporting to him. Throughout the central development office at Alpha, managers emphasized the importance of open communication and taking the time to coordinate complex programs throughout the university. This is one of only a few institutions in the study in which fund-raising managers did not resent or feel conflict about the need to spend time in the actual management of fund raising. Planning and goal setting are well-used tools in this operation, and Alpha has a comprehensive plan for each constituency, each giving program, and each development support area. The mission of the university is clearly articulated and well known. Priorities are clear, and most staff members spoke of both the clarity of communication with senior management and the opportunity for input. A strong sense of shared responsibility exists at Alpha. All staff members emphasized their roles as coordinators of university-wide activities relevant to their respective areas.

The entire development effort at Alpha is characterized by entrepreneurial efforts to develop fund-raising policies and strategies designed to break away from long-standing traditional approaches that no longer meet the needs of this university. The upcoming campaign, the centralization of fund-raising efforts, the president's strong hand in setting fund-raising priorities that address overall university needs, and the up-to-date technologies used in fund raising are all indications of a highly entrepreneurial program.

Institutional commitment to fund raising is also an outstanding characteristic at Alpha, indicated by the president's involvement in setting institutional priorities and the long-range commitment of resources for current and future fund raising. The staff reported that the entire Alpha community learned hard lessons from earlier experiences in cutting back on fund raising after a specific campaign. As a result, as the vice president said, "We will campaign forever." A broad consensus exists at Alpha that more energy must be expended on strengthening the image and identity of the university as an integrated entity.

Less outstanding characteristics at Alpha, but ones that are clearly present, are volunteers' roles in fund raising and staff commitment to the institution. All development staff members at Alpha continue to enlarge the roles of alumni volunteers in direct solicitations for several reasons. One reason is their belief in the effectiveness of peer solicitations. Another is their belief that volunteers can greatly exceed the number of personal solicitations now possible for professional staff members. And the third, and perhaps the most important, reason is their belief that a strong volunteer network is an ongoing asset, influential and useful to the university in numerous ways.

Alpha is not an institution that evokes exuberance and passion from its constituents. From its beginning, Alpha has been respected for its seriousness of purpose and commitment to high-quality education. The fund-raising team at Alpha reflects those institutional values. Although some staff members expressed strong feelings for the institution, most staff members expressed dedication to the fund-raising goals rather than to the institution itself. Staff members were as busy at some other institutions, and in some places seemed more harried, but nowhere else were staff members more interested in what they were doing than at Alpha. There was a "hum" at Alpha that made it different from any other institution we visited. Although staff members were glad to talk about their programs, the seriousness of purpose at Alpha left no time for small talk or informal conversation.

Emerging as strong characteristics at Alpha are the trustees' participation and an emphasis on improved relationships with all constituencies. Systematic and purposeful efforts were under way to develop close, long-term relationships with alumni, donors, and the community and to increase trustees' involvement both as donors and as resources in the fund-raising process.

In summary, what can others learn from Alpha's experiences? The factors we identified as contributing to fund-raising effectiveness at Alpha are as follows:

- Comprehensive detailed program plans and goals for all major donor groups, for all major giving programs, and for all development support areas
- Long-range planning and commitment of resources
- Development of systems and processes to ensure continuity of programs
- An awareness of the need to stay closely involved with donors and recognition that it is the university's responsibility to maintain and nurture relationships with donors
- Clear recognition that however loyal or generous constituents may be, very few will initiate either involvement or gifts
- A balanced effort between current and deferred gifts
- Recognition of the annual fund and alumni relationships as the building blocks for future success in fund raising
- Purposeful, professional, and supportive management of the complex fund-raising enterprise, characterized by clarity of communication and widespread participation
- Professional staff members committed to shared goals and methods for achieving them
- Inspired leadership by the president for the overall advancement of the university
- A perspective that subordinates fund-raising planning to academic planning
- Leadership by the fund-raising staff through education and consensus building for universitywide efforts

3

Encouraging Long-Term Relationships and Involvement:

A Public Research University

> BETA: Some outstanding characteristics at Beta are the director
> of development's leadership, extensive involvement of volunteers,
> the consistent emphasis on good relationships with all constituen-
> cies, and innovative programs in scholarship development and
> alumni affairs.

This public research university, with almost 31,000 students and
educational and general expenditures of more than $348 mil-
lion, is in a major city of a western state. In spite of modest
resources when compared with other institutions of this type,
Beta has impressive outcomes in total voluntary support and
for all donors except alumni. Descriptive statistics for Beta appear in Table 3.1. Figures for all institutional characteristics
are below the median for public research universities, meaning
that this institution has fewer resources than at least half of all
public research universities. Outcomes for all gifts are below
the median, except for nonalumni gifts, which are above the
median. Nevertheless, actual outcomes for total voluntary support, nonalumni gifts, and corporation gifts are substantially
higher than predicted outcomes. The actual outcome for foundation gifts is about equal to the predicted amount, and the actual outcome for alumni gifts is below the predicted amount.
The organizational chart for the development staff appears in
Figure 3.1.

Table 3.1. Descriptive Statistics (1985–1987 Average) for Beta University (Public Research).

| | Range for Type | | | | This Institution | |
	High	Median	Low	Actual	Predicted	Difference
Institutional Characteristics:						
Educational/General Expenditures	$1,492,920,300	$446,411,300	$109,175,100	$348,153,333	—	—
Endowment	$330,666,700	$94,416,800	$26,792,900	$44,105,032	—	—
Expenditures per Student	$127,500	$13,100	$5,500	$11,280	—	—
Cost of Tuition	$3,500	$1,700	$500	$1,196	—	—
Alumni of Record	321,100	185,000	89,300	125,000	—	—
Enrollment	63,100	32,800	2,300	30,864	—	—
Age of Institution	200 years	130 years	70 years	103 years	—	—
Fund-Raising Results:						
Total Voluntary Support	$87,092,200	$30,908,500	$6,097,900	$27,905,093	$20,727,785	+1.35
Alumni Gifts	$185,715,200	$6,574,400	$136,500	$740,076	$2,080,817	0.36
Nonalumni Gifts	$20,002,500	$5,326,800	$2,071,300	$13,575,338	$7,279,485	+1.86
Corporation Gifts	$31,336,900	$11,387,500	$1,298,700	$10,588,008	$6,774,217	+1.56
Foundation Gifts	$22,173,400	$4,520,600	$368,900	$2,978,004	$3,063,635	0.97

Figure 3.1. Organizational Chart for Beta University.

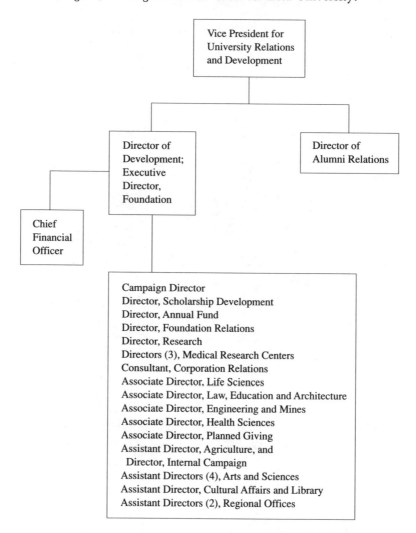

Director of Development

The chief development officer at Beta has the title of director of development and also holds the position of executive vice president of the Beta Foundation. When we asked staff members the reasons for Beta's fund-raising success, they most often cited the leadership and influence of this director. One staff member commented: "The director really has made the difference. He has a hands-off leadership style, and he is never negative. He allows people to be independent and always acknowledges a job well done. If people make mistakes, he encourages them to try again or to do something different. He is also a good recruiter. He identifies and attracts other good people for the team." Another said, "I think he is a man of vision, a very big person. He sees the overall picture, and therefore little things never become big issues with him. There's a team spirit here because of his leadership. That's important, because I don't want to be out there by myself, and I also don't want everyone else I'm supposed to be working with nipping at my heels. He fosters camaraderie and team play."

Staff members repeatedly cited the same characteristics of the director's style, such as "gives support to be innovative and daring," "is a laissez-faire manager who allows us to be creative," and "doesn't do a lot of day-to-day monitoring but holds us accountable." One senior staff member summed up the director's leadership style in this way: "He commands attention, not by his overt actions, but because of his physical presence and the respect people have for him. He doesn't need to exert his power with aggressiveness."

Now in his eleventh year at Beta, the director was Beta's first development officer and functioned for some years as a one-man operation. The professional development staff now numbers twenty-eight, and additional people will be added to the staff until each college has a development officer. Most fund-raising activities are centralized, but, the director noted, "We provide services in a decentralized fashion." Staff members are assigned to colleges and work with deans to set priorities and identify fund-raising strategies, a system that the director believes is preferable to having deans hire and manage their own development officers.

In the director's opinion, a centralized effort better serves overall university needs and also better serves individual colleges because senior management in the development office has more professional expertise in fund raising than the deans do.

The director noted that how well the centralized system works varies among deans, but developing good relationships with deans and faculty members is a high priority for the development staff. The director meets monthly with the deans' development council to increase communication and resolve conflicts.

Currently, all professional development staff members report directly to this senior officer, an arrangement that he indicates has become "cumbersome." In the new structure that will be implemented, three or four senior staff members will report to the director, and all other development staff members will report to these senior managers.

Along with managing this large operation, the director continues to raise funds, emphasizing, "I absolutely would not have it any other way." He works primarily with major donors, many of whom he has been involved with over the years.

A new administration in the early 1970s instituted systematic fund raising at Beta. Although the university had been growing in academic prestige in several disciplines, the director noted, "We had never publicized that nationally. We had no need to cultivate outside interest when federal and state funds were flowing in. Now we're telling our story. Beta is a school that is on the move."

According to the director, Beta's president is an active, able participant in fund-raising activities, even though he had no fund-raising experience prior to his arrival at Beta in 1982. The director said, "The president has prospects to cultivate and solicit, and he does it very well. We make sure that he's involved only with major prospects. That's the best use of his time, and he does a good job." Other staff members also spoke of the fund-raising abilities of the president, whom we were not able to interview.

The director is unusual among the senior managers we interviewed because of his strong position about not setting dollar goals for any unit or individual fund raiser. He explained, "I'm really interested in long-term development, in major gifts. That's what we are, a major gifts operation. I want relationships between prospects and disciplines to develop so that gifts are brought in at the right time. If individuals or programs have to achieve specific goals in any given year, the effort might be so overpowering that we'll lose the donor's interest and confidence. Dollar achievement should be looked at only on a long-term basis, not year by year."

Observing that "the bottom line is only one way to see how people are doing," the director said that "another way is to look at how successful the development officer is in attracting and involving the private sector. Have advisory boards been established and are they active and effective? For us, involving the right volunteers is a strong measure of effective performance. Another measure is the confidence that the development officer gains among faculty members." The director evaluates staff performance annually and rewards good performance. He said, "People who are performing well above the others in all the areas I mentioned, not just the bottom line, are compensated well above the others."

First Major Campaign and Campaign Director

After a few focused campaigns in the last ten years, Beta began its first campuswide campaign, for a goal of $100 million, scheduled to run from late 1987 until 1991. At less than halfway through, the campaign had already raised $74 million.

Under the direction of the president and the provost, a universitywide process was used to develop specific campaign goals. The director of development said, "The goal-setting process was good for the institution and the campaign. Widespread participation in planning helped a lot of people on campus to feel that they had a part in the campaign. The faculty understand the goals and the campaign has their support."

Senior development staff members used outside counsel for assistance in planning the campaign and met with counsel on a monthly basis during the first year of the campaign. After that, meetings occurred on a quarterly basis. The director said, "We made a conscious decision not to have the consulting firm manage the campaign because we wanted to be in control."

No single volunteer is chair of the campaign at Beta, a somewhat unusual situation for a major campaign. Instead, a group of twelve individuals make up what is called the Office of the Chair. The director of development explained: "Any one of the twelve could have served as chair. We didn't want to burden one person with the responsibility of serving as chair for the full five years, so the twelve people share the responsibility. This is an atypical arrangement, but because we know our leading volunteers so well from their long-term relationships with the university, we thought it would work well. We're very pleased with how the arrangement is working."

The campaign director came to Beta in 1987 after serving as president of the local community college for nine years. Although the original feasibility study for the campaign indicated that the goal should be no more than $75 million, at the official opening of the campaign, the goal was announced as $100 million. University and campaign leaders are discussing the possibility of raising the goal to as high as $140 million before the campaign ends. (When campaigns go well, goals are often raised while they are still in progress.) "One reason for the increase from the recommended $75 million to $100 million," the campaign director noted, "was political. Our rival institution was in a $100 million campaign, so some people thought that we should do no less than that."

As many experts recommend for major campaigns, fund raisers at Beta began soliciting what are known as leadership, or advance, gifts before the official announcement of the campaign. At Beta, these solicitations before the official opening of the campaign netted $35 million and included gifts from alumni, friends, and some corporations. The campaign director said, "These results were very gratifying, so the original goal of $100 million seemed obtainable. Our advance gifts made it easier to convince people that they were joining a successful team at a university with wide appeal and support locally, regionally, and nationally." The campaign director stressed that the campaign is expected to permanently change the level and scope of fund raising at Beta, by securing both a greater number of gifts and gifts at higher levels for the annual fund.

Campaign activities closely follow a detailed campaign plan approved by the office of the chair. The campaign director described Beta's campaign plan: "In the first year, we focused on what we called our lead gifts, gifts of $1 million or more. We had twenty-seven such gifts on the gift table, and to date we have received twenty-one of the twenty-seven. In the second year, we are focusing on what we call major gifts, which are gifts of $100,000 or more. When we begin our third year, we will focus on what we call special gifts, which are gifts under $100,000."

To start the campaign, alumni volunteers hosted dinners and receptions locally and in several major cities across the country and along the West Coast. The university had not previously been active outside of its state. The campaign director said, "These events were the first contact we have had with some alumni in twenty years. It is difficult to say hello and immediately ask for money, so we started by talking about the university's accomplishments and mentioned that we were in our first comprehensive campaign. Then I would go back later to set up a committee of key alumni for prospect rating sessions. Our cultivation of out-of-state prospects may not result in major gifts for this campaign, but we expect to see increased results in the annual fund and in long-term relationships."

Beta has a full-time staff person working to increase Beta's coverage in the national media. The campaign director noted that Beta has been more visible in national publications such as *Time Magazine* and *USA Today*. Seeing the university mentioned in these magazines might be just the spark an alumnus needs, he said. "We are getting some unsolicited gifts, which is both gratifying and surprising, and I think they are the result of the national publicity that we are deliberately promoting."

The campaign is funded by a portion of the interest generated by cash gifts. The director explained: "The first six months' interest on cash gifts is contributed to the campaign budget. For example, if the annual interest rate is 10 percent, the budget gets $5,000 from a $100,000 gift. By the fourth or fifth year, as cash gifts come in and interest accrues, we may not need the full six months' interest."

A campaign document emphasizes that volunteer leadership is the single most important ingredient in the campaign.

The campaign director said, "Our volunteer leadership has been the key — having the right people who have a strong belief in the university making the right contacts. Probably 80 percent of gifts are solicited by volunteers. We have approximately forty volunteer committees across the university with an average number of twenty people per committee, so we have 800 potential volunteer fund raisers. Realistically, probably half of those are actively involved in fund raising."

Director of Foundation Relations

The foundation relations staff has developed a computerized data base of 400 foundations for systematic cultivation. The director of foundation relations stressed the importance of good research to identify good foundation prospects, including reviewing the annual reports of foundations. He noted that what foundations say they do in their brochures is not always what they actually do.

This director is optimistic about the future of fund raising at Beta and about the campaign: "The foundation world is growing in this region. We're seeing the proliferation of small family-managed foundations, with $200,000 or $300,000 in assets. Some of these are willing not only to give us commitments over the years for tens of thousands of dollars per year but also to talk about passing the corpus on to us at the end of their lifetimes. That is very fertile terrain. We hope to get $8 million in foundation gifts for the campaign by making carefully targeted solicitations that realistically match university needs with foundation interests. We're at about 60 percent of that right now, so I am confident that we'll be over the goal."

The director described his role as typical in the sense that he represents the university to foundations, but how he works to develop good relationships with faculty members he sees as not so typical. As a former faculty member himself who also worked in faculty development, he understands the faculty members' point of view, and he also understands why development staff members and faculty members may not always understand each other. "Some faculty members don't understand why development can't do everything for them. Sometimes faculty members expect the development office to write proposals, prepare budgets, identify possible funding sources, and then hand them the check. Or faculty members may come in April and say they need money for the summer. I tell them that is virtually impossible, but if they want to talk about *next* summer, maybe we can get something done. Even when faculty members do get around to raising money for their own projects, they have very little time in which to do it, and they are easily frustrated. They usually also think their projects are the most important items."

Policies for submitting proposals to foundations also sometimes cause misunderstanding and conflict between development staff and faculty. As fund-raising activities have increased throughout the nonprofit sector, foundations have been overwhelmed by funding requests, and officials at many of the country's largest foundations now stipulate that they will consider only one request at a time from any particular institution or organization. At Beta, as at many other institutions, this stipulation has resulted in the need for official universitywide policies to restrict, coordinate, and track proposal submissions.

Describing proposal submission at Beta as "anarchic in many ways," the director of foundation relations said, "On a campus of this size, we can't, nor do we want to, thwart faculty initiative. Furthermore, the academic decision-making process is sacrosanct in regard to who submits proposals, so unless a dean says not to talk to someone about a project, we try to get money for any faculty member who asks. Nevertheless, after serious review, we decided that submissions to eighteen foundations need to be managed at the provost's level, with friendly comments from us, because of the foundation's complaints about multiple submissions or stipulations about the conditions under which they will review proposals."

Development staff members drafted guidelines for submitting proposals that were signed by the provost and were distributed to faculty members. The director noted that in response "a dozen or so faculty members who were experienced in raising private money wrote heated letters to the provost, saying they resented the procedure and would ignore it. Some complaints were legitimate. They said, 'For ten years I have had a good relationship with the so-and-so foundation and nobody is going to tell me I can't talk to them.'"

   This director stressed that viewing faculty as a constituency that the development office serves rather than as a competing or hostile faction has helped promote better coordination and cooperation between the staff and the faculty. He feels frustrated "when faculty members think we are gatekeepers who play favorites. We would actually like to reduce the number of foundations requiring clearance, but those demands come from the foundations themselves." The director feels that cultivating relationships with faculty members and educating them about the development process are important. He said, "I have an open door for faculty and I talk to them often. It is important for development staff to be responsible with faculty. I always make sure before they leave that we have an understanding about who is going to do what. Maintaining credibility with faculty is essential because we're not raising money to put into a bank account. We're raising money to see something happen. And where does it happen? With the faculty. They're the ones with the ideas. The development officer is just the expediter."

Director of Scholarship Development

Beta has a veteran fund raiser in the position of director of scholarship development — the only position of its kind in the schools we studied. The director said, "When I first started raising money for scholarships, we concentrated on getting help for the first two years, with the idea that students would find a way to handle financing the next years. That didn't always work. It's dreadful to put students in college for a year and then take that scholarship away. They end up with nothing to show for their time but the $5,000 in loans they have to repay. Now we have more sophisticated donors who want to see students through school in specific programs." The campaign includes a goal of $15 million for scholarships, which has already been exceeded by $2 million.

This director and his staff sometimes find individual donors for students who cannot be helped by the financial aid office. He said, "We still have a few donors who will support these kids from time to time and keep them in school, but this type of donor is becoming extinct. At one time, we had more than twenty such donors we could tap, and now we have only five or six." Another change the director has observed is the increase in scholarships from corporations. "We still get more scholarship money from individuals than we do from foundations or industry, but our industry scholarships are increasing. Often we speak to the personnel or human relations people in corporations — not usually the same people other development officers are dealing with, so we're not competing."

With statesmanship and confidence in Beta, the director was able to promote considerable goodwill for the university as well as generate a sizable amount of annual scholarship money by helping to get a statewide scholarship program under way: "This privately funded scholarship program pays twenty students $6,000 a year for their entire undergraduate careers, to be used at any of the state's three public universities. This program originally started because the foundation providing the scholarships wanted to give us and the other two public universities in this state a certain number of scholarships each year. I suggested that they award the scholarships and let the winners make their own selections about which school to attend. I'll be honest and say I think that was what they wanted me to suggest."

The program has been in operation for three years. Each year so far, seventeen out of the twenty winners have chosen to attend Beta, and, the director noted, "We might get all twenty this year. I thought we'd get the winners and we do. It was a gamble, but I figured that we would get more than 50 percent. I didn't dream we'd get as many as we do."

Director of Alumni Relations

The director of alumni relations said the decision to professionalize and expand all areas of university relations has been critical in Beta's fund-raising success. "We've been fortunate at Beta under our new administration," the director noted. "All institutional advancement areas have grown here because of the understanding on this campus that fund raising can't be successful unless all aspects of university relations are successful."

Having served as an evaluator of alumni operations in several other major public universities, this director has an expanded view of how the separate areas in university relations work congruently to achieve overall university goals. "In every institution the team evaluated," he said, "there was a lack of understanding of the role each unit plays in institutional advancement. Often, the development office got more resources than the alumni association, the public relations office, government relations, and cultural affairs. It was difficult for these units to grow while resources for the fund-raising unit were so high."

The director discussed the growth in alumni programs at Beta. "When I came in," he said, "the alumni association was at the end of a five-year feud with the institution, partially over losing control of scholarship and annual fund operations. We lost a number of active volunteers. My staff and I worked to rekindle the enthusiasm of the remaining volunteers and to recruit new ones. Our current board of directors, which numbers forty-eight members who come from seven or eight different states, is a great group of people." The budget for alumni affairs when the director arrived was less than $400,000 and the staff numbered twelve. The budget at the time of the site visit was $1.2 million, and the staff numbered twenty-five.

The director said that Beta once had a dues program to fund alumni affairs. At that time, the annual fund, the athletic department, and some other units were all making solicitations. "Overall, we were putting twelve pieces in everybody's mailbox every year," he said, "competing basically for the same $50 and communicating in-house confusion to alumni. We concluded that competing at the mailbox was hurting us all, so we dropped our dues program in favor of financing from the annual fund. That was not a popular concept in 1982. My peers were critical and warned that development people would end up running the alumni association. Today, some of those same colleagues are studying our program because they now want to drop their dues programs."

Alumni relations staff members have created some unusual services to keep alumni informed about current events and new developments on campus. One service is a television program that is produced on campus with the help of the local American Broadcasting Company (ABC) station. The monthly program is aired on ABC locally and on cable throughout the rest of the state. Staff members also produce a half-hour radio program that is aired weekly on sixteen stations throughout the state. In both the television and radio programs, Beta faculty, deans, the president, and vice presidents present features on aspects of the university of interest to alumni.

The director described another unusual service provided by alumni relations: "We operate a national call-in computer bulletin board service, which began with a donated personal computer and some software that cost $25. We call it a computer magazine, and it's run by a bright computer student who volunteers his time. Alumni can get information about job openings, sports scores, cultural events, financial aid, and student recruitment." In four years, the computer magazine has received over 40,000 calls from all over the country, and the telephone line is always busy. The number of calls, estimated to be the maximum possible for the time period, "represents just the tip of the iceberg of people's interest in this service," the director said.

Alumni relations staff members assist twenty-eight fully active and numerous "more casual" alumni clubs. The director believes these clubs contribute to fund-raising success by raising Beta's visibility in the communities in which they operate. Active clubs are involved in recruiting students, developing scholarships, arranging club events, and, in some cases, producing their own newsletters.

Better record keeping is another change in the alumni relations area that supports fund-raising efforts. "When I came," the director said, "we were still using an old batch processing system for alumni records. Now, with our own software, we produce directories and questionnaires and even have a campaign tracking program. We've merged many things into our computer system that were kept separately by development people. Deans can get lists, labels, and reports at no cost. Each year for five years we have increased this service to the campus by more than 50 percent. This year we'll exceed 4,000 campus requests from this system."

Director of Internal Campaign

Part of the overall campaign plan at Beta includes an internal program to solicit campaign gifts from faculty and staff members. Although internal solicitations have become fairly common in institutions with major campaigns, the internal campaign at Beta is noteworthy not only because of the careful planning underlying the solicitations but also because the staff member responsible for the campaign serves as an excellent example of how managers can enhance fund raising through imaginative staffing.

The senior staff member responsible for the internal campaign has been involved at Beta in many different capacities throughout his life. "I am almost seventy-six years old, and I have lived here all my life," he said, "so I know a few people. I was born in this city and was an undergraduate here. I joined the faculty for eight years and then went into business for twenty-five years. After I retired from business, the president asked me to come back as an academic dean, which I did for seven years." Two years ago, the former dean attempted to retire again, but another president of Beta persuaded him to remain, this time as the development officer for the college he had attended as a student and then later served as a faculty member and dean. The president emphasized to the dean how useful the dean's extensive community contacts would be in raising money for the college. When he later asked the dean to assume responsibility for Beta's first internal campaign, he used a similar argument, citing the dean's considerable network of internal relationships.

The former dean said, "Being chair of this effort is a particular challenge because I know a certain amount of conflict always exists between faculty and staff members and the administration. I insisted on two conditions for the internal campaign: that donors could specify how their gifts were to be used

and that there be no coercion of any faculty or staff member—
other than administrators, whom I figure I can coerce!"

The dean has suggested three categories for specifying
gifts. The first category includes the official campaign priorities for each particular college. The second category includes
campuswide projects to benefit the university community, such
as support for child care, an endowment for professional staff
development, or an endowment for faculty travel. The third
category includes specific projects in each college that are not
covered by campaign goals. For instance, a college might decide it wants to create a faculty/staff lounge that would cost
$50,000. If the college had fifty faculty and staff members, this
college would set the suggested individual contribution at $1,000.
The dean stressed that he encourages faculty members to desig-
nate gifts for projects they have a personal interest in, but "I
told them we would not accept contributions to themselves or
their own projects. That's not giving."

To start the campaign, the dean wrote letters to the 400
administrators at Beta and the remaining 12,500 members of
the university community. Each college or administrative department has a solicitation committee, with chairs appointed by its
dean or vice president. Committees involve both faculty and
staff, and every faculty and staff member will be solicited by
a peer.

The dean said, "We don't have an official goal for the in-
house campaign. The campaign consultants tried to insist on
a goal, but I said no. If we give the faculty members a goal,
they'll just rebel. Nine people from the faculty and staff have
already given a total of $1.67 million. My own optimistic projec-
tion is that gifts from faculty and staff members will exceed $20
million by the time the campaign ends."

Other Aspects of Fund-Raising Programs

The university recently constructed an attractive building on
campus to house its foundation, most of the development staff,
the alumni association, and the offices of community and public service and federal relations. The building was constructed

without donated funds. The foundation not only needed additional space but, according to the foundation's chief financial officer, "We needed space that made a positive statement about the university and the foundation. You can't bring somebody into a dark cubbyhole to ask them for a substantial amount of money. This building reflects the prestige and importance of the university." The director of development thinks the building helps the fund-raising effort at Beta because development staff members "feel good operating out of this place. They know they are part of a successful organization, and they're proud of that." Most of the development staff members that we interviewed mentioned that being all together in the new building has increased and improved their internal communication.

Advisory Boards. Many senior development staff members pointed out that the relationship between the university and the city figures strongly in Beta's fund-raising success. "Even though this is a large city," the director of development said, "the university has been a primary focus for the community for a number of years. The relationship beteen Beta and the city is very congenial." Many staff and faculty members are prominent in community affairs, and many community leaders are formally involved in some way with the university. The administration at Beta has encouraged the involvement over the last ten years, which, according to the director of development, "has turned out to be very helpful in our fund-raising efforts."

The community is involved in the institutional affairs of Beta primarily through advisory boards. These boards have been in operation in many units of the university for decades. The boards were originally created to advise on the curriculum and other matters. Most of the boards have expanded to provide support for fund raising and other institutional advancement activities.

Advisory boards generally meet quarterly. Deans appoint the members, who are drawn from community leaders with special interest or expertise in a discipline or professional area. Development officers at Beta have played a major role in strengthening existing boards, in helping deans to enhance the functioning of the boards, and in encouraging the creation of boards in new areas. One development officer said, "We don't recruit a group of people and then decide who's going to be the chair. We first recruit the chair, who then helps the dean recruit other members for the board. We do everything we can to make advisory board members feel that they're part of the university, although we make it clear that the advisory groups are support groups, not policy-making boards."

One college development officer described how an advisory board in his college influenced programming: "Development staff members drafted a fund-raising case statement for the heart center and presented it to the advisory board members for their input. Board members know by now that we truly want their suggestions. The board suggested that the center increase its emphasis on prevention of heart disease. As a result, the heart center developed a whole unit in prevention that has been very active and visible in community education." Members of advisory boards also provide support, which can involve making or soliciting major gifts, getting speakers for a meeting, or hosting a private reception.

This development officer said that although some people might think he should be "cranking out direct mail," working with advisory boards is his highest priority. "Soliciting funds is not the first thing to do when starting a fund-raising program," he said. "It's the fourth thing. The first thing is to open an office and get staff. The second thing is to work with volunteers to create an advisory board. While getting your business cards printed, don't worry about sending out direct mail or making a list of foundations. Instead, work to form advisory boards, because they will positively influence everything else you do. The third thing is to develop communications materials such as case statements, pamphlets, fact sheets, videos, and tailor-made grant proposals, all with input from your advisory board. Developing these materials with the advisory board builds consensus and helps to clarify plans. After you finish these three things, you can start soliciting funds."

This development officer, who is a former faculty member in business administration, also said that he plans fund-raising events around advisory board meetings. "I want to keep fund-raising events, which I don't much believe in, from proliferating. One fund-raising event per year for each major unit is enough. Events tend to syphon off effort that should be put into soliciting major gifts." He believes strongly in volunteer involvement as a way to ensure fund-raising success. He added, "If you're selling $100 dinner tickets, it doesn't make much difference what people's interests are or whether you have participation in planning. But if you're talking about major gifts, then you've got to match donor interest and involvement with giving opportunity. People don't give to meet needs. They give to reinforce success, to be a part of greatness. Quality, success, progress, energy, and vision — these are the things people want to be part of and support."

Annual Fund. The annual fund program is in a much earlier phase of its evolution than other fund-raising programs at Beta, and alumni gifts are considerably lower at Beta than gifts from other donor groups. For several years, some deans have conducted their own annual telephone campaigns to ensure discretionary money for their colleges, but universitywide efforts have been sporadic and have had uneven results. The director of development indicated that other factors, in addition to the fact that Beta has not had a comprehensive annual fund program, kept the total for alumni gifts low. He said, "Our alumni body is relatively young because this institution grew rapidly in the 1960s, and until recently, we did not have a strong alumni program to make sure alumni knew they were important. Also, until very recently, gifts could be received in a number of places. A gift to the chemistry department might go directly to the accounting office and never be counted in our totals." To remedy this situation, the president of Beta created a new office for receiving and accounting for gifts. The director of development is now the only person on campus authorized to receive and acknowledge private gifts.

    In 1989, the central office, under the supervision of the new director of the annual fund, coordinated the first universitywide comprehensive telephone program to reach all alumni.

The director said, "Direct mail was our predominant way of reaching prospects for the annual fund prior to last fall. Now we have leased a house close to campus, have hired students to make calls, and have hired a professional firm to manage the phonathon and provide an on-site supervisor. Our rival university, which has had a comprehensive annual fund program for seven years, received $700,000 in pledges for the whole year, while we received over $600,000 in pledges in the first six months of our new program."

The program has a pledge rate of 24 percent so far. The director said this rate was "very good," considering that most alumni had never been called before. About 20 percent of the donors who had never given before made pledges, which to taled $283,000. "Start-up costs are high," the director noted, "because we have a lot of overhead, but we are acquiring new donors. We may only clear $60,000 to $65,000 this year, but we are building a business; we are not just investing for a one-year return. We want to build a foundation of donors to develop prospects for major gifts, so what we're doing this year will pay off for years to come. We use a very segmented approach that we believe will help us to upgrade individual gifts over the years."

The director noted that in some universities unrestricted funds have increased only at the average rate of 10 percent a year, while money for specific purposes has increased 280 percent per year. The director indicated that in addition to working to develop the overall annual gifts program, staff members will also be wrestling with the complex problems confronting annual fund staff members in most institutions: looking for ways to increase the amount of unrestricted funds and to equitably charge the costs for the annual fund to the respective colleges.

Corporate Gifts. Beta's part-time consultant for corporation relations came to Beta after a long career as a program officer in a large corporate foundation. He consults with development staff members on corporate solicitations and also solicits major corporate gifts for the capital campaign. "Industry is growing in this state," he said, "unlike in many other states. Most companies relocating here want to be first-class citizens of the community. Giving money to university development is an important part of getting settled in this area. We are projecting an $18 million corporate goal, or 18 percent of the total for the campaign."

The consultant pointed out that when he began working for a corporate foundation in 1960, public institutions received only about 20 percent of all corporate gifts to higher education. Not only were fewer public than private institutions engaged in systematic fund raising, but many corporations had policies restricting gifts to private institutions on the grounds that the company's tax dollars already supported public institutions. "Currently," this consultant said, "public institutions receive 50 percent or more of total corporate donations." He attributes that increase to three factors. First, many public universities are in the top ranks of the country's research institutions. Second, corporations hire many of their professional people from public institutions. Third, public institutions are doing a better job in soliciting corporate gifts than previously. "At one time," he said, "it would have been common to run up against a corporate donor who didn't believe in supporting public education, but this is happening less and less often now."

Donor Research. Recently, the development research staff has expanded to include, in addition to the director of research, two full-time researchers and three part-time people responsible for managing the computerized prospect tracking system, converting information from an old computer system to the new system, and clipping and filing articles from daily newspapers and periodicals. The research staff uses standard directories to gather information about foundation and corporation prospects. To gather information on individual prospects, the staff uses directories and periodicals from the local area and from other cities and states in which development efforts are focused. The research staff also uses a commercial computer network to secure information from corporate and foundation annual reports and periodicals, but only when time is short.

The director said, "We sometimes operate in a crisis mode, but not as much as we used to because of both better training and better planning. Now we follow our long-range plans and also react to immediate needs." The director tries to anticipate what development officers need by looking at various academic areas and at projects in progress. She thinks about new prospects and attends volunteer campaign committee meetings and major gifts meetings to pass along names of prospects.

Gathering information from development officers, deans, and faculty members regarding contacts with prospects is important in keeping donor records accurate. In many institutions, the prospect research office asks development officers to complete and return a contact report form. However, development officers often do not file these reports in a timely fashion or at all. This director has addressed the problem by asking not for a special report but for "something — a copy of the letter confirming an appointment, or a thank-you letter after an appointment, anything — to document telephone, mail, or face-to-face contact with a prospect. We put that information into our computer system so that we have a record of every contact with prospects. Since we eliminated special forms, we actually get more important information about current contacts, which we can use to follow up for more detailed descriptions of significant contacts with prospects." Research staff members can produce lists of specific development officers' prospects and activities or a chronological list of all contacts with specific prospects.

The research staff also maintains the computerized prospect identification system. Local and regional volunteer committees identify and rate prospects, using a list of factors such as types of assets and identification with the university. Research staff members can produce lists of prospects by ratings or alphabetically, indicating who gave the ratings, when the ratings were given, and where the committee that did the rating is located.

The director of research constantly looks for new sources of information and carefully evaluates the accuracy of information from all sources. She said, "Eventually, I would like somebody to go through the real estate microfiche from the assessor's office and make note of properties that our prospects own. We could also have people investigate more corporations outside the state. And I would love to get involved in the next big alumni survey to make that a source for development information as well as alumni records." The director noted that she continuously reviews options for new lists of prospects but generally finds that the information from commercial services is not current. The director indicated that prospects might be furious if they knew the kind of records Beta keeps, even though the basis of the records is public information. She said, "I don't publicize the fact that we're developing profiles, and I write memos to development officers from time to time to remind them that the profiles are not to be seen by committee members. It is important that we keep information on prospects confidential, and we must also be certain that no information is in prospect files that shouldn't be there. Prospects have the right at any time to ask to see their files. Should that ever happen, I don't want prospects to be offended or to sue the university."

Analysis of Fund Raising at Beta

Outstanding characteristics of the fund-raising program at Beta are the leadership of the director of development, involvement of volunteers in fund raising, and emphasis on constituent relationships. Presidential leadership and institutional commitment to fund raising are also notable characteristics.

The director of development's leadership of the fund-raising staff is the core element in this successful fund-raising program. The director of development is a highly experienced fund raiser with strong management skills and a personal style that encourages fund raisers to work as a team, take risks, and be professionally autonomous. Staff members stressed the impact of the chief development officer's positive influence more in this institution than at any other in the study.

The director of development also has created an emphasis on long-term relationships with multiple constituencies to ensure the best overall and long-term fund-raising results at Beta. In contrast to national urban trends, the population of the city in which Beta is located has grown more than 36 percent over the last twenty-five years. From its earliest days, the university has "belonged" to the community. As both the university and the city have grown, Beta has consciously maintained this relationship. In addition to university trustee boards, numerous hardworking advisory boards have operated in many of the university's colleges and divisions for several decades. When Beta began fund raising in earnest ten years ago, trustee and advisory boards were natural sources for well-placed volunteers and prospects.

At Beta, staff members consistently emphasized relationships in the fund-raising effort, a rather different overall focus than that of the other institutions we studied. Although staff members were fully committed to raising money, they often expressed the belief that dollars raised were the result of nurturing of relationships, both within the university and within the community. Alumni relations programs at Beta are creative and entrepreneurial, and a strong tie exists between alumni programs and fund-raising efforts.

The strength of institutional commitment to fund raising is apparent at Beta in many factors, not the least of which is the president's leadership in fund raising. He advocates processes that support fund raising and participates in the securing of major gifts. Other indicators of growing institutional commitment are the expansion of staff and programs in all aspects of institutional advancement, the careful attention to refining and communicating Beta's image, and the implementation of universitywide processes to set fund-raising priorities and policies.

The overall management of fund raising at Beta is a composite of strengths and emerging characteristics. Within the fund-raising unit, planning is more intuitive than formal (with the notable exception of the campaign) and goal setting is not concrete. The number of fund-raising programs, staff members, and dollars raised has rapidly increased at Beta, and some management practices and systems still reflect the period when fund raising was a much smaller, much less complex operation.

The director of development is responding to the need for a more suitable organizational arrangement (for example, to have professional staff members reporting to several senior staff members instead of to the director), for more formal standards and policies (for example, for gift accounting and acknowledgments, for assigning prospects, and for sharing prospect information), and for better computer systems to address complex needs for information and communication. However, there is no indication that the director of development will change his strong stance against setting concrete fund-raising goals for individual fund raisers and programs.

In spite of rapid growth and change, the fund-raising effort was smooth-running, harmonious, and comprehensive — as a result of both the director of development's leadership and the highly professional staff. Most of the staff members were not Beta alumni, and their commitment to the university was based more on respect than on affection. The fund-raising staff at Beta, an interesting blend of new and experienced fund raisers, includes people who came to their jobs at Beta from senior positions in national politics, the arts, academic administration, and university teaching.

In summary, what can others learn from Beta's experiences? The factors we identified as contributing to fund-raising effectiveness at Beta are as follows:

- Use of existing university strengths and traditions as fund-raising resources
- Strong leadership by the director of development, who encourages teamwork, risk taking, and staff autonomy and who elicits staff support because of his personal style and professional expertise
- Systematic, progressive expansion of the development staff to build comprehensive fund-raising programs for the university and individual colleges
- Centralized fund-raising organization with an emphasis on providing services to colleges
- Emphasis on developing and maintaining positive relationships with internal and external constituencies
- Effective presidential participation in fund raising and leadership in setting institutional fund-raising goals and priorities
- Focus on long-term relationships and long-term results

- Judicious use of outside counsel, combined with internal intuition and knowledge, for campaign planning
- Emphasis on creating a national image for Beta
- Integration of all institutional advancement activities to support fund raising
- Creative and original alumni programming and services
- Carefully planned internal campaign, managed by a development officer with internal relationships that are extensive, long term, and positive
- Strong institutional commitment to provide staff, budget, and office space for development activities
- Recent extensive investment in universitywide comprehensive telemarketing program to enhance the annual fund, with the long-term purpose of developing and identifying major gift prospects

4

Not Afraid
to Break the Rules:

A Private Doctoral University

> GAMMA: Strong leadership at several levels as well as systematic
> planning and management and an outstanding entrepreneurial
> approach are the distinctive features of Gamma's fund-raising
> program.

This private doctoral university, with an enrollment of about
7,500 and educational and general expenditures of more than
$151 million, is located in a small town on the outskirts of a
major northern city. Over the last decade, private support for
this university has increased dramatically, from $4.8 million in
1979 to $34.3 million in 1989, more than a 600 percent increase.

Descriptive statistics for Gamma appear in Table 4.1.
Gamma's tuition is close to the highest for all institutions of this
type. All other institutional characteristics but two, endowment
and enrollment, are also above the median. All voluntary support outcomes are above the median and above predicted outcomes. The organizational chart for the development staff at
Gamma appears in Figure 4.1.

President J.

Everyone at Gamma tells the story about President J. and
Gamma's fund-raising campaign in the late 1970s. Consultants
had advised the president that Gamma could expect to raise
$40 million in a major campaign. President J. said that figure
was much too low. He added a one to the number and set the
goal at $140 million. The campaign, completed in 1985, raised

Table 4.1. Descriptive Statistics (1985–1987 Average) for Gamma University (Private Doctoral).

	Range for Type			This Institution		
	High	Median	Low	Actual	Predicted	Difference
Institutional Characteristics:						
Educational/General Expenditures	=341,917,000	$85,615,100	$22,843,000	$151,323,313	—	—
Endowment	=705,601,300	$100,870,800	$14,108,300	$95,918,856	—	—
Expenditures per Student	$30,300	$10,100	$4,600	$20,408	—	—
Cost of Tuition	$12,500	$9,300	$4,300	$12,088	—	—
Alumni of Record	148,000	56,200	9,800	63,468	—	—
Enrollment	35,300	3,300	800	7,415	—	—
Age of Institution	220 years	120 years	60 years	136 years	—	—
Fund-Raising Results:						
Total Voluntary Support	$42,564,100	$11,534,200	$1,774,700	$20,272,258	$18,011,696	+ 1.13
Alumni Gifts	$25,263,900	$3,275,000	$0	$4,830,422	$3,993,006	+ 1.21
Nonalumni Gifts	$21,922,000	$2,599,700	$439,800	$4,506,203	$2,169,928	+ 2.08
Corporation Gifts	$10,949,000	$3,262,100	$314,000	$4,796,835	$4,532,869	+ 1.06
Foundation Gifts	$17,625,300	$1,707,300	$56,500	$6,138,798	$5,779,479	+ 1.06

Figure 4.1. Organizational Chart for Gamma University.

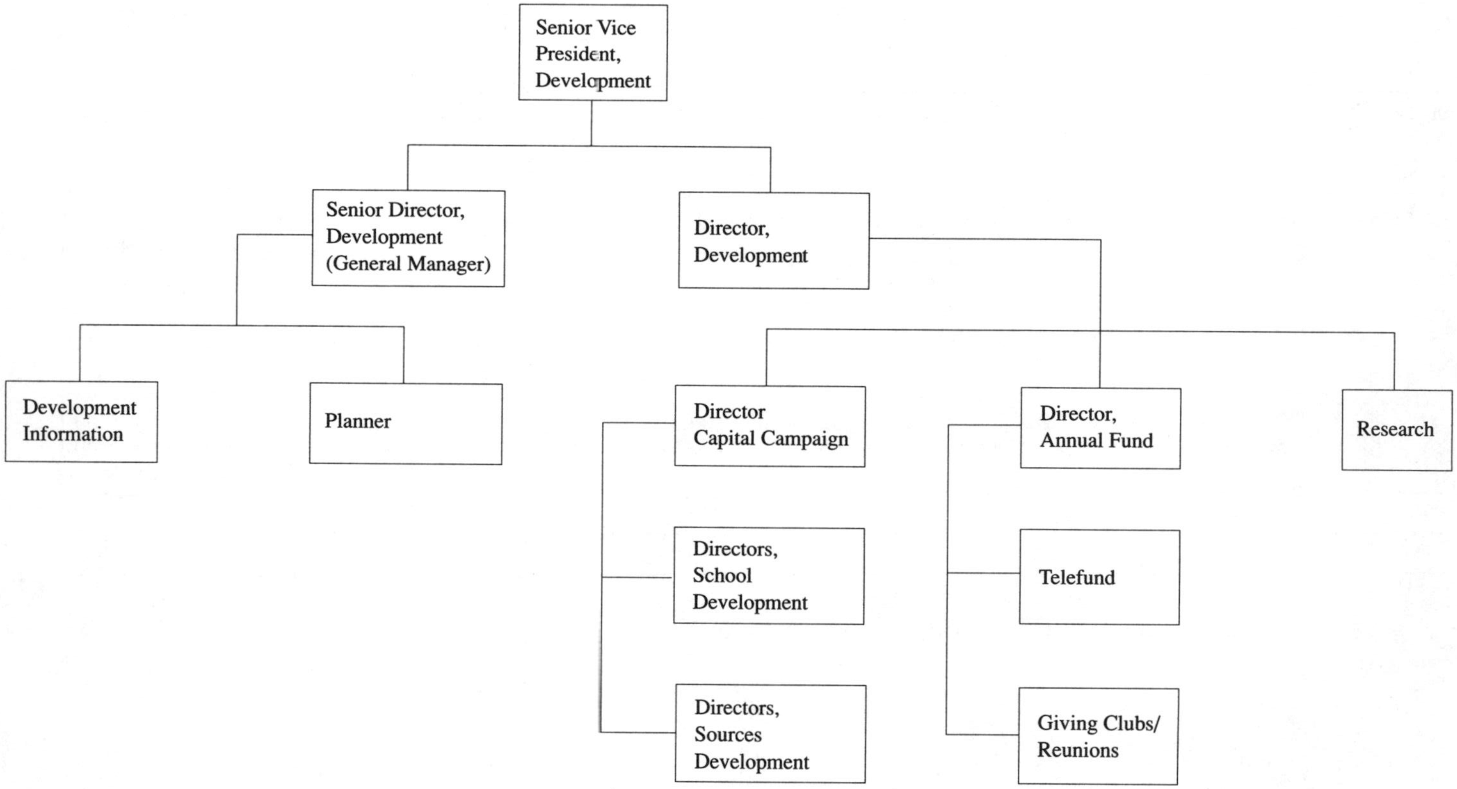

$145 million and laid the foundation for the present campaign for $250 million.

The president indicated that the goal of the present campaign is to increase the annual level of total voluntary support from $30 million to $50 million a year. "During the first campaign," he said, "I was very active in soliciting gifts from the $100,000 level on up. Now I set targets and make sure everybody understands these targets, and I don't get involved in individual fund raising for less than $1 million." He noted that personal contact with donors is the key to large gifts and added, "One of the remarkable things about our previous campaign was that the bulk of large gifts were from people who had no earlier interest in the university but who were persuaded to give through personal contact. By the end of the campaign, alumni had become enthusiastic about what was happening here. I decided we should start a new campaign almost immediately to capitalize on the alumni's new interest. Now we are getting much more money from alumni than previously."

The success of the campaign widely altered perceptions about the university among internal and external constituents. One staff member said, "In our first campaign we found a donor population worth $100 million that we didn't even know we had. Now, we think differently. We assume a prospect base is limited only by our own imaginations."

The president is often given credit for many other positive changes at Gamma, including significant improvements in academic quality, financial viability, and research, as well as the development of numerous international ties and programs. President J. was described as "a great thinker" and "a citizen of the world—the first person I've ever known personally that I think of as a great man."

Senior Vice President of Development

At Gamma, the senior vice president plays a critical role in setting the mission and direction of the institution as well as in leading the fund-raising effort. This vice president has a professional degree, taught for many years in one of Gamma's professional schools, and eventually became the dean of that school. The president said of him, "He had no background in fund raising, but he is a very energetic person and a person I get along with very well. I knew he could do the job and he has." Development staff members indicated that a strong relationship exists between the vice president and the president and that the vice president has considerable authority throughout the university.

One staff member said, "He is a dreamer, a visionary. He is very close to the president and has a great deal of influence on what we do. If he is concerned, for instance, about a certain school, everything stops and everybody works on that school." Another said, "The vice president is a superb fund raiser, but he is not a mentor because we don't really have the personal connection with him that mentoring would require. When we make calls with him, he's not there as a helper or as an adviser. He's an entrepreneur and a connection maker."

The vice president talked about his "training" as a fund raiser. "When I took this job, in 1979," he said, "I put an ad in the *Chronicle of Higher Education* to fill directors' positions in the annual fund, corporate/foundation relations, capital campaign, and bequests. For three months, I learned fund raising from the 120 people who applied for those jobs."

Today Gamma is internationally known, but this was not always the case. "The whole idea of promoting ourselves was unheard of here not too long ago," the vice president said. "It was out of character. I distinctly remember going to other cities and having to explain who we were and where we were located. Now I don't have to do that, and our appointments come easily." The vice president convinced Gamma's administrators to buy a helicopter to fly in out-of-town prospects. "I have not been criticized once for the expense," he said.

The vice president has specific expectations of the development staff and clearly communicates them. For instance, he outlined his expectations when traveling: "We put out guidelines for international travel, such as make sure you've contacted the United States embassy for a cultural briefing and always go to a museum when going to a foreign country before seeing anybody. If you go to a museum, you begin to understand the place a little better. If you're traveling with me, I want five appointments a day. Get a car because we can't waste time hailing a cab. Our productivity goes up if we get a car. Don't talk to me about my third appointment of the day when I'm on the way to my first. And I want to see a good trip report."

The vice president said the quality of his development staff compares favorably with the quality of the development staff at any other institution. "Our turnover last year was almost zero. Right now we have 2 or 3 openings out of 116 positions. We have a good percentage of staff members with master's degrees in business administration and some who have lived all over the world. They could be working at a lot of other places. At staff meetings, I ask the development officers to think about why they work for a nonprofit organization to evoke their sense of pride. I tell them that we're in this as a family and that what we do is important. I remind them of what they've been able to do that no one else thought was possible for this institution. I remind them that what they're doing is extraordinary."

Senior Director of Development

The senior director of development said that ten years ago Gamma was what he would call a traditional university, but it is "much more entrepreneurial now." Using terminology that reflects the fund-raising philosophy at Gamma, the senior director, whose background is in higher education finance, presented an overview of the development division and his function: "My role is basically that of general manager of the division called university development. Under this umbrella we pull together fund raising, alumni affairs, and publications and communications."

The fund-raising unit "is a sales organization, and we behave like one," he said. "We use the same management tools that sales organizations use. We set dollar and activity goals and monitor progress. We train our fund raisers in professional sales techniques and combine that training with traditional fund-raising approaches, such as cultivating donors." At Gamma, fund raising is guided, according to the senior director, "by the four P's of marketing—product, promotion, place, and price. The products we sell are buildings, endowed chairs, and scholarships. To sell them, we need to promote our image as a high-quality institution through publications and communications. Place has to do with our location and how we can use it to interest donors, locally and elsewhere. Price applies to the cost for an endowed chair, which is now $1 million. Someday the cost will be $1.25 million or $1.5 million. We tell people that they have to endow the chairs before we raise the price. It works."

The senior director noted that Gamma uses approaches other institutions might not be comfortable with. "For instance," he said, "we have cold called prospects interested in animal welfare to solicit donations for the veterinary school, a practice that many people would frown on. But our veterinary school spends a great deal of its time and resources on animal welfare. We were also one of the first universities to be aggressive in telemarketing at a time when many people thought it was heresy to train and pay students to do telemarketing."

The senior director indicated that, unlike a sales organization, the university does not pay commissions or bonuses to fund-raising staff members but has considered this practice. He said, "It is a controversial issue. We raise the question, every now and then, in discussions with the chairman of the finance committee of the board. We think it is appropriate to have financial incentives based on achievement for development staff members, but our board isn't ready for commissions. We do reward people based on performance with varying levels of annual salary increases."

The trustees' decision to provide a seven-year campaign budget of $42 million is a reflection of institutional commitment to fund raising, the senior director said. Early projections indicated that Gamma might actually spend about $2 million less than that sum.

In response to a question about increased competition in fund raising, the senior director said, "The tough competition is not so much for dollars as it is for good fund raisers. Many fund raisers are now leaving higher education to become vice presidents of fund raising elsewhere and to earn higher salaries. Hospitals, for instance, in some cases promise to pay university fund-raising personnel salaries that are 25 percent higher than what colleges and universities can pay."

Director of Development

The director of development is the chief operating officer of development at Gamma. All staff members with direct fund-raising responsibilities report to him, either directly or through other managers. He is the ranking officer with direct fund-raising experience and the pivotal person in Gamma's blending of the art of fund raising with sales management techniques. He said, "One of my responsibilities is to set and meet fund-raising goals and the other — which I see as my primary responsibility — is to build a long-term, viable development program for this institution. I have tried to instill in the institution and its constituencies a sense that the future of the institution is tied directly to the success of its development program — to show how the institution and program are linked and to show that both have enormous potential for continued growth. I do some direct fund raising, but I cannot be out on the road much because my administrative responsibilities are critical. The time that I spend with prospects is almost an indulgence."

Noting that he is influenced by the philosophy of Gamma's president, the director said, "I have always taken my cues about organization and direction from our president. The way the development department is organized follows very closely what the president admires and has strengthened in the university — a strong central core with strong independent school components and programs and an emphasis on shared effort and cooperation."

The director explained that Gamma did not have the classic, or traditional, fund-raising history of many of America's private universities. He said, "Gamma was founded by a group of faculty members from an Ivy League school to educate the sons and daughters of the local community. It was considered to be to Gamma's credit that it didn't cater to the rich. Gamma was independent and paid its way through tuition, earned income, and the subsidies that low faculty salaries and deferred building maintenance provided. The university community felt considerable pride in that attitude of independence, and that attitude carried Gamma for 100 years."

After the inflationary years of the 1960s and 1970s, Gamma began to decline. The current president took office in the late 1970s and began to draw the university out of this period of considerable insecurity and instability. When the director of development arrived in 1979, the university was "fiscally very weak, with a poorly maintained physical plant and very little tradition of professional fund raising," he said. "It appeared to alumni that this institution didn't need philanthropic support because it had never asked for it. We had no significant established donor base—in those days, $1,000 was a large gift for many board members—but we were told to raise $140 million, with no planning, no precampaign period to raise advance gifts, nothing. One day the president said, 'The campaign has begun.'"

There was no time "to identify, cultivate, train, and change the philosophy of the constituency we had at hand. When that campaign was over, we saw that the consultants, who had said our potential was to raise $40 million, had been absolutely right in one sense. We raised just about that amount from the only constituency that the consultants had considered—our alumni. Most of the rest of the money came from unaffiliated individuals." The director thinks that consultants tend to be traditionalists, trying to replicate what has been done in the past. "They tend to operate by formula and the formulas tend to lag behind the real world. This world is changing so rapidly that strategies and programs have to respond to the needs of each particular institution. Consultants really can't get under the skin of an institution in that way."

The director's management philosophy reflects a strong belief in individual responsibility. "In our case, the development officer is the core of the development program," he said, "because we don't have a strong volunteer infrastructure. The professional development officer carries a great deal more of the burden than may be the case at other institutions. Our school directors own their programs, and it's very important that they do. They have a considerable amount of latitude for independent action within the structure we set, which involves quite a lot of rules, guidelines, goals, and strategies. We also monitor their progress very carefully, watching activity as well as achievement."

The director said that the most important thing he tries to convey to professional staff members is the need for communication and coordination. He said, "We must all have the fervent belief that each person's success is intimately bound up with the success of everybody else. We must share ideas and information, with no barriers to this sharing."

The director promotes communication and coordination between staff members through frequent meetings. "Every Friday morning I have a breakfast meeting open to anybody on the professional staff," he said. "There's no set agenda, and the meeting is a good opportunity for staff members to talk to each other and to raise issues with me and other management staff. Two to three times a week, we have an 8:00 a.m. meeting to discuss a single prospect. All staff members who have an interest in or knowledge of that prospect, including people from research, sit in." Other meetings include a full-day staff meeting once each month for professional fund raisers and division-wide staff meetings three times each year.

The director was asked to provide the rationale for the high fund-raising goals set for this institution. He replied, "If your campaign is for $10 million, you can't ask somebody for a $10 million gift. If your campaign is for $250 million, you can ask somebody for a $25 million gift. Also, if you ask somebody who is capable of a large gift for $1,000, they'll give you $1,000 and may laugh at you. If you ask somebody who is capable of a large gift for $1 million, they'll swallow hard but may give you $250,000. Setting high goals and falling short is better than setting the goals low and reaching them. We ask for $5 and $10 million gifts to get $1 million gifts. Occasionally, we'll be surprised and get what we ask for, and then we're ahead of the game."

Taking a controversial position, the director noted, "If I had my way, our campaign would have been for $500 million, not $250 million. That would have made it, at the time, the second largest campaign ever. I would have included public funds in the goal. The actual task would have been no different than it is now because we expect to receive more than $200 million in public funds during this period. The difference is that the *New York Times* would have had a banner headline saying, 'Gamma University Announces Unprecedented $500 Million Campaign,' which would have been invaluable publicity for us. As it is, a $250 million campaign isn't bad for a little place like this."

The director has an unconventional attitude about the role of volunteers in fund raising, one that grows out of his conviction that fund raising is professional work. "We are the professionals," he said. "We are the people who make it happen. In our first campaign, we had no volunteers. The time and effort required to service large volunteer committees were not commensurate with the return we would get from them."

The current campaign includes eighteen volunteers. When asked about this change, the director said that although the goal for the present campaign had increased over the goal for the last campaign, his budget had not been increased proportionately. He decided to include volunteers to increase effectiveness without increasing costs. He said, "We have one volunteer for each major university area and donor group. We established extremely strict criteria that we spelled out and wrote down. We told potential volunteers that we expected them to make a gift of $1 million and to make three solicitations a year. A lot of people said no. Those who said yes knew what they were being asked to do, and they have done it. To my surprise and delight, they have absolutely fulfilled their mandate, in part because our expectations were very clear. I'm still opposed to diluting the effectiveness of a good professional staff by servicing large groups of volunteers."

"This is business, not a charity," the director concluded. "This is a corporation with a $6 million annual budget and 120 employees, most of whom are highly skilled. We will turn a 600 percent profit this year. Our alumni and donors have come to respect that."

Development Officers

In a group interview, five development officers at Gamma discussed Gamma's recent evolution, emphasizing the leadership of the president and senior vice president. One said, "The president and vice president created a self-fulfilling prophecy that this is a world-class institution. We laughed in the first campaign about the idea that Gamma could be a world-class institution, but it is all coming true. Based on coverage in the national and the international press and in Nobel prizes and Rhodes scholarships, in recent years, Gamma has had outstanding recognition. We are not yet equal to our chief rivals, the schools we have overlapping admissions with, but perception breeds reality in higher education."

Another staff member said, "The president and vice president made the conscious decision to change Gamma radically in a short time. They didn't have the time to convince the 60,000 members of the university community or to get their help. They went to people who did not need to have their minds changed. Seven of the twelve biggest donors in the first campaign were people who had no previous ties to Gamma. They went to many corporations and foundations that Gamma had never approached before. They said, 'Here's our vision of the future,' and people gave like crazy. Most people start campaigning with their alumni, but we came to our alumni last. The alumni now see a very different institution and want to invest in it. It took a lot of guts for the president and vice president to bypass the only friends we had at the time — a remarkable act of faith in Gamma's potential on their part."

While entrepreneurial leadership abounds at Gamma, day to day support by management is sometimes in short supply. "At times," one staff member said, "I find management very helpful. I get good advice or help in cutting the red tape in the administration. At other times, it's impossible to get somebody's attention, which has encouraged development officers here to be self-reliant." Since senior managers at this institution are "thinking in tomorrow," development officers find that it falls to them "to make sure that today's tasks get done," the staff member said. "Organizing solicitations, managing the fund-raising goals, and making projects work are our responsibilities. We play a bigger role in day-to-day operations at this university than our counterparts do in many other places."

"We've recruited a staff that is very self-starting, that

bristles under too much management and oversight, and that expects to talk on the phone with a chief executive officer of some corporation and go see him or her without a senior university officer or volunteer," another development officer said. "Dealing directly with donors enhances our images of ourselves as professionals. I came from an institution at which a volunteer was always between me and the donor. Here I feel like a builder. These are my projects, my bricks that get stacked together; this is my new professorship, too. It's something that I'm responsible for and make happen in a very direct way."

The development officers related the challenges, rewards, and personal costs of working in this environment. One staff member said, "Everybody has too much to do. Remember the guy who used to spin plates on sticks on the Ed Sullivan Show, keeping them all spinning at the same time? That's what it's like here. The university's needs are insatiable and our potential is unbelievable. The university will need more when this campaign is over than it did when it began. Some days management says, 'Yes, you got a million dollars yesterday, but what about today?' This attitude can be a very negative or a very positive influence, depending on how things are going."

Another staff member said, "I'm glad that we're succeeding, but the inability to satisfy needs despite running at 100 miles an hour can be frustrating. I go from being excited and challenged to exhausted, but those of us who have chosen to stay here thrive on that. I looked very hard at a senior position at another institution last year and the real reason that I didn't go is because they couldn't tell me what they needed. I went into a dorm at night and talked with students and said, 'If you were talking to the new vice president for development, what would you say the college needs?' There was a long silence and somebody finally said, 'Well, the sailing team needs new boats.' If you asked *anybody* at Gamma, you would get a soliloquy for an hour."

A third staff member commented, "I was asked to speak to a local professional group last year about new fund-raising styles. I said, 'I know that you invited me here because you all think the way we do things at Gamma is weird.' There was nervous laughter because to some people at other institutions, we are pariahs. They're used to their old-boy network, which is fabulously successful, and we envy them because we don't have one, but they're curious about what we are doing. We are raising almost as much money as they are without doing any of the things they swear by. It's a shock to both them and us."

Planner and the Planning Function

A notable aspect of the development operation at Gamma is the systematic, formalized planning process. A senior staff member with the title of planner reports to the senior director of development. She participates with senior management and development officers in creating a comprehensive annual master plan. The plan is approximately eighty pages long. It is printed in July of each year and is a working tool for the fiscal year. An abbreviated list of contents from a recent year's plan demonstrates the thoroughness of the plan and the planning process. Specific goals for activities and outcomes are established for most of the areas in the list.

> Fund-Raising Goals by School and Source
> Gift Table for Annual and Capital Gifts
> Activity Measurements
> Staff Activity Standards
> Projected Capital Asks by Source and School
> Capital Prospect Identification Goals
> Narrative Operating Plans by School and Source
> Annual Fund Operation Plan
> > Giving Clubs
> > Direct Mail
> > Matching Gifts
> > Senior Class Gift
> > Club Counts
> > Telefund
> > Reunion Gifts
> > Corporate Affiliates
> > Schools and Sources

Phone-Mail Prospect Pool
Support Activities—Research, Parents Program, and
   Stewardship
Fiscal Year Monthly and Year-to-Date Totals

A section of the plan spells out standards and specific goals
for fund raisers. "The standards", as stated in the plan, "represent
an effort to give development officers the tools they need to establish certain disciplines for fund-raising activities." The fund
raisers' standards include adding forty-eight new prospects likely
to give $25,000 or more to the donor pool per year and sub-
mitting forty-eight written proposals ("asks") per year. In addition, specific goals are set for source directors, school directors,
and associate directors. Directors have goals for larger gifts than
associate directors, but the number of asks is the same for all.
Fund raisers understand that the suggested goal of four new
prospects and four asks per month will not be distributed evenly
throughout the year. Senior managers monitor the activity of
the development staff and fund-raising results monthly and hold
formal quarterly reviews with all staff members. The plan also
contains narrative operating plans for each school, each of which
includes goals and program details for the annual fund, capital
gifts, and special projects.

Not all staff members are comfortable with the planning
process. One senior staff member said, "We depend too much
on charts and statistics. Having so many asks a month may help
motivate people, but it may also cost us money. People may
get frantic and make a premature, unsuccessful ask for a gift
they might have gotten if they had waited six more weeks. When
our system of monthly asks and goals became public, we became the laughingstock of the development community throughout the area. They said, 'Did you know those people at Gamma
have goals like used car salespeople?'"

The role of the planner (the only such position we encountered in any development office in our ten institutions) is
to help development officers and senior managers set specific
quantitative goals and standards and to provide the data necessary for close monitoring of activities and progress. To set final

goals, the planner said, "We sit down with each development officer and say, 'This is where we think you can go next year.' Setting the numbers involves a lot of discussion. Key development staff members go to the deans and explain our thinking, so that when the plan is published, we have central development management plus the school administration on record."

Gamma has used this method for four years, and, according to the planner, "It seems to be working, but the process is only effective as long as it is treated by management with a healthy skepticism. Measuring the things we can easily count is only one way to assess what's going on. Minimum standards are important because we need to maintain our sales orientation. What do good salespeople need to do to be successful? They need to have prospects in the pipeline and they need to be working with them. This [setting specific standards and goals] is a pure sales management tool to encourage the development officer to do the hardest part of the job—to go out on the road."

Analysis of Fund Raising at Gamma

In a program with many notable characteristics, an entrepreneurial approach to fund raising is the most outstanding characteristic at Gamma. The *American Heritage Dictionary* (2nd College Edition) defines *entrepreneur* as "a person who organizes, operates, and assumes the risk for a business venture." In current popular usage, the word often means a person who is especially talented at seizing or creating an opportunity to do something that others would consider too risky, either because there is too slight a likelihood of success or because failure would cause considerable loss or harm. *Entrepreneurial* is often used to connote a situation in which decisions made or actions taken are outside of or contradict conventional practice. All of these definitions describe fund raising at Gamma.

Some of the entrepreneurial practices and actions in the fund-raising program at Gamma include:

- Discarding of consultants' recommendations for both campaign goals and focus because the recommendations were contrary to the president's expectations and judgments

- Pursuing a challenging course at a time when many people thought the university's resources and capabilities for succeeding on such a course were at their lowest
- Launching an ambitious major campaign without several features experts say are vital: a long-term planning period, a carefully staged kickoff and announcement of advance gifts, carefully designed campaign publications, and mobilization and involvement of trustees and key alumni
- Using management practices more often associated with business than with higher education administration or fund raising, such as setting explicit goals for dollars raised, providing in-house sales training for fund raisers, speaking of traditional benefits to donors as "products" with "prices" that will increase as time passes, and encouraging donors to "buy while the price is low"
- Looking beyond traditional constituencies, developing new constituencies, and "sidestepping" alumni and volunteers
- Restricting involvement of volunteers and defining highly explicit expectations of people who serve as volunteers
- Selecting a chief development officer based on entrepreneurial abilities rather than on experience in development
- Focusing systematically on the most productive use of the staff members' and major donors' time (for example, buying a helicopter to facilitate donor involvement and presence on campus)
- Undergirding an action and results orientation with methodical, organized planning and monitoring
- Encouraging staff members to be risk takers and promoting a high level of staff responsibility and autonomy
- Appreciating the ongoing necessity to "sell the vision," both internally and externally
- Defining and communicating explicit expectations for staff performance

Other outstanding characteristics at Gamma include leadership of the president and senior vice president, institutional commitment to fund raising, and emphasis on goal-oriented management of the fund-raising function. The president was responsible for initiating the campaign that changed Gamma's history as a fund-raising institution. He continues to have a direct and powerful impact on fund-raising goals and on staff members. The senior vice president, in an authoritative position in relation to the entire institution as well as among development staff members, is primarily responsible for the entrepreneurial and enterprising culture in the fund-raising unit at Gamma. Together, the president and the senior vice president have demonstrated that adhering to current or traditional beliefs about fund-raising practice may be less effective than relying on intimate knowledge and understanding of the history, strengths and weaknesses, potential, and aspirations of the institution in charting a fund-raising course.

Because of the history of this university, the fund-raising program at Gamma did not have a "classic" evolution, which is perhaps a sufficient argument by itself for the abandonment of classic fund-raising techniques. A consistent finding in all of our research on fund raising is that classic approaches work best in institutions that are themselves classic in some way. As the glow from the considerable success of the first fund-raising campaign recedes under the passing of time and the urgency of new demands, Gamma is building a fund-raising program that incorporates solid fund-raising traditions and planning and monitoring mechanisms that are more detailed than any we saw elsewhere. Institutional commitment to fund raising, strongly influenced by the president, is evident in adequate resource allocations, institutional priorities and fund-raising policies, and the continuous effort at Gamma to define its niche and refine and communicate its image.

Senior development managers at Gamma appreciate the need for planning and evaluation of staff and programs. Yet, although there are strong management controls, staff members have considerable latitude in day-to-day operations and input into overall decision making and program planning. At Gamma, of all the institutions we studied, expectations of the staff are most clearly specified, staff performance is most closely monitored, and programs are most systematically evaluated. Gamma was also one of the few institutions that emphasized staff training.

Less than outstanding characteristics at Gamma are trustees' participation in fund raising, staff commitment to the institution, and emphasis on constituent relations. There is no
direct, organized effort under way to substantially change the
degree of the trustees' involvement in fund-raising activities. This
is an area in which Gamma continues to act in opposition to
a conventional fund-raising rule. However, as the senior vice
president indicated, the composition of the board at Gamma
is changing. As the university grows in stature, scope, and
resources, board membership will undoubtedly both reflect and
facilitate those changes. Increasingly, trustees will probably be
major donors, if not direct participants in fund raising.

Staff commitment to the institution is not an outstanding characteristic when compared to the degree of commitment
we found in some other institutions. At Gamma, as at Alpha,
for instance, staff members were more committed to the success of the fund-raising enterprise than to the institution itself.
It was not that staff members at Gamma were uninterested in
the institution or had negative feelings; rather, staff members
believed that if they did what they were charged with doing,
Gamma's continued prosperity would be assured. As explained
by the development officers, the pace at Gamma is fast, the mood
upbeat, the excitement contagious, and the rewards gratifying.
Staff turnover is quite low at Gamma. Most development staff
members were at Gamma years longer than the present average for the field of two to three years. Nevertheless, professional
staff at Gamma reported, in general, a higher level of stress than
did staff members at most other institutions we studied. It is
almost certainly true that some professionals prefer and function best in a high-stress environment, so the necessity to hire
staff with the right "fit," especially for a program with as strong
a personality as Gamma's, emerges as a critical management
responsibility.

As we have indicated throughout, Gamma has no long-
standing tradition of close relationships with donors and does
not have an identity as a regional institution. Nor do volunteers play a significant role in Gamma's fund-raising success.

In summary, what can others learn from Gamma's experiences? The factors we identified as contributing to fund-raising effectiveness at Gamma are as follows:

- Entrepreneurial fund raising influenced by the external environment and intimate knowledge of the institution, rather than by traditional fund-raising practice
- Sharply defined orientation toward results, with strong management controls
- Distinctive, authoritative leadership by the president, senior vice president, and senior managers
- Emphasis on effective planning and concrete goal setting and actual use of a planning document as a working tool, one result of which is explicit expectations and standards for staff members
- Awareness of the reciprocal growth between institutional quality and reputation and fund-raising progress

5

Teams and Champions in a Decentralized Environment:

A Public Doctoral University

> DELTA: Delta is a national leader in successful annual giving programs among public universities, although in many ways the overall fund-raising program at Delta is in an early developmental stage. Recent major changes both at the institutional level and in the development area resulted in what some staff members at Delta called a revolution. Delta is adjusting to major changes while continuing to increase fund-raising results.

This 120-year-old state university, with an enrollment of about 15,000 and educational and general expenditures of more than $201 million, is located in a small town near the coast of a western state. Descriptive statistics for Delta University appear in Table 5.1. Institutional characteristics are all above the median for public doctoral universities, except for tuition, which is near the median, and enrollment, which is below the median. Outcomes for voluntary support are above the median for institutions of this type. Actual outcomes for total voluntary support, alumni gifts, and foundation gifts are all substantially higher than the predicted amount for these donor groups. Actual outcomes for nonalumni gifts and corporation gifts are about equal to the predicted amount. The organizational chart for development appears in Figure 5.1.

Delta Foundation

The Delta Foundation was incorporated in 1947. Until 1989, university development staff members were foundation employees.

Table 5.1. Descriptive Statistics (1985–1987 Average) for Delta University (Public Doctoral).

| | Range for Type | | | This Institution | | |
	High	Median	Low	Actual	Predicted	Difference
Institutional Characteristics:						
Educational/General Expenditures	$438,312,300	$116,648,500	$45,711,900	$201,560,110	—	—
Endowment	$889,209,900	$14,610,800	$937,400	$22,558,600	—	—
Expenditures per Student	$149,600	$8,200	$4,200	$12,760	—	—
Cost of Tuition	$3,500	$1,600	$800	$1,506	—	—
Alumni of Record	210,000	83,200	7,600	97,101	—	—
Enrollment	40,500	19,100	1,600	15,229	—	—
Age of Institution	200 years	100 years	20 years	120 years	—	—
Fund-Raising Results:						
Total Voluntary Support	$42,505,100	$5,872,300	$1,442,000	$13,301,650	$9,711,497	+1.37
Alumni Gifts	$15,790,900	$1,134,400	$10,300	$3,199,486	$2,073,370	+1.54
Nonalumni Gifts	$6,640,500	$1,383,300	$172,400	$2,053,034	$2,075,479	0.99
Corporation Gifts	$18,387,300	$2,047,300	$281,300	$3,613,717	$3,671,762	0.98
Foundation Gifts	$8,160,200	$939,500	$0	$3,012,171	$1,438,347	+2.09

Figure 5.1. Organizational Chart for Delta University.

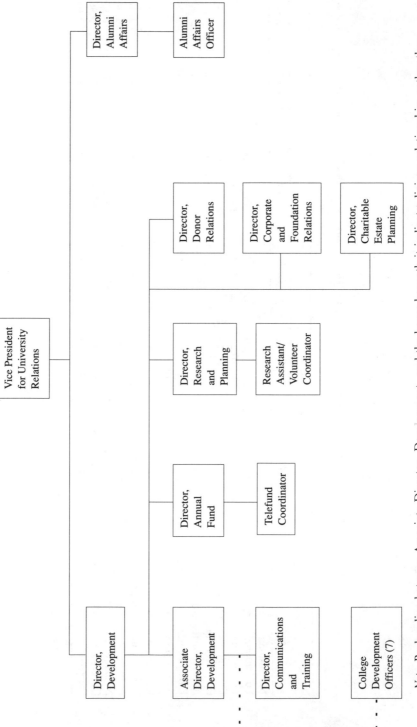

Note: Broken line between Associate Director, Development, and the boxes beneath it indicates liaison relationship, rather than direct reporting relationship.

To meet operating expenses, the foundation levies a one-time charge of 2 percent on all gifts at the time of donation and charges for managing endowment accounts. The foundation's practice of levying a charge on gifts to finance foundation activities is controversial on the Delta campus. One staff member said, "Taxing gifts makes people crazy. Frankly, I don't understand why people cannot recognize that this operation needs to be funded. The charge started out at 10 percent, and so many people screamed that the administration backed down and lowered it to 2 percent, but people are still grumbling. There is a surcharge on research dollars to help fund the research office, but nobody seems to object too much to that."

Fund-Raising History

Delta has had formal fund-raising programs since 1963, when the former director of development (recently retired) was first hired. The former director, who agreed to be interviewed, was the first development officer for the university overall. When he arrived, the alumni and athletic associations were raising small amounts of money for their own programs. A few faculty members or department chairs also occasionally raised funds for their programs. The former director made an early decision to focus on planned gifts, not only because it was a fruitful area that promised long-term benefit to the university but also because "it didn't interfere with anyone else's turf."

One senior staff member credited the former director of development with much of Delta's present fund-raising success. "He had been here for so long," she said, "and he made many friends for Delta who thought he was terrific. In a quiet way, he put the university on the fund-raising map. His work continues to benefit Delta because he secured bequests that are going to come in for many more years."

While continuing in his role as chief development officer for the university, the former director assumed the responsibilities of chief operating officer of the Delta Foundation in 1967. He filled both roles until his retirement, when the foundation and development offices were separated. In the early 1970s, the central development office assumed responsibility for the annual fund, which has since achieved substantial growth and considerable success. The former director observed that attitudes and understanding about fund raising have "matured" throughout the campus, and, in his opinion, the university "has a better handle than ever before" on the need to set universitywide fund-raising priorities and policies. The former director is optimistic that Delta could be successful in a major campaign but is not certain about how soon the university would be ready to proceed. He stressed that the success of such a campaign depends not only on a sophisticated, professional campaign but also on educated donors, and he is not sure "even yet if the fruit is ripe enough for picking."

Need for Leadership. At the time of the site visit, Delta was searching for someone to fill the position of vice president for university relations, a position vacant for over a year. The former vice president left this post to assume a college presidency at a time when Delta was contending with a severe budget cut. The president of Delta said, "We stated publicly that we would not fill the position at that time. We suffered for a year — and suffered is exactly what I mean — in so many ways related to university relations. People who were against filling the position a year ago are begging us to fill it now. We do need this kind of person, someone who can see vacuums and charge into them — a champion." A campus newsletter reported that the deans were now unanimous in their support of filling the position.

The new vice president will oversee alumni affairs, development, information, publications, conferences and special events, public affairs, and marketing services, making the position, in the president's words, "one of the toughest jobs at the university. What we really need is someone at the highest administrative level who is an expert at assessing how the public will react. If we are going to be successful in our public relations, we're going to need a champion."

The "Revolution." The word *revolution* was used by several fund-raising staff members at Delta to describe recent changes in the development area. Staff members used this word to convey the drastic nature of the changes and the significant impact these changes have had. The changes began when President J. arrived in 1985 and created a new organizational structure for executive administrators of the university and introduced a new management style (these broad changes are discussed in the section on the president).

The university development office, once under the auspices of the university's foundation, has recently been placed under the university's control in order to separate fund raising from fund management and distribution. Furthermore, fund raising, historically totally centralized at Delta, is now decentralized, with development officers in five colleges who report solely to their deans. Moving the development office to university control resulted in a thorough reorganization of the central development staff and changed operating relationships between development and foundation staff members, who still share the same offices. Decentralizing fund raising created new roles for central staff members vis-à-vis the colleges and complex new relationships between college development officers and central staff members.

Many staff members view these changes as highly disruptive; they spoke of how stable and effective the development process once had been. A few staff members were skeptical that fund raising would continue to be as effective under the new circumstances. Because of these changes, the fund-raising unit at Delta was the most "troubled" of those we studied. Nevertheless, several staff members also believed that "the worst" was over, that adjustments and renegotiations of roles and turf were under way. They thought that fund-raising results would continue to improve. The director of development was optimistic that during 1989 the university would generate the highest fund-raising totals not related to a campaign it had ever achieved in one year, possibly as high as $15 million.

Delta's development program provides an excellent example of a development program struggling to modernize and expand, build on its considerable past successes, and take care of the daily business of raising money while contending with traumatic changes and considerable ambiguity. Given the state of flux at Delta and the fact that many staff members were troubled, the president and the director of development are to be commended for their willingness to participate in our study.

Fund-Raising Campaigns. Delta has not had a universitywide major campaign but has had three specific campaigns. Each of these campaigns was successful, and most staff members thought that the campaigns provided some important fund-raising lessons.

Delta's earliest major fund-raising campaign, started in 1978, raised money for the construction of an auditorium. President J. said, "When a symphony or ballet came to town, they performed in our basketball court, which is right next to the railroad tracks. Almost without exception, during the quietest movement of a Mozart symphony, a train would come through. So we decided to build what we were calling the Great Hall, which was to be not only for the university but for the entire community." The building as originally conceived would have cost $10 million, but consultants advised Delta that it could expect to raise only $4 to $5 million. "So halfway through the campaign," the president said, "we changed the plans and ended up with a building that cost half as much. We call this the Cultural and Conference Center. The building is used constantly and is exactly what we needed. Getting that advice from our consultants was one of the luckiest things that ever happened to us. From that experience, we learned that we must make sure that our fund-raising efforts are carefully matched to what the university really needs as well as based on good assessments beforehand of what is possible for us to raise."

A campaign launched in 1983, in its final stages at the time of the site visit, had an overall goal of $18 million. In 1983, no one thought that Delta was in a position to undertake a universitywide campaign, so this campaign was designed to focus on three interdisciplinary areas that are particularly strong at Delta (materials research, gene research, and marine sciences) and the humanities. One senior staff member said that although a number of campuswide committees were involved in deciding which program areas to include in the campaign, the campaign continues to evoke heated debate across campus.

The campaign is controversial because most university areas are not included in it. One staff member said, "This approach to fund raising was wrong for Delta at a time when faculty members and academic administrators in all areas were more aware than ever of the need to acquire voluntary support. Furthermore, Delta had recently hired some very aggressive new deans in some programs not in the campaign who think fund raising is a large part of their responsibility. So we have aggressive new deans and a major campaign that excludes them." Deans from the excluded colleges are distressed when major donors or prospects for their colleges are solicited for gifts to support other areas of the university.

Another staff member suggested that some university administrators and foundation board members did not understand what motivates donors to give and had limited appreciation of the fact that the donors "ultimately decide where to put their money." Also distressing to those people not included in the campaign was the desire on the part of some influential foundation board members to avoid setting specific goals or a specific time period for the campaign and to keep the fund-raising efforts open ended and ongoing.

The campaign will close with results far exceeding original goals for marine sciences and gene research and at or above goals for materials research and the humanities. The director of development said, "It was an extremely positive experience for the faculty members and units that benefited from the money we raised. And this campaign established six and seven figure gifts as reasonable expectations for Delta because we acquired our first gifts at that level in this campaign." The university's first endowed chairs also came from this campaign, and several foundations and corporations that made their first sizable gifts to the university during this campaign have continued to make large annual donations.

Another major fund-raising effort was a campaign for athletic programs in 1987–1988 that overlapped with the campaign for selected academic areas. In the 1980s, after women's athletics were mandated in higher education institutions by federal legislation, many states allocated specific funds for these programs, but Delta's state did not. Higher education athletic programs in this state were and continue to be funded almost entirely through private support and earned revenue. Delta's campaign, designed both to raise money and to increase public pressure for state support for college athletics, was initiated at a time when university administrators and senior athletics staff members felt they had to act quickly in order to keep athletic programs operating. The development staff was given responsibility for the campaign only after it had been publicly announced.

A senior staff member said, "This fund-raising campaign was an example of everything you should not do. First, donors don't want to give money to a stopgap measure to save something. They want to put money into something vital and positive. It was difficult to cast the campaign in positive terms under that negative banner. Second, announcing a campaign without adequate planning and without advance gifts is difficult, and it was also difficult for development staff members to step in after staff members in athletics expected to handle the campaign on their own." The problem for the central development staff, a senior development officer noted, was "one of responsibility without clear authority." Additionally, since this campaign overlapped with the campaign for academic programs, confusion and controversy arose over who had "rights" to specific donors and about which fund-raising effort had priority.

One staff member said, "It was an extremely frustrating and time-consuming campaign." Nevertheless, some results were beneficial, including the opportunity for university and foundation administrators to learn less divisive ways to implement complex fund-raising programs. The director of development said, "There is indeed more awareness now of the financial situation of athletics at our state institutions and the campaign did find 1,400 new donors for athletics, which gives us a much expanded base to build on. We also had a number of new major donors, and athletics had never before sought major gifts."

The president appointed a committee to evaluate Delta's readiness to undertake a universitywide major campaign in the near future. The committee was given ten months to prepare its report; our site visit occurred roughly midway through this period. The committee, chaired by the dean of the business school, included several other deans, university vice presidents, and members of the development staff. The committee's task was to evaluate what internal resources in personnel, organizational structure, computer facilities, and budgets a campaign would require and to assess the current status of the resources at Delta. Committee members consulted with senior development managers from other universities with experience in major capital campaigns to learn what they did right and wrong, benefits and problems, costs and budgets, and the role of volunteers. They visited other institutions to study campaign practices and results.

Everyone we interviewed at Delta believed that there would be a universitywide campaign, except one committee member. This person pointed out that everyone across campus took it for granted that a campaign would be started just because the committee had been appointed, forgetting that the president's charge to the committee was to evaluate the feasibility of having a campaign. This committee member said the committee had not yet made its final decision about whether to recommend that a campaign be initiated. Conversely, one senior university officer said there would be a campaign for about $100 million and that it would take about two more years for Delta to prepare for the campaign.

President J.

President J. was a faculty member and a department chair at Delta before leaving for a position elsewhere. He returned to Delta in 1985 as president and made major changes in the organizational structure and management practices of the university. When he assumed office, twenty-nine senior administrators reported to the president, but as President J. noted, there were "no vice presidents, not even a chief academic officer. Therefore, we had strong deans who operated independently of one another. This management style is more appropriate in a much smaller institution, which we once were. The institution was managed as if it were still small."

Upon the advice of consultants, the president instituted an organizational structure including five vice presidents to whom all other senior administrators report. The president said, "This is not an original or innovative structure, but for Delta it was revolutionary." Another major undertaking was the implementation of a long-range strategic planning process, the first such effort at Delta since 1969. President J. said, "We got everybody—faculty members, administrators, alumni, staff members, students—into the act. We came out with a set of goals that was too comprehensive, but we did identify priorities."

The president also made changes in budget allocation procedures. "Historically," he explained, "if the university got a 2 percent increase in funding, every college and unit got a 2 percent increase. If we got a 2 percent cut, everybody tightened up 2 percent. I decided we would allocate funds in the best interest of the university, which may not mean giving something to everybody. Under my system, our colleges have received increases of from 1 to 6 percent, and we can put some money into the library, computing, and the educational opportunities program."

As a consequence of new allocation procedures, people across campus are more interested in securing private support. Prior to the recent changes, fund raising was totally centralized— "officially," that is, but as President J. said, "People in the barn and behind the barn and under the hayloft were all raising money on this campus. I know because when I was on the faculty, I was one of them." To coordinate and expand fund raising and to respond to the preferences of deans, Delta hired fund raisers for the five largest colleges instead of hiring more staff members for central development.

The president indicated that many positive developments at Delta are the result of "champions" and the private support they attract. He said, "When we get a little money, we attract a faculty member who becomes a champion for a new program." As an example, he cited Delta's status as a sea-grant university, one of only about twenty in the country. "That never would have happened," he said, "without our oceanography program and a certain faculty member who kept pushing to secure out-side grants to make it happen. One champion got things mov-ing. I'm a firm believer in champions."

President J. is certain that Delta has not "scratched the surface" of its potential for fund raising. He said, "Several months ago, I had a call from an alumnus I had never heard of. This alumnus said, 'I keep responding to my alumni mail, but you aren't paying any attention to me and I'm well off. Why aren't you paying any attention to me?' I said, 'Let's start now. Tell me how you spell your last name.'"

The president said this particular alumnus was "just hun-gry to be involved" at Delta, and, unlike other affluent alumni with an interest in the university, this alumnus initiated the con-tact. "We have some outstanding alumni, and until now we haven't paid the right kind of attention to them," the president said. "We have to identify our prominent alumni and cultivate rela-tionships with them prior to starting a universitywide campaign." For the president, the question is not whether Delta will initi-ate a major universitywide campaign but when the campaign will be and for how much.

President J. defined his fund-raising role as the "tradi-tional" one, saying, "The donor wants the president to do the asking for a big gift because that says the gift is important to the university." He noted that he does more direct fund raising now than previously. He said, "Earlier, I couldn't devote much time to developing external relationships. I had to stay close to home to be sure we didn't throw away the baby with the bath-water. But now, our vice presidents know the university, and we have matured in our ability to know what is critical to main-tain and what must be changed."

President J. observed that within the next five years, "Delta will evolve into an organization in which the provost and vice presidents run day-to-day operations. The president's in-ternal job will be to manage the values of the institution, but most of the president's time will be spent making sure the legis-lature provides money, looking for federal opportunities for fund-ing, and working with alumni and friends to increase volun-tary support."

Director and Associate Director of Development

The director of development was hired in 1987 by the former director of development because of his expertise in raising major gifts. He has probably felt the impact of the changes in the department more than anyone else. Since he joined the staff, both the vice president and former director of development have left, making him the senior member of the development staff. Additionally, as we have already noted, the development office was separated from the university's foundation and fund raising has been decentralized. The director said that 1987–1989 "has been a tough time. We've been through a lot of changes and will be in transition for another two years. Then we'll be into raising advance gifts for a major campaign, so we will be in new territory for the next four to six years." The director was surprised that Delta had been selected for this study, saying that he believes that the fund-raising program currently is not as effective as it is going to be in the upcoming years.

The associate director of development was originally hired as the university's first college development officer (for the agriculture college). She initially focused more on alumni relations than fund raising until she learned from development officers for agriculture colleges in other state universities how successful they were in raising funds for agriculture programs. She convinced the dean that her time would be better spent in fund raising than in alumni relations. During a five-year period, she helped to increase the endowment assets of the agriculture college from $10,000 to over $8 million. She assumed her position in the central office shortly after the decision was made to separate the development office from the foundation.

In addition to raising major gifts and overseeing the administration of the central office, the director and associate director have responsibility for coordinating college fund raisers with the central office, training staff members, and setting university policies as members of the campaign preplanning committee.

Overseeing Administration of the Central Office. The central development staff holds an off-site yearly retreat to prepare annual plans. Each of the teams devises formal plans and sets concrete goals for their areas, and the combined staff creates an overall plan. Individual staff members are also required to develop formal plans and set goals for their own areas of responsibility.

Staff members' annual performance evaluations and merit-based raises are closely connected to their achievement of their goals. The central office directors believe that setting definite goals is a prerequisite to successful fund raising, primarily because goal setting helps to clarify priorities and set direction for effective performance.

These directors facilitated the shift of the department from foundation to university control. In addition to voluminous paperwork, they also had to face the negative feelings that many staff members in the central office had about becoming state employees. The shift involved the reclassification of several positions to fit state personnel categories. Some employees felt a loss of status associated with "becoming a number" in the vast state system.

The development staff continues to be housed in the foundation offices, and the two, now-distinct, units share data bases, files, and equipment. A single unit has been divided into "we" and "they" factions, which has required not only skillful handling and good management decisions by administrators but also considerable patience and tolerance in handling employee dissatisfaction and conflicts. One staff member said, "When we were all one happy family, we had better cooperation. Now, we're at odds about the functions we share and maintain jointly, such as coverage of the phone and reception area and our data bases." As we noted earlier, some staff members are uncertain that either of the now separate functions will ever work as smoothly as they did when they operated as a single unit. Nevertheless, senior managers from the development office and the foundation believe that the turbulence is easing and conflicts are slowly being resolved.

Coordinating College and Central Office Fund Raisers. One of the directors noted that it is "a fundamental structural flaw right now in our program that the college development officers have no reporting relationship with this office." This problem will be addressed in the coming fiscal year through the leadership of the business school dean, who is also the chair of the committee to study campaign possibilities. This dean believes that both his school and the overall development function will fare better if his development officer has a joint reporting relationship with him and the central office. He will create a joint reporting relationship next year for his development officer, even if no one else on campus does. The director said, "We're hoping other deans will follow his lead."

The other director pointed out, "We've gone to a decentralized structure in a short period of time. The college fund raisers often are reporting to deans who think they have a much better understanding of fund raising than they actually do. Even when deans are knowledgeable about fund raising, they all think they should have first priority and that their projects are the most important. It is their job to do that; and it is our job to be able to say, 'Wait a minute. The college of such and such has priority and here's why.'"

The directors indicated that probably the most difficult aspect of their jobs is the coordination of activities between the central office and the college fund raisers. One of them noted, "We try to get people to share information. We want everybody to have the opportunity to cultivate prospects, but not all at the same time. We try to broker information and direct traffic so we don't step on each other and, more importantly, so we can present the university to donors and prospects in the best possible way."

A major problem in information sharing and coordination is the limited access college development officers have to the computer system. One of the directors said, "The bigger your data base and the more powerful your system, the more complex and the less user friendly both become. Our computer can do everything, but when our system was originally designed, it was created for use by a limited number of people because the office was centralized then. We are working with college development officers to increase their access to the system, but, unfortunately, it is taking more time than anyone would like."

Noting that there is no "higher authority to settle our differences," one director said, "Everyone must be part of the solution, and we're all still learning how to do that. Some people think that the new vice president is going to come riding in on a white horse and solve all of our problems. I think the new vice president's expertise will help, but we all have to be part of the answer."

Training Staff. The associate director of development has organized training seminars for all university development staff members as part of the effort to coordinate universitywide fund raising. Central staff conducted a survey to identify topics of interest and resources available for the training. College development officers, central development and foundation staff, deans, the president and vice presidents, and secretaries in development offices were all invited to the training seminars. Attendance has ranged from twenty to sixty people at seminars on topics such as planned gifts, real property gifts, understanding donor motivation, new directions in annual giving, marketing nonprofit organizations, donor recognition, and computer training. Seminars were held monthly for a year, but will be decreased to quarterly. The seminars were recorded on videotapes and are kept in the central office for use by new staff members.

Setting University Policies. In 1988 the associate director chaired a committee of central and college development officers to draft university policies. Although the committee was charged with a specific concrete task, several staff members indicated that the process of developing university policies had done as much as anything else had to create more positive relationships between staff members in the central office and in college development. The committee sought extensive input from deans and faculty members in drafting the policies and then presented them to the president, who made them official in 1988. The policies cover approval of projects and their priority and clearance of prospects. These policies address issues staff members face in every large institution we studied.

The purpose of the policy on project approval and priority

is to determine the level of support provided by the development office and president for each project. Each college or unit outlines fund-raising projects and priorities and submits them for review by the development priorities committee (comprising vice presidents, the director of development, and other staff members appointed by the president). The committee works with the president to assign a priority to each project, based on the relationship of the project to unit academic plans, the impact the project would have on the university budget, and the potential for finding interested donors for the project. Fund-raising projects are assigned priority according to the following scale:

> Maximum priority — president, university officers, and development office raise funds
>
> High priority — appropriate dean and development office raise funds
>
> Special priority — development office assists faculty member in raising funds
>
> Standard priority — college or unit raises funds without assistance from development office

The policy on prospect clearance has two parts. One involves submission of proposals to a select group of foundations and the other involves cultivation of major gift prospects. At present, Delta submits proposals to eleven foundations that require an institution to submit only one proposal at a time. A committee appointed by President J. reviews preliminary proposals and decides which of those can be developed, and in what order, for submission to the select foundations.

The second part of the policy is designed to coordinate solicitation of major gifts, identify a limited number of prospects who will be solicited only by the president, and allow a university representative the opportunity to cultivate a major gift prospect, knowing that he or she is the only representative from the university cultivating that prospect. A prospect for a major gift at Delta is defined as a prospect likely to give at the level of $10,000 or more. In assigning clearance to cultivate the prospect, the committee considers the prospect's interest in the university, potential giving level, affiliation or ties, giving record, and other interests. The committee also considers university priorities, the unit's past history with the prospect, and the amount of the request. Development officers request clearance of a prospect for specific projects but may also be given open-ended clearance for certain prospects.

Annual Fund Staff

Delta fund raisers have been using a phone-mail program to contact alumni for annual gifts since 1970, placing Delta among the first institutions of its type to conduct comprehensive annual fund solicitations. They have also conducted regional annual fund drives in as many as thirty cities since the early 1970s. The success of the annual giving program brings national recognition to Delta. More than 30 percent of Delta's alumni give to the annual fund, a participation rate among the highest in the country for all public institutions. In 1987–1988, the annual giving program generated over $1.2 million, with gifts from over 25,000 donors.

One factor contributing to the overall success of the annual program is the parents' fund, which developed from a time-honored tradition at Delta to involve parents in university affairs while their children are on campus. For many decades, the university has invited parents to campus for two special weekend events, Dads' Weekend and Moms' Weekend, which features programs designed for students and parents to attend together. More than 3,000 fathers usually attend Dads' Weekend, and more than 5,000 mothers attend Moms' Weekend, making this the busiest, most popular weekend of the year, "even more popular than homecoming," the annual fund director said.

When development managers first suggested that Delta might capitalize on parents' interest and support by asking parents for donations to the annual fund, university administrators were concerned that parents would be critical and object that they already supported the university through taxes. Nevertheless, the decision to solicit donations from parents prevailed.

Direct mail solicitations were sent to parents beginning in 1973, and phone solicitations were started in 1982. Currently, the parents' program solicits about 6,000 families per year and receives gifts from about half of them. In a recent year, donations from parents totalled almost $88,000, placing Delta among the top five public doctoral institutions in parent contributions.

Director of the Annual Fund. The director of the annual fund, a veteran at Delta with more than seventeen years' service, first worked in the registrar's office and moved to development eleven years ago. He said that the alumni office "has done a tremendous job of tracking alumni and providing current addresses and phone numbers, so only about 10 percent of our alumni are lost. We've used outside firms who use social security numbers to find addresses for lost alumni. About 35 percent of previously lost alumni pledge when we reach them. We're working on finding another group of lost alumni by looking up parents' addresses. I believe we will eventually have our lost alumni down to 5 percent, which is the kind of figure private schools have."

Prior to 1986, the annual fund solicited gifts for unrestricted use, but since that time, the program has been directed primarily toward "constituency-specific asks." The director pointed out that although the general pool of unrestricted funds has decreased since Delta adopted a constituency-based approach for the annual program, gifts to colleges and the student foundation have increased. Some programs traditionally funded by unrestricted money, such as faculty development and student programs, are now funded directly by the units involved with the additional resources they are acquiring.

The central annual fund staff has also been involved in defining roles of college development officers. The annual giving program is designed to serve the entire university, constituency by constituency, and the annual fund director believes that college development officers should focus on major gifts instead of functioning as annual fund program administrators for their areas.

The director discussed goals set for the annual fund:

"Right now we have goals to stimulate unrestricted gifts, to increase donors by 2,000, donations by $100,000, the participation rate by 1½ percent, and the average gift by 50¢. Generally, these goals are based upon our previous history." The director stressed that it is important for Delta to maintain the high level of functioning of the annual program. "In the mid-1980s," he said, "we poured as much as we could into increasing the number of first-time donors. We spent more in 1983 than we spend now. We have a very lean organization today with a very focused solicitation, but if we don't keep up our work over the next twenty-five years — first, soliciting for money, and second, making sure that our information base remains good — we'll be left in the dust."

Telefund Coordinator. The telefund coordinator, a Delta graduate and a former student volunteer in the annual giving program, has been in her paid position for about two years. At the time of the site visit, the telefund program operated with 450 student callers, both volunteers and paid employees. Student volunteers call all alumni who have made donations in the past two years in what is called the Super Telefund, which has a pledge rate above 90 percent.

The telefund coordinator explained how student volunteers are recruited and trained: "Volunteering for the telefund provides visibility for the sororities, fraternities, dorms, and clubs that participate. We train volunteers for the Super Telefund in only two sessions, but since they're calling people who are very much interested in Delta, they usually do a good job." She added, "Fortunately, we always have some experienced callers who come back, and they help spread the word around campus that we need volunteers."

Throughout the rest of the year, paid student callers, about 110 over the course of a year, solicit donations from lapsed donors and alumni who have never made donations. They call on Monday through Thursday evenings "because we think calling on weekends infringes on donor privacy a little more than calling on a school or work night. We know we're calling in a competitive market so we try to be as courteous as possible," the coordinator said. Callers are prepared to provide information or "be sounding boards if alumni want to make comments. If an alumnus has a complaint, the student writes it down, and we forward it to the right office." The telefund coordinator reported that paid student callers secure gifts from 2,000 to 3,000 new donors each year.

A comprehensive training manual for student volunteers and paid callers includes sections on duties, procedures, conversations, responses, and mail appeals. Also included is information for student employees about the pay scale and how performance will be evaluated. Students earn specific bonuses for each completed pledge from previous donors and nondonors, for matched gifts, and for pledges of $100 or above. "Although it is not uncommon anymore, I think we were one of the first public universities to pay student callers," the telefund coordinator said. "It's a way to help students, and it's a great way to orient students to the university's need for private support. I hope that we've been able to open some students' eyes so that their perspective about supporting Delta is different than it might have been."

Decentralized Fund-Raising Staff

The site visit at Delta included a group interview with the alumni affairs officer and four college development officers.

Alumni Affairs. Since the early 1900s, Delta's alumni program was funded by dues; in 1961 the dues program was discontinued in favor of an annual giving program run by the alumni office. In the early 1970s, the president centralized all fund raising. The alumni affairs officer said, "He thought that the foundation development staff was better equipped to run an annual giving program and that the alumni affairs staff would be free to focus more on public relations activities. We've come full circle recently in that it's now again necessary for us to do our own fund raising, so we are starting a new membership program. It makes sense in the context of a more decentralized fund-raising approach overall that we raise our own money, too."

The alumni affairs officer is confident that the membership program will do well because of the success of the annual
giving program. "I think we have a core group of alumni who
are extremely loyal. Compared to other schools in this part of
the country, we have good attendance at alumni activities and
athletic events. From comments that we get, we think our alumni
are very interested in receiving the alumni publication, which
will now be restricted to dues-paying members only. Also, our
travel programs and merchandise offers usually have gotten
higher-than-expected results."

In 1988, the executive committee of the alumni board set
a goal to acquire 10,000 dues-paying members within eighteen
months. The alumni affairs officer said the goal was established
as a result of the suggestion from "a highly respected alumni
director from another school, who said we would get an auto-
matic 10 percent response from our first mailing. That would
be about 7,000 alumni. We decided we ought to be able to bump
it up another 3,000 within eighteen months." The alumni affairs
officer thinks this goal may be too ambitious but is nevertheless
confident that a membership program will be successful at Delta.

College Fund Raisers. College development programs are fi-
nanced by a percentage of voluntary support revenues to the
college. A portion of each college dean's salary, calculated to
reflect the amount of time the dean spends in fund raising, is
also taken from total private dollars raised. One development
officer said that educating the faculty about the need for development activities is an uphill battle in some colleges in which
"the faculty think their programs would be better off if they could
just spend money to hire more teaching assistants instead of
spending money on fund raising." The development officer believes that resistance to spending money in order to raise money
is fairly widespread on public university campuses and does not
see Delta as unusual in this respect.

Nevertheless, understanding of the long-term and incremental benefits of comprehensive development efforts is growing at Delta, nurtured by experienced fund raisers and some
enterprising deans. One college development officer who is a

leader in educating faculty members was a provost and, before that, a faculty member at another institution. He has a deep understanding of the faculty point of view and is also experienced in dealing with faculty attitudes toward administrative functions.

The dean of the business school, who will shift part of the responsibility for supervision of his development officer to the central office in the next fiscal year, has established a development council for his school made up of prominent volunteers and donors. Other deans are considering creating similar councils for their schools.

For the most part, fund-raising programs in the colleges are all still in their early developmental stages. Although some college development officers have had extensive fund-raising experience elsewhere, most of them are new to Delta. The college development officers were impressed by the loyalty Delta inspires in its graduates. One said, "I've never been any place where there is the feeling of support and the alumni loyalty we have at Delta. I think these have played a great part in Delta's fund-raising success." Another said, "I think this university has throughout its history been recognized as a very friendly and caring place but also a university with a straitlaced image. All of this tends to create a very intense loyalty."

The college development officers discussed with us how changes at Delta have affected them. One said, "The last eighteen months have been a very unsettling time because there are new players and new rules. We—and I emphasize we—are making up the rules as we go. Our fund-raising policies are new territory, developed through a grass-roots effort and approved all the way up the line and then put in force." Another college development officer said, "The regular meetings we have with central staff members to decide policies and resolve conflicts are very important, but they are difficult, too. I usually come out of those meetings depressed, and I know there are other development officers who also feel that way. But the meetings are the only way we're going to get things resolved, so I'll keep attending."

A major problem for the college development officers, as indicated earlier, is access to information in the computer data bases. One college development officer said, "Maybe they shouldn't have hired us until they had the computers and support ready for us. I've spun my wheels quite a bit because of not being able to get accurate data in a timely manner. But everybody here somehow manages to keep a good spirit about it." Another officer said, "College fund raisers have been put in an awkward situation and have worked extremely hard to maintain good ties and to work as a team. Some good people in the central office are also trying hard to make sure that this is a team effort. We've had some good cooperation. We've also had people pounding their fists on the table, saying, 'This isn't going to work' or 'I don't like this,' but it's very healthy when people aren't afraid to speak up."

Analysis of Fund Raising at Delta

The outstanding characteristic of Delta's fund-raising program is the strong commitment to the institution expressed by almost all the people we interviewed, even those new to the university. This is one of the four institutions that we studied that evokes exceptionally strong loyalty and affection in students, graduates, and staff members. Related to this commitment to the institution is the determination of most staff members to get through this difficult time — to work out the problems and to make the new structure work. People on this campus take seriously the future of their much-loved institution. Although some are distressed by current conditions, almost everyone is confident that Delta has great potential to substantially increase voluntary support.

Other strong characteristics of the fund-raising program at Delta are presidential leadership, institutional commitment to fund raising, and several aspects of management in the central office. President J., colorful and energetic, is a strong leader with a vision for Delta. Committed to making necessary changes while remaining sensitive to long-standing traditions, the president hopes to increase Delta's stature as a research university and its contribution to improving the economy of the state. He exudes confidence but also acknowledges that moving Delta forward is a learning experience for everyone involved. We were particularly impressed by his awareness of the need for his role to continue to change as Delta changes.

Institutional commitment to fund raising has substantially improved at Delta in recent years. As the president explained, the organizational structure and management style had not changed as the university grew, and central leadership and coordination were lacking. By adding vice presidents to the organizational structure, implementing a universitywide planning process, and redesigning budget allocation procedures, the president made it clear that Delta will operate under stronger centralized control. The recent decision at Delta to expand the fund-raising staff by placing college fund raisers under deans' auspices is somewhat at odds with this new direction and perhaps is a compromise with deans to offset other areas in which they have had to give up some autonomy.

Through trial and error, Delta has learned the importance of universitywide coordinated effort in fund raising. People on campus are aware that fund raising was successful in the past because of the hard work of some people, the basic soundness of the institution, and the affection and respect the institution evokes in its constituents but not because of strategic and skillful planning and design. Key participants are excited about Delta's fund-raising potential and have both a new respect for the complexity of fund raising and a new understanding of the importance of long-term planning and coordination in fund raising. These attitudes are evident in the decision to fill the position of vice president for university relations, in the expansion of the fund-raising staff across campus, and in the work of the committee to study campaign possibilities. Earlier fund-raising experiences have made several key players on campus wiser about fund raising, and some leaders are emerging among deans and fund-raising staff members.

Managers in the central development office use planning procedures and produce documents that are as well conceived and designed as we saw anywhere and better than most. Some staff members complained that the planning and goal-setting processes were only formalities. However, we saw that the use of plans and goals in day-to-day operations provided structure and cohesion in a situation that might have been even more turbulent without these supports. Additionally, Delta was one of only two institutions that we studied in which managers talked directly about staff development and training and had actual programs in operation to address these needs.

Some staff members at Delta are distressed and have low morale because of recent organizational changes. In general, employees everywhere have limited tolerance for the turbulence that major changes cause, and adjustment to these changes almost always takes longer than people think it should. This often causes people to conclude prematurely that the changes were mistakes. These conditions require the kind of courage and strong management commitment to provide concrete assistance and support to staff that are evident at Delta.

Throughout our research, all the fund raisers we met who also have significant management responsibilities were ambivalent about spending time managing when they might be out raising money, and that ambivalence was very strong at Delta. The senior central development managers were doing a highly creditable job in managing in this difficult time, yet it was also clear that their passion was for raising money. Delta needs committed fund raisers and also needs managers who are devoted to minding the store. Delta and most other institutions might be better served by turning such passionate fund raisers loose and turning the management over to staff members who thrive in management positions.

In summary, what can others learn from Delta's experiences? The factors we identified as contributing to fund-raising effectiveness at Delta are as follows:

- The emergence of creative thinking about how to use Delta's capacity for generating intense loyalty to benefit the university in direct ways
- Strong, visionary presidential leadership of the fund-raising process
- A newly articulated universitywide strategic mission that emphasizes overall needs and directions

- Increasing acceptance of the need for all institutional advancement efforts to be universitywide and to be managed by a high-ranking university officer
- Good planning and goal-setting procedures and products in the central development office
- Strong traditions and programs for annual and planned gifts
- Careful, deliberate assessment by campus representatives from diverse areas of the possibilities for a comprehensive major campaign
- Well-developed policies for prospect clearance and proposal submissions

6

Planning for
the Long Range:

A Private Comprehensive University

> ZETA: Strong presidential leadership, close integration of fund
> raising and university planning, and a commitment to long-term
> results are characteristics of the fund-raising program at Zeta.

This private comprehensive university, with an enrollment of
5,500 and educational and general expenditures of almost $40
million, is located in a midsized, midwestern capital city. Descriptive statistics appear in Table 6.1, and the organizational
chart appears in Figure 6.1. Zeta is at the median for expenditures per student, cost of tuition, and age and above the median for other institutional characteristics. Outcomes are above
the median for institutions of this type for total voluntary support, and for gifts from all donors but nonalumni individuals.
Actual outcomes are higher than predicted for total voluntary
support, alumni gifts, and corporation gifts and lower than
predicted for nonalumni gifts and foundation gifts.

Until recently, fund raising at Zeta was limited primarily to corporate donors. As one senior staff member observed,
"Since the dollars coming in from corporations during the last
campaign looked good, we didn't see what was getting away from
us." Under the direction of the current vice president, institutional advancement activities at Zeta have expanded considerably and now include comprehensive programs for marketing
and communications, fund raising, alumni and parent relations,
and special events. Specific fund-raising programs operate for
the annual fund, planned gifts, major gifts, and gifts from all

Table 6.1. Descriptive Statistics (1985–1987 Average) for Zeta University (Private Comprehensive).

	Range for Type				This Institution	
	High	Median	Low	Actual	Predicted	Difference
Institutional Characteristics:						
Educational/General Expenditures	$133,432,400	$21,509,400	$1,773,000	$36,669,032	—	—
Endowment	$264,888,400	$12,493,300	$811,100	$17,820,274	—	—
Expenditures per Student	$26,400	$6,500	$2,800	$6,665	—	—
Cost of Tuition	$15,500	$7,200	$700	$7,530	—	—
Alumni of Record	126,700	19,000	2,900	52,951	—	—
Enrollment	13,900	3,000	200	5,502	—	—
Age of Institution	190 years	100 years	30 years	107 years	—	—
Fund-Raising Results:						
Total Voluntary Support	$31,165,000	$2,907,700	$103,000	$4,935,811	$4,717,427	+ 1.05
Alumni Gifts	$12,111,700	$677,000	$4,200	$1,835,408	$1,544,451	+ 1.19
Nonalumni Gifts	$11,223,400	$930,600	$28,700	$781,309	$163,576	0.47
Corporation Gifts	$19,345,900	$399,400	$13,800	$1,800,306	$822,676	+ 2.19
Foundation Gifts	$6,941,100	$384,200	$18,700	$518,788	$757,986	0.68

Figure 6.1. Organizational Chart for Zeta University.

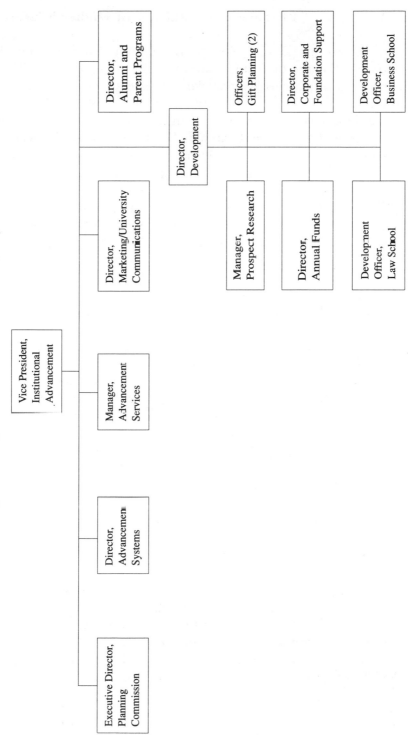

donor groups (alumni, nonalumni, corporations, and foundations). For the first time, development activities are fully integrated with universitywide planning and are guided by a major
committee of the board of governors, with special subcommit-
tees for areas such as special, planned, and annual gifts and relations with alumni and parents. The institutional advancement
staff prepares a comprehensive master plan that states the staff's
overall mission and goals and specific goals and action plans
for each area.

Under the direction of the current president, the university has overcome a serious decline in enrollment and financial
stability. A senior staff member said, "Over the last three years,
our entering freshman class went from 620 to 750 and then to
more than 900. An almost 50 percent increase in enrollment
is remarkable in the face of the demographic decline we're dealing
with, and both our tuition and admissions standards have gone
up. These successes have been mainly due to the president's
charisma, energy, and ability to make the community aware
of Zeta's strengths and a very competent admissions staff. Now
we need to make the same dramatic leap in development. Admissions has a fresh crop of recruits each year, but there aren't
many new potential million-dollar donors turning up every year,
so our work is cut out for us."

At the time of the site visit, Zeta's development staff members were securing advance gifts for a capital campaign with
a goal of $115 million that was soon to be announced. The presi-
dent said, "Many challenges are ahead for the university, but
we are making good progress. If someone had said when I arrived that in four years we would announce a campaign for $115
million, I would have said, 'No way,' but thanks to everybody's
pulling together, we're going to do just that."

This chapter describes how the university is building on
past fund-raising performance to secure Zeta's future. An early
period in Zeta's fund-raising history also provides an illustra-
tion of how a fund-raising program can reach goals and generate statistics that look good on paper and still not serve the institution well.

President M.

President M. assumed office at Zeta in 1985 and spent his first two years working to stabilize the financial base of the university. One major aspect of his work was to streamline and reorganize academic programs. In a relatively short time, he helped to condense nine colleges into six, eliminate thirty degree programs, and add fourteen new degree programs to sharpen Zeta's focus and mission. Other changes fostered by the president include the use of more creative marketing and promotion, the reorganization of the board into a more effective structure, the creation of the position of vice president for institutional advancement, and the expansion of the institutional advancement staff. The president described his first two years as "exciting because although it was a difficult time, the university was ready for a change. Faculty members were excited about making changes and were willing to take some risks and accept that we had to discontinue programs not central to our mission."

Planning Commission. In 1987, after the major restructuring of the overall academic program, President M. convened a national commission of 330 people from education, business, government, the arts, health care, and the nonprofit sector to develop strategic plans for Zeta and to set priorities for future fund-raising programs. The executive director of the commission was a senior member of the institutional advancement staff.

     This director said, "We invited over 550 people to join the commission. I said to the president, 'Why don't we just select 100 people?' He said, 'No. We can't do that, because then it's our list. If we extend the invitation and people choose to accept, they will develop a sense of ownership.' Of people invited, 330 accepted. About half of those were from the Midwest, but the rest were from all over the country."

     Members of the commission were organized into eleven task forces — one to represent each of Zeta's six major academic units and five major administrative areas. They were asked by the president to "listen to our specific plans, our hopes, and our needs. Let us know whether you think our plans make sense, whether we have taken a realistic assessment of our goals in light of the resources that are available or might be forthcoming. Challenge our assumptions. Make sure we are moving in directions that benefit our city, state, and nation. And prod us when necessary to raise our aspirations for quality programs." This commission presented its final report to the board of trustees only nine months after its initial meeting.

The vice president for institutional advancement said, "The commission was to decide what Zeta would do in the next decade and the next century, but they were not to talk about costs. We wanted them to talk about quality, academic programs, and strategic direction." Each task force made specific recommendations, from which the board developed Zeta's strategic plan.

Board members and senior university administrators worked at a three-day retreat, "turning recommendations into goals and strategies, still not talking about dollars at all," the vice president said. No recommendations were eliminated, but the group determined that some recommendations were more urgent than others. Finally, after program goals were set, the vice president said, "The board attached dollar figures totaling over $100 million to program items. If we had talked about costs any earlier in the process, no one would have dreamed that Zeta could even begin to do something of that magnitude. What resulted is a program that is ambitious yet realistic, and the responsibility for setting fund-raising goals and for making a commitment to fund raising started with the board, not with the president and not with the development office."

When we asked him why he selected this model for planning, President M. said, "We needed more people to understand our strengths and weaknesses, and we had to be more open to criticisms and suggestions. Earlier in our history, we involved all internal constituencies in strategic planning, but people outside the institution were uninformed about what we were doing. Even though Zeta is a private institution, we are located in a capital city that expects us to behave as if we were a public institution. The more people who understand Zeta and are involved with us, the better."

The planning process was completed in a much shorter time than a consultant had told the president was possible. When we asked how Zeta could do in a year what experience suggested would take more than two years, President M. explained that Zeta had already accomplished some of the academic planning and internal assessment the planning model required. He said, "We had demonstrated previously in our decision-making processes that we were able and willing to make changes. We didn't have to spend six months getting our faculty members to agree that this was a good idea. Also, Zeta didn't have a lot of time. In two and a half years, the train might have been too far down the track to catch, so we had to move. It was a risk, and no one could be certain of the outcomes, but we had to chance it."

The president secured a foundation grant to fund the planning project. "At the time we did not have a balanced budget," he said, "and this was going to cost anywhere from $100,000 to $200,000 — money we didn't have. I told one of our enlightened board members why we had to take these steps and why I thought the plan would work. Fortunately, he agreed, and his foundation provided the money. Without those funds, it would have been harder to accomplish in that short period what I said we had to do."

Fund Raising. President M. had been involved in developing legislative relationships and securing state funds before he arrived at Zeta, but he did not have experience in fund raising in the private sector, which he now finds "very rewarding and enjoyable." He said, "I have to be visible and involved in fund raising even though our institutional advancement staff is extremely talented. Donors want to see the president, especially from an institution that has not cultivated them over the years. If I'm not out there meeting prospective donors, they'll assume I'm not interested." The president estimated that in earlier years he spent one-third of his time in fund raising. At the time of the site visit, he said that he spent half of his time in fund raising. He projected that soon he would spend two-thirds of his time in fund raising — an amount of time that most experienced development officers may find unusual. "Frankly," the president said, "I expect to spend this much time in fund raising after the campaign, too. In the foreseeable future, the president at Zeta, whoever that may be, will be very heavily involved in fund raising because the responsibility will not end when this campaign ends."

When we asked him whether he was concerned about the increased activity in fund raising by public institutions, President M. responded, "Not at all. For all institutions, securing funding from all sources is more competitive, but it's something we can live with. We just have to be increasingly creative and aggressive in getting our story across. People will support private institutions if we don't just sit back. I don't think it would help to sit in a chairman's or CEO's office and criticize that person or complain about public institutions."

Recalling a meeting at a corporation that had recently dropped its policy not to give donations to public institutions, the president said, "I think I was sensitive to why they believed they needed to support the public universities in this state. At the same time, I made it clear how Zeta is important to them, too. We walked out of that session with a very nice gift that I was not so confident we could secure when we walked in." The president emphasized that "making sure that Zeta has a story worth telling" is as important as telling that story.

President M. said that he received a negative orientation to fund raising from other presidents. "When I started looking for a chief development officer, I was told that it would be difficult because there are not that many good people in the area of development. Several presidents also said that I would not find loyal people because development professionals move on quickly. They also told me that I would find people with showy résumés, making exaggerated claims about what they had done. I had never hired a development person, so I was concerned after hearing these things. As it turned out, that was not my experience in recruiting development staff members. I am very pleased with our chief development officer and the staff he's attracted."

The president noted that "although there are stories of abuses, if you look at the tremendous record of philanthropy to higher education, a lot of people must be doing some marvelous work." Now, he discounts many negative stories about the fund-raising field and considers the motivation of the people who tell these stories.

He went on to say, "I think development people — now I am doing the stereotyping — are optimistic, outgoing people, confident about their abilities and what they can deliver, and I think there will always be tension about fund raising. For example, our faculty members, in general, do not understand why the development staff has not already raised all the money we need. When we talk about our fund-raising campaign, we must make sure that the faculty members understand that although we have commitments of $51 million, we do not have that money in the bank. We must educate people about these things and be careful about how much we promise."

Staff members in institutional advancement expressed strong regard for President M. and what he has accomplished at Zeta. A senior development staff member said, "In 1984, public opinion and perceptions of the university were the lowest I had ever known them to be, and I have been a student, employee, or volunteer since 1946. Our campus and grounds had even started to look a little unkempt. Our momentum began to build when our new president arrived, and now attitudes are very different. Some faculty members returning from sabbaticals could not believe the difference. A lot of work still must be done, but we're going in the right direction. A new, energetic president can do wonders, especially one who is perceived as favorably as our president is."

Another senior staff member said, "Presidential leadership is essential in long-term fund-raising success. Our commission on the future was a classic example of how to involve trustees in a significant way in the life of a university without compromising the academic decision-making process one whit. President M. is an exceptional leader, not only in his ability to communicate his vision for Zeta but also in his ability to get things done."

Vice President for Institutional Advancement

The vice president had been in his position for less than three years at the time of the site visit. Prior to his arrival, fund raising at Zeta was characterized by a strong focus on the local corporate community, and little attention was paid to individual donors. The 1981–1984 campaign to raise $25 million raised 52 percent of gifts from the corporate community and 17 percent from alumni and friends.

The vice president said, "The campaign was successful in reaching its goal, but when the campaign was over, the university was not really any better off. They built some new buildings, but the foundation for continued fund raising was not any stronger than it had been before the campaign. Some alumni and local corporate leaders actually criticized Zeta's lack of focus in fund raising and said we weren't asking for large enough donations. For instance, in the campaign, the law school solicited every graduate for an endowment gift. They asked for pledges of $1,000 over a ten-year period at $100 a year—from lawyers! Such requests encourage donors to give below what they are able and willing to give. We are changing that."

The average gift at Zeta in 1988 was $34, which, the vice president indicated, "is absurd for a university of this magnitude when the national average for private universities is well over $100. Seventeen percent of our alumni gave donations then, but now 23 percent give, and I expect 27 percent to give this year. Our ultimate goal, based on my reading of the loyalty people feel to this institution, is 50 percent."

The vice president said that fund raising must be supported by programs that involve donors, particularly alumni, in the life of the university, but that such programs had not been stressed at Zeta. "Our homecoming activities were meager," he said. "Until last year, we only held class reunions for the twenty-fifth and fiftieth years. If you are an alumnus who doesn't get invited back until you've been out for twenty-five years, we've lost you. The more we care for and nurture our alumni, the better we'll do in fund raising."

The vice president said that in preparation for the upcoming campaign, Zeta is "asking for magnificent gifts from board members and alumni used to giving $50. We are talking to many board members about seven-figure commitments. Before we ever announce this campaign, all twenty-eight board members will make commitments that will end up being more than the entire goal of the earlier campaign. We will have pledges or cash totaling about $50 million before we go to the public to announce a program for over $100 million. It's standard in the business to have 30 to 50 percent up front before you announce a campaign, and we need close to 50 percent here since Zeta has not done this kind of fund raising before."

The vice president said he does not believe in using "slick case statements and fancy brochures. Zeta will not produce a flashy document that describes the entire program or locks it in concrete. I want to provide each major gift prospect with a personalized document, a document in progress, so that the prospective donor becomes part of the design rather than a person who gives an amount that I established. I want to help donors see what the university's needs are and then help them determine how they want to be involved."

The vice president said, "This institution could not raise a dollar unless great things were being done here by great people in the classroom. The advancement program is an extension of that fact. Zeta needs $2 million in annual support a year. We are putting money, time, and talent into permanently increasing the annual fund because the fund is the future of Zeta's fund-raising success. Initially, we may spend as much as 55¢ on the dollar to do that, but that will help secure big gifts that may cost 2¢ on the dollar."

The vice president continued, "I'm talking about a long-term program, not a quick fix. This staff is working very hard to build a fund-raising foundation, unique to this institution, reflective of this institution's needs, history, and goals. This foundation will be built on continuing close relationships with alumni and others who care about the university. Long after this president and the rest of us are gone, the foundation for fund raising will still be here."

"I don't like the word *campaign*," the vice president said. "People think, 'Zeta's in a campaign and I've got to give because it's the big one.' I want donors to know that this is a major fund-raising effort, but I also want them to understand that five years from now we are going to ask for another gift and that in the meantime we want them to be involved with us."

"Many development officers come to a school knowing

they are going to move on in three years," the vice president said. "That doesn't do the institution any good. Our profession has to take seriously the need to establish programs that undergird the future of the institution. That involves continuity and commitment. We do a disservice if we come in, apply the quick fix, and move on." Pointing out that institutions also have some responsibility for staff turnover, the vice president said, "It's cheaper to pay more to keep good staff members than it is to hire new people every three years. It seems to me that this is not well understood at many schools."

Teamwork and wide participation in goal setting and planning, reflective of the president's management approach, are two prominent aspects of the vice president's management style. Each year, for what he calls "the most important four days of the year for our office," the vice president holds a planning retreat, primarily for senior development staff members, although all staff members participate for some of the days.

The senior staff members create a comprehensive calendar for all major activities that they use throughout the year as a working plan. They review last year's progress, identifying strengths and weaknesses for every program and activity. Directors have already evaluated their own programs, and this group process provides them with feedback from other team members. The senior staff members also develop new annual goals during this meeting. The vice president said, "I participate in setting goals, but the directors are going to carry out the programs, so they must have ownership. I think encouraging team ownership, along with letting the directors know they have someone to lean on if they need help, is extremely important."

Director of Development

The director of development assumed her position nine months prior to the site visit. She had been a college development officer in another institution. All fund-raising staff members report to this director in the central office, and each staff member has an assignment as liaison for a specific college. "At Zeta we have a centralized program," the director said, "but we are dealing with alumni constituencies that identify with their colleges. It's very important to avoid the suggestion that some constituencies are not as important as others. Over time, we will either have a development officer for each college or have development officers in regional areas with heavy concentrations of alumni. We must make sure that we have specific development officers for all constituencies."

The director said, "We need annual support from our constituencies to supplement our budget. In addition, some special projects fall outside the budget, and we need to build our endowment. For these reasons, we're spending a tremendous amount of energy in strengthening our annual program."

The annual fund has two key characteristics: face-to-face solicitation by volunteers of donors with the potential to give $1,000 or more and a systematic mail-phone solicitation of all other prospects. Annual fund staff members recruit as many alumni callers as they can and then augment that group with paid student callers. Three alumni-staffed phonathons operate in regions outside the local area, and more are planned for next year. A telemarketing company solicits alumni who have never made donations and long-lapsed donors and provides data to plan future solicitations. The director said, "If alumni have not made a gift in twenty years, it is clear they're not going to make one, so we have to question any strategy for soliciting their support that represents much of an investment."

Zeta hired an outside firm for prospect screening. "For gross screening," the director said, "the firms all use the same things, but each one uses different specific refinements, so we had to consider which were best for us. One firm used indicators of linkage to the institution, such as giving record and involvement with the alumni board; we rejected this firm because Zeta has not had much alumni involvement in the past. Another firm created indicators of giving behavior over time from fifty institutions; we rejected this one because we did not think Zeta was similar enough to institutions used to develop the criteria."

The firm they selected combines census data, sociological patterns, and rating scales to measure a prospect's potential to give. The cost for screening the 45,000 names of Zeta's alumni, parents, and friends was $19,000, which also included updates of addresses and phone numbers.

The director also said that Zeta is developing a prospect research and tracking system based on her study of tracking programs in use at other institutions. To supplement the screening provided by the outside firm, the director has created the management of advancement prospects system (MAPS), which is a committee made up of all development officers. "Through MAPS," the director explained, "we identify prospects, develop specific cultivation and solicitation plans, and coordinate multiple requests to approach a given prospect. Each college's liaison is the advocate for that college and is responsible for keeping deans fully apprised of progress with donors they're interested in."

All development staff members are recruiting alumni to serve the institution in ways they have never been asked to do before. Staff members are consistently surprised at the positive response they get and the interest "long-neglected alumni" have in serving the university.

This director, similar to the vice president, favors a team management approach and understands that management is critical. She spends only 20 percent of her time in direct fund raising, chiefly with major donors. She said, "Most of my time so far has been spent in recruiting and hiring staff members, which is a very demanding task. People are everything in this field. I have put a lot of effort into building a team."

Indicating that success as a fund raiser is no guarantee for success as a manager, the director said, "Being an effective manager of human resources — keeping the staff well integrated and supportive of one another — takes real skill, which I am working to develop and improve. One of the most important and useful seminars I've ever attended for my own professional development was the one on effective human resources management sponsored by the Council for Advancement and Support of Education (CASE). I also attended the CASE seminar on executive management. I recommend these seminars."

The director follows the lead of the president and vice president in involving others in planning. She said, "I'm a firm believer in planning and in wide participation. Last week, we met off campus for two full days to begin to develop a strategic plan. We started the retreat with some team-building work, facilitated by the university's director of human resources, who is herself quite a resource. I keep telling the staff members that we can enjoy this journey we're on, in addition to working hard and making important things happen, and also that I need their help in remembering that myself. Fortunately, a couple of the staff members are great at helping us all to relax and have fun. We are committed to regular social outings together. We think social activities support our commitment to build something permanent for Zeta."

Analysis of Fund Raising at Zeta

Zeta's fund-raising program is one of both substance and style. Most of the characteristics from the list in Chapter One are outstanding characteristics of the fund-raising program at Zeta, including trustees' participation, which was not an outstanding characteristic at many of the institutions we studied. Leadership, by both the president and vice president, is the core outstanding element because all of the other characteristics seem to have been directly influenced by this leadership. Styles and values of top leadership in any institution filter down through organizational levels. The influence of the styles of the president and vice president for institutional advancement are visible at Zeta in the emphasis on teamwork, wide participation in planning and goal setting, and open evaluation and in the willingness of staff members to give each other credit for Zeta's achievements. We were impressed by the combination of statesmanship and entrepreneurship in the leadership at Zeta. We were particularly impressed by the president's attitudes toward competition in fund raising and stereotypical images of fund raisers. With these attitudes, the president provides leadership not only for staff members at Zeta but also for higher education overall.

Institutional commitment to fund raising is also an outstanding characteristic at Zeta, indicated by adequate current and long-term resource allocation for fund raising, efforts to increase awareness among Zeta's internal and external constituencies both of the need for greater voluntary support and Zeta's potential to secure it, and the extensive effort to set overall institutional priorities and fund-raising goals.

Also noteworthy among Zeta's many outstanding characteristics is the candid approach to marketing. If management is still considered to be a not-quite-respectable activity in higher education, marketing may be considered even less respectable. Nevertheless, although most institutions are engaged in marketing, most are not as direct as Zeta about it. One director at Zeta has the term *marketing* in his title, the only director who has such a title at the institutions we studied. Under the leadership of President M., staff members are working to define Zeta's niche, to improve Zeta's quality overall, and to communicate Zeta's image effectively across the country.

Management of fund raising is also outstanding at Zeta, characterized by team efforts to plan and evaluate all programs. Systematic efforts are under way to enlarge and improve information systems, and managers value taking the time to ensure good communication. At Zeta, the consensus is that a sophisticated and complex fund-raising program will not work in the long run without skillful professional management. This is the only institution we studied in which professional human resource staff members were used to help enhance fund-raising performance.

There is an optimistic, positive climate at Zeta. Staff members are committed not only to professional standards and reaching their goals but also to another value, that of creating a long-lasting foundation for future fund-raising efforts. Volunteers' roles in fund raising and an emphasis on constituent relations are emerging as strong characteristics at Zeta.

In summary, what can others learn from Zeta's experiences? The factors we identified as contributing to fund-raising effectiveness at Zeta are as follows:

- A president with vision, ability, skill, and strong interest in fund raising
- Well-crafted strategies for fund raising and university growth

that are integrated among all levels, from the board to the frontline practitioners

- Serious, substantive commitment to long-term and cumulative results
- Detailed, comprehensive programming and staffing for fund raising and strengthening relationships with all constituencies
- Emphasis on customizing programs to reflect Zeta's strengths and needs
- Emphasis on teamwork and wide participation in decision making as a way to ensure staff commitment and ownership
- Ambitious and realistic goals
- Efforts to strengthen external involvement and participation in Zeta's growth, locally, regionally, and nationally
- Awareness of need to educate constituencies and to be patient with slow but steady progress in this education process
- Strong professional standards and expert know-how in management and fund raising
- Investment of adequate resources and careful selection of methods and approaches new to the institution
- Open evaluation of all activities

7

Building on
Its Position
as a Source
of Regional Pride:

A Public Comprehensive University

> THETA: Using existing strengths—the greatest of which is the
> devotion alumni and staff members feel toward this institution—to
> build new ones is the distinctive feature of Theta's fund-raising
> approach. Also outstanding are leadership by the president and
> chief development officer and an emphasis on constituent rela-
> tionships.

This public comprehensive university, with an enrollment of
more than 15,000 and educational and general expenditures of
more than $108 million, is located in a small southern commu-
nity. Formerly a state teachers college, Theta became a university in the late 1960s and opened its medical school in the late
1970s. This university has a strong commitment to provide service to the region. As one senior development officer said, "We
are not only the focus of attention educationally but also eco-
nomically, socially, and politically. Our president not only leads
the university but also leads the entire region."

Descriptive statistics appear in Table 7.1. Figures for
Theta fluctuate over the ranges for institutions of this type. Theta
is at or near the higher end of the range for educational and
general expenditures and expenditures per student, above the
median for alumni of record and enrollment, at the median for
age of institution, and below the median for endowment and
cost of tuition.

Table 7.1. Descriptive Statistics (1985–1987 Average) for Theta University (Public Comprehensive).

| | Range for Type | | | This Institution | | |
	High	Median	Low	Actual	Predicted	Difference
Institutional Characteristics:						
Educational/General Expenditures	$108,253,800	$41,489,600	$8,105,600	$108,250,000	—	—
Endowment	$15,918,300	$2,281,300	$5,900	$1,081,400	—	—
Expenditures per Student	$7,800	$3,900	$2,300	$7,091	—	—
Cost of Tuition	$2,200	$1,300	$700	$842	—	—
Alumni of Record	115,100	30,000	6,100	56,500	—	—
Enrollment	31,100	9,100	1,900	15,300	—	—
Age of Institution	180 years	80 years	20 years	81 years	—	—
Fund-Raising Results:						
Total Voluntary Support	$6,154,400	$1,690,000	$81,700	$4,700,000	$3,300,000	+1.43
Alumni Gifts	$1,221,300	$339,700	$0	$540,100	$390,100	+1.38
Nonalumni Gifts	$2,019,500	$340,100	$23,700	$2,019,000	$866,700	+2.33
Corporation Gifts	$4,724,600	$273,000	$9,300	$1,243,000	$1,630,000	0.76
Foundation Gifts	$1,481,900	$83,900	$0	$860,300	$267,000	+3.22

All voluntary support outcomes for this institution are above the median for type. Nonalumni gifts are higher for this university than for any other institution of this type. Actual outcomes are substantially higher than predicted outcomes for total voluntary support, alumni gifts, nonalumni gifts, and foundation gifts. The actual outcome for corporation gifts is somewhat below the predicted amount for this donor group. The organizational chart for Theta appears in Figure 7.1.

Three major universities are located in the same region of

Figure 7.1. Organizational Chart for Theta University.

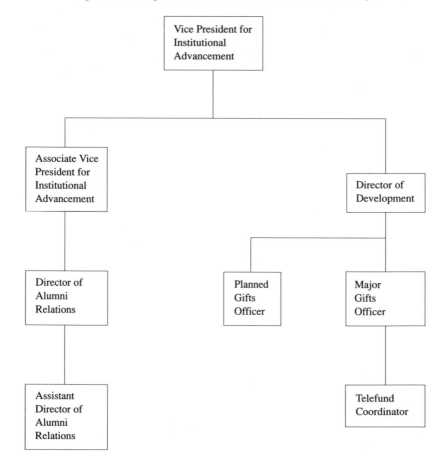

the state as Theta is. Theta's loyal alumni and friends are not discouraged by frequent unfavorable comparisons between Theta and these other institutions. One staff member insisted, "We try harder because Theta has always been the underdog in the state. The others may beat us in dollars raised but not in energy and effort." All but one member of the professional development and alumni staff are Theta alumni. The nonalumni said, "When I came here, everyone I talked to — alumni, people in the community, students, faculty members, staff members — expressed strong commitment to the institution and quickly made a convert out of me. It is wonderful being with people who feel so deeply about their institution. The university I attended is a fine academic school, but its alumni have little depth of feeling for the school. I am constantly amazed by the dedication I find here."

The atmosphere that motivates staff members to "try harder" and elicits great loyalty is a distinguishing characteristic of this institution. One staff member stated, "All of us have a great vision for this university and a personal stake here as well. Each one of us has a strong feeling for the university. Not only do we have a job to do, but this is our heritage. We love this school and want to help it be all it can be."

President R.

President R., in his position for two years at the time of the site visit, is an active participant in fund raising at Theta. When he first arrived at Theta from an administrative position at a midwestern university, he deliberately avoided fund-raising calls. "We thought it would be harmful for me to meet people with my hand out. I tried to meet people first so that it would not be a signal that when the president makes an appintment he is always coming to ask for money."

Theta has been successful in fund raising, in his opinion, primarily because of the strong role the university plays in the region and the resulting commitment to the school people feel. "A lot of generous people who have never attended the school support Theta. Some have never gone to college at all, but they nevertheless see us as their university." The need to generate increasing amounts of private support is clear to President R. "If we are to be a high-quality institution, we have to find people willing to invest in us," he said. "Improvements are not going to happen if we depend on the state to fund them."

President R. observed that commitment to institutional advancement is building throughout the university. One indication is the participation of faculty members and deans as volunteers in the annual telefund. However, a state regulation prohibits the withholding of donations from paychecks, a regulation that the president believes inhibits annual gifts to Theta from faculty and staff members. President R. is especially impressed by "the outstanding allegiance and generosity of retired faculty members," many of whom stay on in the community.

Soon after he arrived at Theta, President R. learned that many people in the region, some in very influential positions, had "an image of the university that was at least twenty years out-of-date." The university had not paid enough attention to how it was perceived in the community. "At one time, I put all the university publications out on my desk and recognized immediately that the university did not have a standard visual identity. We had some extraordinarily good and some extraordinarily bad materials and everything in between. A consistent visual image helps people to think of a university in a more refined and deliberate way. I don't promote image as opposed to substance, but we're a better institution than our materials reflected, and we want people to have a contemporary image of the university." The president created a new office reporting to the vice president for institutional advancement to oversee all university publications.

President R. spends 10 percent of his time in direct fund raising. During the peak months for annual fund solicitations, in addition to taking his turn at the phones during special solicitations, he speaks at as many as ten alumni or athletic association functions per month. He estimated that he will be spending between 40 and 50 percent of his time on fund-raising activities when Theta undertakes a major campaign.

The vice president expressed strong praise for President

R.'s leadership and fund-raising abilities: "Our president has a very distinct idea of who we are and where we ought to go. He has excellent personal skills, his instincts are right, and he is not afraid to ask for gifts. If we could have looked the world over, we would not have found a better person for this time in our history."

The president and vice president are working to increase trustees' involvement in Theta's advancement. The vice president said, "Historically, the board did not have fund-raising or public relations responsibilities, and presidents did not have a lot to do with forming the board. Recently, we have suggested names to the board of governors and have been able to get some people named to the board who will help in fund raising. When I arrived, most board members were not donors. Now all trustees are members of the President's Society, which means they have made a commitment of $10,000, and four or five trustees have made or helped secure gifts of $100,000 or more." It is not just actual donations that Theta needs from its trustees, as the vice president noted: "We need to build their sense of ownership in the university and our fund-raising success. It is our responsibility to make sure they are involved and active."

Vice President for Institutional Advancement

Three university foundations raise money for Theta: the academic foundation, the athletic foundation, and the medical foundation. The vice president for institutional advancement is the chief development officer for the university and has oversight of fund-raising programs for the academic foundation. The fund raisers for athletics report to the athletics director; the fund raiser for the medical foundation reports to the dean of the medical school. Since these fund raisers do not report to the vice president for institutional advancement, they have been omitted from the organizational chart. Staff members from the three foundations meet several times a year to review activities with mutual prospects.

Institutional advancement (which includes development, alumni affairs, and university publications) and the public service office report to the vice president for institutional advancement. The public service office provides services to regional businesses and nonprofit organizations. The vice president said, "Having the public service component in my area provides some advantages. It gives me another reason to talk to people so that I am not always asking for money. We try to avoid doing a project for someone and then coming back a week later to ask for money, but our client companies do become prospects."

Theta has had formal fund-raising programs for only ten years and has recently enjoyed rapid advancement. In 1985, Theta received its first $100,000 gift, the largest gift up to that point. Theta acquired its first $500,000 gift two years later and its first $1 million gift in 1988. The vice president said, "We've been lucky, but, then, I'm convinced that the harder you work, the luckier you get. We have simply worked harder and smarter at focusing our efforts."

The only organized fund-raising campaign at Theta for an academic program was conducted in the mid 1980s for the business school. The goal for that campaign was $2 million; Theta raised $2.2 million. The university is currently in a campuswide planning process, expected to result in a major fund-raising campaign in the next several years with a goal that may be as high as $50 million. One factor indicating that it is a good time for a major campaign is the changing composition of the alumni body. The vice president said, "Eighty percent of all alumni have graduated since 1960. For so many years, most of our graduates were teachers with limited financial means. Now we have business and technical graduates from the late 1950s and early 1960s who are at an age when they can afford to give."

Another factor favoring a major campaign is the qualitative growth of the university, as described by the vice president: "During our growth years, many people saw Theta as a brash, not entirely acceptable second cousin in relation to other public institutions in this state. We were growing fast but were not seen as having the academic quality that other schools had. Some people still think of us as they did twenty-five years ago — a party school but not a good place to get a serious education. That is an inaccurate view because we now have a medical school and our business school is one of the strongest in the state. We are excellent in the arts, music, and the performing arts. These areas of the university are now recognized as among the best in the South."

Although each institutional advancement unit completes an extended annual report, which includes an analysis of the year's accomplishments and projected goals for the coming year, the vice president said their focus has been on short-term goals. "We have been relatively limited in staff and resources and, by necessity, have focused on what we have to do today. After we draw some broad outlines of what we want to accomplish, we give a lot of leeway and responsibility to individual members of the team. This approach works because of the strength of our staff. We have not had guidance from an overall university plan. We have not been as effective as we will be in the future in planning across the university and within the department."

Advancement managers praised the vice president's management style, citing his ability to provide both direction and autonomy. One said, "We are fortunate to have him. He encourages us to put as much of ourselves into the job as we can, and we don't have to try to guess what he's thinking. We know what he expects."

The vice president explained that both his management style and his fund-raising philosophy come in part from his former experience in business. "I look at donors as customers," he said. "We are selling, obviously. We don't give cars or insurance policies in return for donors' investments, so we work hard to figure out what is important to donors and what will make them feel involved in the university. Much of what we have been doing so far is building relationships. One of our strengths is that our staff people have such good relationships with individual donors. We try in a very direct, honest way to establish the expectancy that we'll ask for another gift. We tell donors, 'We certainly appreciate this $1,000 gift. We will be good stewards, but we are going to come back to you, and the next time we are going to ask for $10,000.'"

Regarding a recent "serendipitous" $25,000 gift to the business school, the vice president said, "We are just beginning to receive that type of gift. When I say 'serendipitous,' I don't mean we haven't worked hard for the gift, but we made no specific solicitation. One day last fall, a corporate vice president who is on some of the university's advisory boards said, 'I have requested that $25,000 a year be set aside for the next three years for Theta.' Some of our donors are just beginning to think like this, without our having to ask each time. These are the real victory stories — the ones that make me want to fall down on my knees and say, 'Thank you, Lord! We must be making progress.'"

Development Staff

The professional development staff includes the director of development, the telefund coordinator, the major gifts officer, and the planned giving officer. Commitment to the institution is the outstanding characteristic of staff members at Theta. The vice president for institutional advancement repeatedly described the staff as "very professional and very committed." As one staff member put it, "I don't know anybody on staff who is here temporarily, waiting for something better to come along. Everybody here is dedicated to what we're doing. Any of us could be somewhere else if we wanted to be." Another staff member said, "What makes us successful is that we have all made a commitment. We might gripe once in a while, we might be tired, especially when we've worked fourteen days in a row and we have to get back up on Monday morning, but we've all made a commitment because we love this institution. Personally, I don't know if I would feel that way somewhere else. Somewhere else, it might be just a job."

Fund-raising staff members in all areas of the university are unanimous in thinking that the greatest barriers to raising money for Theta are the limits of time and staff. The director of development explained: "The university has a certain amount of money in its budget for personnel, including faculty members. The president may have to decide between keeping a faculty member in the math department or getting another employee for institutional advancement. He can't do both, but he recognizes our needs and the value of what we do."

Saying that "program budgets are not bad at all," the director of development pointed out a situation common to many advancement offices in public institutions: "The state does not recognize advancement as a legitimate function, so they don't give us money for new personnel. To add staff members, we have to use money we raise, which defeats the purpose of raising money. If the state would help us with money for more staff members, we could prove in dollars and cents that our department is a good investment."

All staff members we spoke with indicated that they could not see all of Theta's prospects each year and that Theta's donors expect personal contact. The assistant vice president for institutional advancement, who directs alumni relations and has fund-raising responsibilities, said he gets complaints from people who are upset because no one has been to see them, but he has never had any complaints from people who are annoyed about being solicited. "Our greatest problem is in getting to all the people who really want to see us," he said. "They're waiting and they're not going to give significant gifts until somebody comes."

The director of development said of the assistant vice president, "He has built up so much capital in relationships during his twenty years here. If we could turn him loose full time to call on all of those people, the return would be incredible."

The vice president stated that fund-raising results have tripled in some areas in the last five years with staff and budget essentially unchanged. He said, "We are working at or over capacity in some areas. You can do that for a while, but you just can't expect people to give 110 percent day in and day out."

A long-term plan to alleviate staff shortages includes hiring fund raisers for each of the professional schools. These new staff members will report to both the institutional advancement office and their respective deans. Suggesting that "serving two masters" can be problematic, one manager observed, "but these are good problems to have. They are the problems you run into as your program grows and becomes more sophisticated and more complex."

Ten paid student callers and 175 student volunteers, representing thirty campus organizations and residence halls, are involved in the telefund for annual gifts. Additionally, faculty and staff volunteers, including the president, conduct a special telefund for $1,000 donors, and volunteers from a parents' association call other parents.

The telefund coordinator said, "We finally have office space for a permanent telefund bank of twenty-five telephones. We eventually hope to increase our paid callers to twenty-five, but we will still rely heavily on student volunteers and still have our special solicitations by staff and faculty members. We have been segmenting our prospect groups so we can make solicitations more appropriate for each group. We're trying to duplicate in house what an outside telemarketing firm would do."

The director of development noted, "Right now we get gifts from about 23 percent of the alumni we reach. A very sore spot for all of us is the number of alumni for whom we do not have valid addresses. Staff members struggle to keep their heads above water day after day just maintaining the records we do have, so there is never any time to find lost alumni. It's very frustrating."

The major gifts officer explained that she is on the road two to three days each week visiting prospects who have the potential to make a $10,000 commitment — $1,000 a year for ten years — for membership in the President's Society. She initiated area campaigns, "one of the best things we've ever done," in 1988. She explained, "We get a committee of alumni or other volunteers together in certain areas to look at our lists of prospects. They identify people who can give $1,000 or more. Then these volunteers call the identified prospects. In the first year, everybody on the committees joined the President's Society, and then they identified new prospects. Some of them set up and made calls with me, driving me from place to place to save time. Our alumni had never been asked to help in these ways and their response was wonderful. Each week I had more prospects than I could see." Although prospect research is improving, she said, "the goals we set for individual gifts are probably more often too low rather than too high."

The director of development thought Theta could improve gift levels from corporation and foundation donors, although the potential for these gifts has some built-in limits. He said, "A limited amount of corporate money is available within a seventy-five-mile radius. We are young in this business and haven't yet developed strong contacts with foundation and corporation directors. Also, our alumni are just now rising to top corporate levels and sitting on boards, so a lot of potential is building out there."

Current responsibilities of the planned giving officer include scholarship and trust administration, which will eventually be delegated elsewhere to leave the officer with more time for developing the planned giving program. With support from the voluntary planned gifts advisory council, Theta raised almost $1.5 million in deferred gifts in 1987–1988. In addition to quarterly newsletters, prospects for planned gifts receive specialized mailings on such issues as gifts of appreciated property, year-end giving, and explanations of tax implications.

The director of development commented on the importance of the university planning process to the development effort and articulated a problem familiar to many development officers. "The university's first strategic planning process," he said, "will result in more formalized definitions and better prioritizing of university needs. Hardly a week goes by now that I don't have someone come in with a new project that they want us to raise money for. Some of these projects are not terribly promising, but it is not my responsibility to say that a particular project won't work. Deans or department heads are supposed to clear projects and set priorities, but I have yet to see anything that was not a priority. All of these 'minicampaigns' dilute our efforts. When we have more focus, we will be more successful."

The president began the university planning process by asking faculty members to specify their departmental needs and the costs associated with them. The director observed, "We'll wind up with a list worth $500 million, which we certainly cannot satisfy, but that will be condensed into a realistic set of priorities to be the basis for our capital campaign. Faculty members will have a stake in the campaign because they will have had a part in deciding what the money will be raised for. By the end of the campaign, everyone associated with the university will have greater understanding of institutional advancement. A successful planning process and campaign will have a long-term beneficial effect for us."

The development staff indicated that the management style of the director of development contributed to their success. One fund raiser said, "The way in which we are managed is a real plus. We can try any reasonable idea, and his door is always open for guidance. We are treated like professionals, which has a lot to do with how we feel about ourselves. I've made some errors along the way, but he's the one who has taken the heat. That kind of support really brings out the best in us."

Alumni Affairs

Theta has thirty-six regional alumni chapters. Some alumni affairs programs are homecoming; outstanding alumni and service awards; publications; student recruitment; travel, insurance, and merchandise; teaching excellence awards; President's Club; and parents' programs. Of special note are programs for student ambassadors, university scholarships, and transcripts to alumni. In a recent year, the alumni association allocated over $168,000 to university programs, including eighty $1,000 scholarships, four $3,000 scholarships, and twenty additional scholarships.

Student ambassadors are student volunteers who provide various services throughout the campus under the auspices of alumni affairs. The student ambassadors have brought national recognition to the institution. They competed successfully to host an upcoming national convention of student organization members.

The alumni association is also involved in a program to assist the registrar's office in responding to requests for transcripts that arrive without accompanying payment. Instead of withholding transcripts and responding that a fee is required, the registrar's office sends the transcripts and informs former students that the alumni association is underwriting the payment for the transcripts as a service to them. The alumni are asked to reimburse the association and are invited to become involved if they are not current members.

The alumni affairs unit maintains alumni records (making about 1,800 changes in the alumni data base per month) and supports fund raising through the quality of the events it sponsors. One fund raiser said, "After my mother attended an alumni function here and one at her own alma mater, she said that the difference was unbelievable, that they acted cold at her school because they felt they could rest on their laurels. We don't do that. We put a lot of effort into meeting people and making them feel welcome. Now, my mother gives us money, but she doesn't give to her own college."

Medical Foundation

The executive director of the medical foundation has held that position since the medical school was founded in 1977. The foundation was established initially to raise money to supplement state funds for equipment and faculty members' salaries. The purpose of the foundation has been expanded to include providing seed money for research and special projects. The medical foundation now raises about $1.5 million per year. The director is the only fund raiser. Part-time staff members produce an alumni magazine and conduct donor research. The director explained that he and the medical school dean collaborate to set the fund-raising agenda and goals. He said, "I have never had to work under a regime with someone telling me I had to raise 2 percent more from X and 10 percent more from Y."

In 1988, the medical foundation spent $85,000 from interest on endowment funds for direct fund-raising costs, publications, and salary for a research associate. Although the director solicits funds from all major donor groups, he indicated that most gifts to the foundation come from nonalumni individuals, foundations, and corporations. "We've been raising cause-specific funds from friends since we opened the door," the director said. "We didn't have any alumni, and our faculty members were all poor. Most of our alumni who are still in residency training are still poor, but before they graduate, we ask them to pledge to get them in the habit of giving. Last year's class of fifty-three graduates pledged $55,000. They're on the right track."

The director organized a parents' group, which raised $100,000 for long-term emergency loans to students. The success of this group reflects parents' desire to be involved in their sons' and daughters' medical school experiences. "Can you imagine a parent flying here to give me $1,000 for the parents' fund? Somebody did. It cost him $1,000 to get here, but he wanted to be involved. These people inspire me. Sometimes the most inspiring people are those who don't have a lot of money to give. I want to include them, so I'll go see parents who give $25 and tell them how their son or daughter is doing." Although the director's immediate purpose is to involve all parents, this kind of personal treatment may benefit the foundation later through gifts from successful physicians.

The director of the medical foundation noted that his personal involvement in the community is important to his success as a fund raiser. Unlike a fund raiser at another institution, who said that being involved in other community affairs represents a conflict of interest for him, the director said, "I'm on every committee possible. So is my wife. That's what it takes to thread yourself into the community. You have to give of yourself, not just ask other people to give all the time."

The high visibility this director has in the community has been useful in raising money but also brings added responsibility. "If people have resources and you convince them that this is a good place to invest, they'll want to give you the money. 'Let me write you a check,' they say, 'you'll know what to do with it.' You have to say, 'No. You can't do that because of the tax consequences. I don't really want to be responsible for this million dollars, so talk to your financial adviser, and then make the check out to the university.' What that proves is that people give money because of who you are, not because of the 'case.' You're the one who came by and drank tea with them. You're the one they give the money to."

Athletic Foundation

Theta competes in Division I football and basketball. The football and basketball teams have not had a winning season since

1983. But private support has not decreased, which surprises the two fund raisers for the athletic foundation. The backbone of the athletic foundation is the forty-chapter athletic club, with a membership of about 4,200 that is increasing at the rate of about 8 percent each year. There are nine membership levels, ranging from $50 to $5,000. Six years ago, the athletic foundation raised about $350,000 a year. In 1988, the fund-raising goal was $2 million. A portion of the money raised, projected at about 22 percent for 1989, is used to cover fund-raising costs.

The director echoed his fund-raising counterparts elsewhere at Theta, saying "Whatever success we have had is because of the tremendous pride people have in the university. People really care about Theta. That fact overrides any great theories I might come up with to explain our success. In spite of what we've accomplished, we haven't even touched our full potential. We have volunteer support that is invaluable. A lot of our people have a kind of pit bull attitude — we're sinking our teeth into the goal of being successful academically and athletically, and we are not going to let go."

The athletic foundation conducts numerous fund-raising events throughout the year. The biggest event, attracting about 25,000 alumni and nonalumni, is a spring weekend event, publicized via radio, television, and billboards within a sixty-mile radius of the campus. The highlight of the weekend is when "everybody from the president to the janitor is auctioned off as a golf partner," the director said. This event, which netted $50,000 in 1988, increases community and regional identification with the university, generates goodwill, and undoubtedly lays the groundwork for future successful solicitations.

The director emphasized the importance of personal contact with Theta donors. "Our donors respond better to a personal contact," he said, "than to a mail campaign or even a telephone request. Our donors really seem to enjoy being together and meeting the people who lead our various athletic programs. Our banquets and spring tours bring a lot of people together who get excited about what's going on, and then they give back to the university."

Asked whether the three university foundations compete for donors, the director replied: "We do compete for some segments

of our donor pool and probably eat a little of each other's pie.
But, in fact, we tell people that we don't want them to stop giving to some other segment of the university because we care
about the entire university, as opposed to caring only about our
individual programs. There is some competition, but it makes
us all do a better job."

Like his colleagues elsewhere in institutional advancement
at Theta, the director said that the potential for increased revenues from private support is as yet untapped. "We're a young
university, with graduates who are just now stabilized in their
careers," he said. "We anticipate a tremendous return over the
next ten years. Our growth, barring any severe economic down-
turns, should be astronomical. My excitement about our potential keeps me awake at night."

Analysis of Fund Raising at Theta

Outstanding characteristics of the fund-raising program at Theta
are the leadership of the president and the vice president for
institutional advancement, the commitment of staff members
to the institution, and the emphasis on constituent relationships.
Institutional advancement staff members and executive leaders
have worked hard to make creative use of Theta's strengths. Because of this, Theta presents an excellent example of how to
use existing institutional strengths to build a foundation for a
formal professional advancement program and, conversely, of how
institutional advancement efforts increase institutional strengths.

Theta's outstanding strength as an institution is its ability to elicit enormous affection from its constituents. (At Theta
and other institutions we visited where constituents are passionate in their loyalty, which is not universally a characteristic of
higher education institutions, we found it surprisingly difficult
to pin down the institutional factors underlying such strong feelings. People are curiously inarticulate about what aspects of an
institution evoke such depth of feeling.) As Theta has grown
from a state teachers college to a comprehensive university with
considerable regional impact and the scope of its influence and
alumni body has increased, Theta has acquired more—and more

ardent — admirers who have been encouraged to put their money where their heart is only in the last several years. Institutional advancement staff members at Theta are not involved in efforts to interest people in Theta, as may be the task at some institutions with new advancement programs, but to reach all those who already have great affection for the university.

The president and the vice president of institutional advancement do an outstanding job at articulating Theta's strengths and aspirations. They have a vision of Theta's potential but also clearly see the developmental work (for example, universitywide planning and fund-raising goal setting) that Theta needs to continue to do, to improve as both an academic institution and a fund raiser. They have effective interpersonal styles that generate commitment and consensus.

Some factors that are assets in institutional advancement at Theta were not deliberately designed for that purpose. The present executive managers did not create many of the resources that provided the foundation for successful fund raising at Theta. Some of these resources are intrinsic to the institution, and some are the result of past administrative decisions. The ability of the current administration to channel those strengths, seize opportunities, set direction and priorities, and mobilize staff members is its distinctive contribution. For instance, the location of university regional service centers under the vice president for institutional advancement was a carryover from an earlier organizational arrangement. This vice president's skill in this atypical structural arrangement enables Theta to carry out its service mission, perceived across the campus as one of its most important responsibilities, with maximum advantage for the advancement office. The administrators' entrepreneurial styles and their openness to others' innovations have considerable influence on Theta's success.

The president and vice president both share and communicate the understanding that fund raising and university growth go hand in hand. They know that their vision for Theta is dependent upon increased private support and that the university must continue to mature (such as through completing its comprehensive planning process) to support fund raising.

Theta's executive leadership gives credit for fund-raising success to alumni and staff members. Theta's staff members give credit to alumni and executive leadership. We appreciate the remark of the Theta manager who said that it is good to be among people who have positive feelings for their institution and, we would add, for each other.

There is no false modesty at Theta. They are proud and confident. They were surprised and pleased that Theta was selected as an institution with an effective fund-raising program, not because they are not aware that they are doing well but because they are so familiar with being overshadowed by their more prestigious neighbors.

We consistently noted that the objective of the institutional advancement staff at all levels was to help the university, and staff's strategy for doing this was to raise money. In some other institutions that we studied, staff members seemed to be more focused on being successful in raising money — not an unworthy, but a different, aspiration. They had less of a personal stake in the achievements of the institution itself. Although members of this advancement staff function under a considerable amount of frustration, with a sense of never being "caught up," they willingly work long hours and seven days a week with limited compensation. Nevertheless, we encountered a great deal less work-related stress and employee dissatisfaction at Theta than we encountered elsewhere. We attribute this not only to the staff's love for Theta but also to the way in which staff members are managed and to their regard for each other.

Emerging strengths at Theta are trustee and volunteer involvement, institutional commitment to fund raising, and emphasis on management of the fund-raising process. A concerted effort is under way to interest and involve trustees in all aspects of fund raising, and fund-raising staff members are delighted by the willingness of volunteers to expand their involvement in fund raising. University leaders reflect the institution's commitment to fund raising through efforts to refine and better communicate Theta's niche and image and to establish university-wide fund-raising priorities. Fund-raising managers at Theta were all cited by the staff members who report to them for their management skills, notably for providing support and good information about expectations for the staff. Staff members reported unanimously that they feel encouraged to be risk takers. Efforts to improve computerized information systems and the planning process within the institutional advancement division are also in progress.

In summary, what can others learn from Theta's experiences? The factors we identified as contributing to fund-raising effectiveness at Theta are as follows:

- Executive vision for the institution and increasing clarity about its assets and markets
- Executive awareness of the developmental, internal work that needs to be done to not only create but live up to an enhanced image
- Highly effective management that includes hiring the right staff members, setting challenging goals, and holding people accountable, while encouraging reasonable risk taking and staff autonomy, with back-up support if an effort fails
- Focusing of limited resources on the most productive or desirable areas
- Implementation of a multifaceted approach to increase understanding of institutional advancement among all constituents
- Recognition of the need for incremental steps and a determination to bring about enduring long-term effects rather than adopting a "quick fix"
- Demonstration of the conventional wisdom that maintains that achieving widespread internal support strengthens the case for external support
- A case for support based on Theta's worth, rather than its need or "right" to private support
- Respect for donors and genuine appreciation of gifts at any level
- The progressive education and development of volunteers, increasing their involvement in higher-order fund-raising activities
- Contact, contact, and more contact with donors
- Long-term cultivation of relationships and directness with donors about expectations for further support

8

Combining Faith and Know-How:

A Private Baccalaureate College

> KAPPA: Effective presidential leadership of long-tenured staff along with never-say-die attitudes and a lot of professional know-how have made Kappa successful in fund raising. Also contributing to this success is the staff's clarity about the institution and its constituents.

This private baccalaureate college, with an enrollment of just about 1,000 students and annual educational and general expenditures of about $5 million, is located in a small city in a southwestern state. Although affiliated with a religious denomination, the college has never received revenues from its church. Kappa has raised private support, vital to the survival and prosperity of the college, from traditional donor groups through traditional fund-raising methods. Fund raising at Kappa has been an uphill climb, so strenuous that the president said, "Sometimes the fact that we've always had such a struggle here makes it hard to feel successful, but when I look at what the odds against us were, I feel very successful." In spite of what has been at times the direst need, the fund-raising programs at Kappa have for many years emphasized Kappa's worth and accomplishments and have focused on developing strong support among constituents who share Kappa's religious and family-oriented values.

Descriptive statistics for Kappa appear in Table 8.1. Kappa is below the median for institutions of this type for every institutional characteristic, indicating that Kappa has fewer resources than at least half of the institutions in this group. Total

144

Table 8.1. Descriptive Statistics (1985–1987 Average) for Kappa College (Private Baccalaureate).

	Range for Type			This Institution		
	High	Median	Low	Actual	Predicted	Difference
Institutional Characteristics:						
Educational/General Expenditures	$43,278,200	$9,439,400	$3,010,200	$4,773,537	—	—
Endowment	$256,011,900	$9,222,400	$247,700	$1,026,814	—	—
Expenditures per Student	$40,600	$8,200	$400	$4,590	—	—
Cost of Tuition	$12,800	$6,700	$2,100	$4,350	—	—
Alumni of Record	37,400	10,500	1,300	8,500	—	—
Enrollment	7,000	1,300	300	1,040	—	—
Age of Institution	250 years	120 years	20 years	30 years	—	—
Fund-Raising Results:						
Total Voluntary Support	$17,565,100	$1,958,500	$119,300	$1,949,507	$1,154,785	+ 1.69
Alumni Gifts	$13,450,400	$572,700	$6,600	$160,747	$217,598	0.74
Nonalumni Gifts	$5,040,300	$578,800	$26,300	$1,366,775	$815,508	+ 1.68
Corporation Gifts	$1,232,900	$268,800	$33,400	$178,109	$192,332	0.93
Foundation Gifts	$3,445,900	$298,200	$5,100	$243,876	$176,262	+ 1.38

voluntary support and foundation gifts are about at the median, alumni gifts and corporation gifts are below the median, and nonalumni gifts are above the median. The organizational chart for Kappa appears in Figure 8.1. Nevertheless, outcomes for total voluntary support and all donors but alumni are above or about equal to predicted outcomes, indicating that Kappa is making effective use of its resources for fund raising.

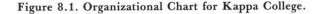

Figure 8.1. Organizational Chart for Kappa College.

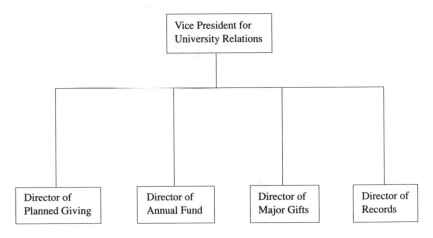

At every other institution we studied, when staff were asked how they accounted for their institutions' fund-raising success, they usually identified one or more of the characteristics listed in Chapter One. At Kappa, when asked the same question, they replied that they have been successful because Kappa would not have survived if they had not been. One staff member put it this way: "We didn't have any choice. We had to have money to operate the institution. We have operated this institution on faith to an extent that you would not believe. You can't imagine the amount of faith it takes to be the business manager here." When we persisted and said that not all needy institutions survive, we discovered a characteristic that has been even more influential in Kappa's fund-raising success than Kappa's need: the development staff's deep, personal commitment to

Kappa and the real sense that each of them plays a direct and critical role in keeping Kappa's doors open.

Kappa began as an elementary and secondary school in 1954. In 1957, it admitted the first junior college students. At that time, Kappa had 110 students and sixteen faculty members, and the campus consisted of dirt roads and temporary buildings. In 1972, when the first bachelor's degrees were awarded, Kappa began what staff members referred to as its "second chapter," with 750 students and twelve permanent campus buildings. By that time, the college had successfully completed several fund-raising campaigns and had surpassed the million-dollar mark in annual voluntary support. The "third chapter," involving the evolution of Kappa from a college to a university, has recently begun. This step is the direct result of past fund-raising success and a step that will result in a broader base for increased future support since many corporations and foundations have a greater interest in the more complex missions and goals of universities than in the missions and goals of colleges.

President S.

President S., a Kappa alumnus, was in his seventh year as president at Kappa at the time of the site visit. He was formerly academic vice president at Kappa. He told an inspiring and sometimes poignant story of Kappa's struggles to survive. President S.'s mission throughout most of his tenure has been "to firm up the financial infrastructure" of Kappa, which in the past was very precarious. "Currently," he said, "we need $500,000 to $600,000 in unrestricted dollars to stay afloat—that is, to balance our operating budget and service our debt. Seven years ago, we needed $1 million for these purposes, so our actual need for unrestricted dollars for operations is less than it was six or seven years ago. Our net worth is considerably higher, and our debt-to-asset ratio is much improved. We have accomplished these things through increased revenues from voluntary support and through frugal spending. We are less panic-stricken about raising money now and more confident about the ability and willingness of our constituents to provide what we need."

All other staff members we spoke with expressed high regard for President S., citing his leadership, his gift for bringing out the best in everyone, and his ability to generate what he himself described as the chief criterion of presidential success in fund raising: confidence in the institution. One staff member said, "President S. has been invaluable in helping us raise money. After they attend a meeting with him, people are usually waiting at home, with their checkbooks in hand, for us to show up." Another staff member noted, "People in the community who do not have the same religious interests as us at all respect what we are doing here and have so much respect for President S."

The president's fund-raising goal for Kappa is to raise the average annual total of private support to $2 million, with $650,000 to $700,000 in unrestricted funds. Although he thinks that is "asking a lot," he said, "with our present austere habits," that amount would meet immediate needs and provide some discretionary funds for improving institutional quality. His first priority for discretionary money is to use it for salary increases, "to use it for the people who have been with us in this struggle for so long. We need to improve facilities, but before we focus on the library, we need to focus on the librarians."

President S., who spends "at least 50 percent" of his time raising money, entered his position fully aware that fund raising would be a critical responsibility. "The trustees who interviewed me asked if it had occurred to me that I would have to raise money," he said. "I said that I thought presidents are always the chief fund raiser, although they may not personally raise the most money." He believes that communicating confidence and generating confidence in the institution are primary requirements for a president to be a successful fund raiser. He said, "Everything a president does has an impact on gift income. Some presidents are more aware of their impact than others. Some presidents raise money without consciously trying because they communicate confidence, and people see them as exciting leaders. Presidents can also make a difference in a more direct way, by overseeing fund raising and actually asking for gifts, which is the style I've used. Unfortunately, some presidents have a negative impact on fund raising. An institution can deteriorate rapidly if the president provides no real leadership and does not promote confidence in the institution." As for his own fund-raising ability, the president said, "I have been able to get the confidence of some people whose gifts have made a difference, but, in general, when it comes to asking for a major gift, I'm not as good as members of my staff."

The president said that fund raising at Kappa has not been rigorously planned or evaluated but has been dictated by the college's urgent needs: "We have never said, 'This year we are going to raise X amount, and next year we are going to raise this much more.' We've done very little statistical analysis or evaluation. We've just said, 'We have to put out every ounce of energy to bring in as much money as we can because our needs are so great.' We do need to become more systematic in our operations, which a recent staff reorganization will help us to do."

President S. is aware that Kappa's less precarious financial condition has complex ramifications for the college. After noting that "our vulnerability has been an asset," he added, "People have seen us as brave, maybe even heroic, and they wanted to reward that. Now we must move our constituency from thinking of survival to thinking of quality. I hope we won't lose their support when we point out that, if the war is not exactly over, a cease-fire has been called."

Everything at Kappa is changing, including the role of the president. "I have long had an interest in Winston Churchill, particularly in his capacity as a wartime leader," the president said. "He became my model when I took this job. When Churchill's war was over, a lot still needed to be done, but the chemistry between him and the people was different. There is a difference between being a wartime leader and a peacetime leader. I'm trying to make that adjustment myself."

The role of the college trustees has also changed as Kappa has become more financially stable. The president explained that Kappa's trustees, who currently contribute about $300,000 per year, have had "the two traditional roles in fund raising: getting money and giving money." However, the trustees' participation in the institution has decreased in recent years, partly due to the increasing stability and prosperity of the college. Recently, the trustees' function in fund raising has been only as donors.

The president said that in the 1970s "a couple of trustees had a lot of cards to call in from this community, and they called them in for Kappa. Back then, our administration went to trustees and said, 'Here are our problems — what should we do?' The trustees would say, 'Do the following and report back to us.' Because we were always in crisis, trustee meetings always involved anger, frustration, and loud voices and could be pretty entertaining, so attendance was excellent. Some trustees came because they didn't want to miss anything."

The president's approach at trustee meetings has been to focus on what is going well. He said, "I say to the trustees, 'We have so many assets here — our fund-raising success, increased enrollment, faculty honors, and so on. Now, by the way, to solve some problems, I propose this, this, and this. How do you vote?' When I first started doing this, the trustees sat back and said, 'Okay. So you're going to take care of things now. We vote yes.' Now, at meetings the trustees say, 'Well, what wonderful things do you have for us today?'" The president wonders sometimes if he has "oversold the positives or given trustees a false sense of security. We must achieve the right balance of trustee involvement or ultimately, our fund raising will be affected. To maintain donor interest over time, it is just as important to keep donors involved as it is to get their gifts. If donors are not excited and involved with us, the money is not going to continue to come in."

Fund-Raising Programs

A recent reorganization of the development staff — probably the most significant staff reorganization in Kappa's history — was brought about by the retirement of the former vice president for trusts and bequests, who had been in that position for twenty years. The new structural arrangement was put in place just two weeks prior to the site visit. Current professional staff positions are vice president for university relations (admissions, development, public information, and alumni affairs) and directors of planned giving, annual fund, major gifts, and records. The vice president for university relations oversees all development activities and works with President S. to cultivate donors and solicit gifts of $5,000 or more and to expand membership on the board of trustees and the president's community advisory board. The vice president, at Kappa for eighteen years but new to development, is optimistic about continued fund-raising success at Kappa, primarily because of the "visionary leadership of the president."

Campaigns. The new director of planned giving had been Kappa's director of development for most of the past thirty years. He was involved in Kappa's first campaign in 1959 to raise $500,000 to build the administration building and in "almost every campaign the college has had since." In that first campaign, initial prospects were church members and local businesses. Currently, contributions from local businesses constitute about 50 percent of funds raised.

The director reported that Kappa hired consultants for some campaigns, but he thought that Kappa "did just as well without professional counsel as with it," indicating that sometimes Kappa's fund raisers have had "the wrong advice from consultants. Once consultants suggested 'For a Debt-Free Campus' as a campaign slogan. It sounded good, but people began to ask why they should get the college out of debt when they were in debt themselves. We have reached our goal in every campaign but that one. For another campaign, consultants said our major effort should be in five big cities and we should ignore the small towns, but I knew that wouldn't work. They said that if we wanted to take the campaign to small communities we would have to do it on our own. So, while they were in the cities with big dinners and highly publicized speakers, we had little dinner meetings in about forty-five small towns. I predicted that we would raise more money in these little towns than they raised in the big cities, and we did."

Kappa has a campaign every four years, with a focus on getting three-year pledges. That schedule, the director said, "gives people a year's rest, and then we ask them again." The director stated that Kappa's chief competition in fund raising is from sister colleges with which Kappa has potentially overlapping constituencies, rather than from the big public university in the same town, which has a very different constituency. From his vantage point of thirty years in the field, he also observed that "competition for the gift dollar is stiffer than ever. This is getting to be a profession that needs some ethical standards. Some of the highly publicized televangelists have thrown a pall over things."

Kappa successfully completed a campaign in 1986 that raised $6.2 million, which was above the projected $5.8 million goal. This campaign, one for which Kappa hired outside consultants, followed a feasibility study that identified dollar goals for various constituencies. Part of Kappa's campaign strategy was to recommend to individual donors that they give 2 percent of their annual income each year for three years. Specific case statements were developed for alumni, trustees, and prospects in three geographical regions. When the campaign was announced, Kappa had already secured $232,000 in pledges from faculty and staff members (all Kappa campaigns start with solicitation of gifts from faculty and staff members, a constituency described by the director as "one of our most generous donor groups"), $1 million from trustees, and $800,000 from local residents and businesses.

The present campaign, in its second year at the time of the site visit and operating without outside consultants, has a goal of $12.2 million. Phase one of the campaign raised $7 million. To kick off phase two, a major foundation made a challenge grant of $1.2 million to raise an additional $4 million.

The director said that Kappa at one time aspired to an enrollment of 5,000 students, but "in the 1960s, something happened that we hadn't planned on — all those junior colleges began to crop up, and we are just surrounded by them now. We soon saw that our original plan to be a larger institution with a broader focus was unrealistic. We needed to settle down and find our niche as a small institution catering to a specific population and to develop our fund-raising constituency from that.

Our donors live in small towns and are country people who want to see us succeed. A lot of personal solicitation is the key. Our nonalumni donors are conservative people who think, 'My $50,000 would be a drop in the bucket at some big place, but it would mean a lot at Kappa.'"

Entrepreneurial Fund Raising. The director of planned giving explained that Kappa began soliciting planned gifts more than twenty years ago. "We are proud that we got into estate planning early. We were the first college in this area with a vice president for estate planning. I've read that about 35 percent of all voluntary support to higher education comes from estate planning, but our total is closer to 50 percent. We have about $9 million outstanding in wills, mostly from people in places most consultants never heard of."

Although Kappa's former planned gifts officer was an attorney, the present director said he did not think it was necessary for a planned gifts officer to be a lawyer. "My job," he said, "is to sell people on our cause and introduce the methods and then strongly encourage them to consult their own lawyers to work out the details."

This director plays an entrepreneurial role in helping to stimulate institutional growth. His current project is "to sell our people on expanding our business administration department to include an international component. Business people have to understand the deutsche mark and the yen and the peso. Programs to train business leaders to operate in other countries and cultures are needed, and I'm convinced that we could get funding." Instituting and developing such a program would broaden the institution as well as the base for private support.

Annual Fund. The recently appointed director of the annual fund has been a fund raiser for Kappa for ten years and served for seven years as a member of Kappa's faculty. His primary focus for increasing the annual fund is to develop alumni relations programs. His philosophy is to concentrate on people who have given in the past.

Kappa's annual fund is loosely planned. "In February,

we call alumni donors," the director said. "Other development staff members and I make the calls. In November, we all roll up our sleeves—we don't have any executives around here— and lick envelopes to get our year-end letter out. In December, we call LYBUNTS [donors who gave last year but unfortunately not this year]. Otherwise, we try to respond as opportunities arise. For instance, last year a foundation said that they would give us $5,000 for scholarships if we could match the money. I called 115 preachers on our donor list and raised the money in less than a month."

The management information system at Kappa is state-of-the-art. It is maintained by the records staff, which includes the director, two staff members, and five students who work part time. A sophisticated computer program is used to record gifts, generate reports, maintain donor records, and produce acknowledgments for gifts. The research/records director is a Kappa alumna and the parent of two Kappa alumni who described the school as "small, young, and poor" but also as an institution that people "dearly love."

Analysis of Fund Raising at Kappa

The fund-raising program at Kappa is outstanding in presidential leadership, institutional commitment to fund raising, and staff commitment to the institution. The president's personal commitment to Kappa and his ability to meet his own criterion for successful presidential leadership—instilling confidence about the institution in others—are basic to his success in leading and inspiring Kappa's fund raisers. His disclosure about using Winston Churchill as a model for his leadership role and his regard for people at Kappa indicate a conscientious approach to leadership. His awareness of the need for his leadership to change as Kappa changes is particularly insightful.

Institutional commitment to fund raising is outstanding at Kappa because fund raising has been a priority for all of Kappa's leaders, and loyal faculty and staff members are aware of the extent to which Kappa depends upon voluntary support. The recent elevation of the chief development officer to the vice presidential level and his involvement in institutional affairs reflect both current trends in staffing for institutional affairs and Kappa's continuing institutional commitment to fund raising. (Because of the recent reorganization of the development staff, we could not assess at the time of the site visit how the vice president for university relations carries out his roles in helping to set institutional goals and in providing leadership to the fund-raising staff.)

Kappa's steady growth has brought continuously changing demands and challenges. At a critical period in Kappa's history, astute leaders began to focus more on strengths and values and less on overall institutional growth. Since that time, Kappa's leaders have emphasized Kappa's special role in the regional educational community. The result is a very clear, widely shared understanding, both internally and externally, of what Kappa stands for, whom Kappa serves, and to whom Kappa can appeal for support. This clear message and the fund raisers' continual adoption of new concepts and techniques in fund raising have supported Kappa's fund-raising efforts.

The development staff members (excluding the new major gifts officer) and the president have a combined total of about eighty-five years at Kappa, an average of seventeen years per person. The commitment of fund-raising staff members to Kappa is obvious in what they say and do as well as in their long tenure. This staff is a model of the devotion and long service many institutional leaders would like to see in their own development offices, but which exists less and less frequently among highly mobile fund-raising professionals and in fast-changing development offices. Love for the institution, commitment to the values Kappa stands for, as well as real pleasure in the challenge and adventure that fund raising has always been at Kappa, result in high personal and professional satisfaction for these staff members.

Entering this tight-knit group could be difficult for someone with no previous ties to Kappa or someone with less of a personal stake in the institution. One staff member said, "A key to whatever success we've had is that we have loyal people who came and stayed. Our most difficult time in fund raising was when we brought in outside people for a short time to head development. They were not dedicated to this institution. People who come in, view this as a job, and do well enough to find a better job somewhere else are not the kind of people we need."

As one of the institutions that we studied capable of generating fierce loyalty and affection in its constituents, Kappa can probably continue to staff the development office indefinitely with people who are already connected in some meaningful way to the institution without sacrificing professional competence. Our study of Kappa, along with some of our other studies, demonstrates how important it is to hire the "right" people and how what is "right" for a given institution goes far beyond a candidate's professional skills and accomplishments.

As focused as Kappa is in its fund-raising efforts, it has never been provincial. Fund raisers and presidents have been creative, rational risk takers throughout Kappa's history. One director's discussion of his attempts to influence academic planners at Kappa to develop programs in international affairs is one of the best examples in the entire study of a fund raiser who thinks entrepreneurially about the connection between institutional growth and effective fund raising. (What we call entrepreneurial one fund raiser at Kappa preferred to call "acting on faith.")

Shared values and purposes, considerable overlap of roles, and continuity of efforts and staff members have substituted for many formal management procedures at Kappa. Formal planning, goal setting, and evaluation have not played much of a role in Kappa's fund-raising success. The college has no formal short- or long-term action plans and no written mission statement for fund raising. However, Kappa has an up-to-date computer system for maintaining good records and providing access to management information.

Fund raising at Kappa has depended very little on an organized volunteer effort. But donors, especially those who are personally solicited, become resources to help in the identification of new prospects for this enterprising staff.

Kappa was founded and has developed as an institution in which the mission is to respond to the needs and values of

a very specific constituency. The institution has earned the
respect and support of the entire community. However, fund
raisers at Kappa have not had much time to devote to alumni
relations or donor recognition programs (beyond routine acknowledgments of gifts). Staff members, including the president,
identified this area most frequently as the development area most
in need of improvement. Although these fund raisers know that
good constituent relationships enhance fund-raising efforts, they
expressed a genuine regret about not honoring alumni and
donors in a way that went beyond the recognition of missed opportunities to enhance fund raising.

    Almost all solicitations for gifts occur in personal inter-
actions between donors and Kappa staff members. (Although
we do not have figures to prove it, this institution probably has
a higher rate of face-to-face solicitation for all gifts than any
other institution we studied.) Personal solicitation of gifts from
most donors by the same staff member year after year provides
a good substitute for formal recognition efforts and alumni
events. It may also be that this kind of contact and recognition
is more in keeping with the values of austerity and good financial management that Kappa shares in common with its donors.

    In summary, what can others learn from Kappa's ex-
periences? The factors we identified as contributing to fund-raising effectiveness at Kappa are as follows:

- Intense staff commitment to the values the institution stands
  for and to the survival and prosperity of the institution
- Leadership by the president in promoting and supporting
  fund raising as well as skillfully participating in it
- Refinement and expansion of institutional strengths and traditions in fund raising
- Emphasis on modest goals and steady, incremental progress
  and growth
- Regular, continuing solicitation of previous donors along
  with continual (if not formal) efforts to identify new prospects
- Sharp clarity regarding what Kappa is and can be and regarding who will care about this institution and its well-being

- Emphasis on Kappa's worth and contributions rather than on its needs
- Acute awareness of the push/pull nature of the relationship between fund raising and institutional progress
- Combination of contemporary fund-raising approaches and technology with warm personal contact and genuine respect for donors

9

Learning by Doing:

A Public Baccalaureate College

RHO: Fund-raising success at Rho, until recently, has been largely the result of faculty contacts with external constituents. A new central staff is working to build on present strengths and increase fund-raising efforts and results across the institution.

This public institution, with an enrollment of 11,000 and annual educational and general expenditures of about $53 million, is located in a small town in a midwestern state. When we selected institutions for the study, Rho was a public baccalaureate college but has since become a comprehensive university. (The public baccalaureate college as a type of higher education institution is disappearing as more and more four-year public colleges become comprehensive universities. Of the thirty-nine institutions listed as public baccalaureate institutions in the 1984 report from the Council for Aid to Education, the first year for which we collected data, twenty-two were listed as public comprehensive universities in the 1989 report.)

Descriptive statistics for Rho appear in Table 9.1. The organizational chart appears in Figure 9.1. Rho has the highest figures for institutions of this type for educational and general expenditures, alumni of record, and enrollment. Other institutional characteristics are above the median. Outcomes for total voluntary support, alumni gifts, and nonalumni gifts are above the median. Corporation gifts are the highest and foundation gifts the lowest for all institutions of this type. Actual outcomes are substantially higher than predicted outcomes for all donor groups but foundation gifts.

At the time of the site visit the presidency of Rho was

Table 9.1. Descriptive Statistics (1985–1987 Average) for Rho College (Public Baccalaureate).

	Range for Type			This Institution		
	High	Median	Low	Actual	Predicted	Difference
Institutional Characteristics:						
Educational/General Expenditures	$53,379,600	$13,107,800	$3,354,600	$53,379,600	—	—
Endowment	$64,608,400	$502,600	$54,700	$1,831,700	—	—
Expenditures per Student	$10,300	$3,700	$700	$4,850	—	—
Cost of Tuition	$4,100	$1,400	$200	$1,900	—	—
Alumni of Record	47,200	9,832	2,900	47,200	—	—
Enrollment	11,005	3,000	1,300	11,005	—	—
Age of Institution	200 years	80 years	20 years	103 years	—	—
Fund-Raising Results:						
Total Voluntary Support	$7,755,600	$417,800	$49,400	$1,791,591	$1,020,531	+1.75
Alumni Gifts	$3,987,500	$41,600	$0	$256,046	$137,354	+1.86
Nonalumni Gifts	$2,393,600	$95,100	$8,500	$380,656	$149,049	+2.55
Corporation Gifts	$1,123,500	$85,600	$2,600	$1,123,519	$847,385	+1.33
Foundation Gifts	$760,800	$39,800	$1,200	$1,200	$290,984	0.00

Figure 9.1. Organizational Chart for Rho College.

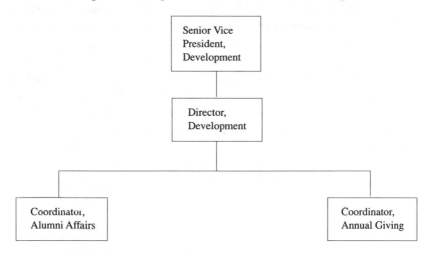

vacant. At the time of the site visit the vice president for finance had been acting president at Rho for seven months. The announcement of the new president at Rho was made about four weeks later. Rho is unlike any other institution that we studied because it is very new to the business of organized, systematic fund raising, in spite of its impressive showing among public baccalaureate colleges. Approximately half of the voluntary support Rho acquires is in noncash gifts of materials, supplies, and equipment, such as the new automobiles damaged in shipment that are donated to the automotive program, or the reams of paper that are given to the printing program, or the up-to-date radiology equipment that was given to the allied health program. These gifts are direct consequences of the relationships academic administrators cultivate and maintain with industries hiring Rho graduates. Rho provides an excellent example of how new central staff members can work to implement programs and educate internal and external constituents about the need for organizationwide efforts in development.

The development office staff consists of the senior vice president of development, the director of development, the coordinator of annual giving, and the coordinator of alumni affairs.

All the staff members are relatively new in their positions. The current staff members have been involved in creating the mechanisms for systematic fund raising, including the basics of office staffing and organization; updating donor records; and debugging a computer system — all very time-consuming tasks. Presenting themselves to the Rho community as consultants who can help rather than as experts who have all the answers, they are also working to define their roles and establish relationships with internal constituencies. They have implemented a new program to raise unrestricted annual gifts and are working to increase overall annual gifts and to develop programs to solicit major gifts, planned gifts, and gifts from foundations. In addition, they are in what one staff member called "the very early talking stages" of a major campaign.

Although Rho has had an institutional advancement officer at the vice presidential level in the past, the function was structured differently. One previous vice president, for instance, was concerned primarily with governmental relations. No sustained effort was made prior to now to implement a central institutionwide development program. Until recently, the central office only coordinated and assisted individual schools and programs in their phonathons for annual funds.

Participation in the annual fund has been (and still is) at the discretion of each dean or program director. Those schools that participate plan their own phonathons, but the central office pays all costs and provides everything but actual callers. One unit recruits alumni volunteers to make calls. Another school uses alumni to call other graduates from their own classes. Some units use only faculty members and program directors to make calls, and some use only student volunteers.

Rho is the only public institution that we studied without a foundation for receiving gifts. Interest on campus for creating a foundation is limited, a consequence of both the autonomy that characterizes units within the institution and the successful individual fund-raising efforts to date.

Senior Vice President of Development

The senior vice president of development, in the office for eighteen months at the time of the site visit, has held nine different positions at Rho over the past twenty years. Prior to this appointment, he was vice president for academic affairs. His experience in that position and his long tenure at Rho have made him an articulate spokesperson for Rho. He described Rho's academic mission saying, "We are not and we don't pretend to be anything other than a vocational technical institution that trains people for jobs. Only 4 percent of our graduates go directly to graduate school. The rest go directly into the job market. All of our programs have advisory committees made up of knowledgeable people in that field, and our curricula are all closely matched to the needs of local and state employers. Our students are prepared to perform on the job from day one. It is not atypical to see in newspaper employment ads throughout the state 'Rho Graduates Preferred.' We are very proud of that."

The vice president explained that "faculty members work with advisory committees and students in off-campus internships, and they are out in the field quite often. They are very aware of the need for and availability of gifts. The donors get tax write-offs, and we get products we cannot function without."

The vice president pointed out that currently deans and faculty members are not expected to acquire private support for their programs. The vice president said, "They realize that Rho cannot provide funding for the quality they want in their programs, so many deans and program chairs have taken the initiative to go after what they need. A universitywide campaign will be entirely different, though, and each academic unit will have specific expectations and formal goals."

The vice president explained the fund-raising history at Rho. "In the 1970s," he said, "our president did not even like charging for tuition, so he had no interest in raising private support. He thought the state should provide whatever was necessary. Our next president saw the need to expand our base of support and started some traditional things like donors clubs."

Originally, membership in the President's Club required a $10,000 gift or a commitment of $1,000 a year for ten years. That figure was raised to $35,000, and another club for $100,000 donors has been established. "About 40 percent of the members of the President's Club are Rho employees, which," the vice president said, "is a good statistic to be able to cite to prospects.

Donors like to know that you can get support from your own people." Other members are alumni and people from local businesses. Corporations make up most of the members of the $100,000 giving club. Membership in both clubs is expected to grow as central staff members identify and solicit donations from new prospects more systematically.

The entrepreneurial president who initiated membership clubs was also responsible for Rho's golf management program. He persuaded a retired corporate vice president to donate land for Rho's eighteen-hole golf course. Rho was the first institution in the country to offer a program to train golf course managers.

Rho has received two large bequests, "one of which just fell into our laps," the vice president said. "We were recently notified of a bequest of $600,000 from someone who lived thirty-five miles from here. I cannot tell you why this donor made the gift, but I am going to meet with her lawyer to try to find out. Our first large bequest, which we received several years ago, was from someone who was a student here in the early 1920s. Her gift, which amounted to $4.5 million, wasn't serendipitous — it was the result of the hard work of the vice president for development at that time, who cultivated her interest in the institution." The vice president emphasized that expansion of solicitation of planned gifts was a priority for the central staff.

Rho's fund-raising history includes one recent formal campaign, which, although not entirely successful, has helped staff members identify what they will *not* do in their next campaign. A campaign to raise money for a building, the vice president explained, "was undertaken with a commitment from a group of corporations critically in need of technicians. They said they were eager to invest in our building because we could ensure future well-trained employees. Thirty people from leading manufacturing companies promised that their firms would fund the entire project, so the president turned the project over to the dean who had all the contacts with these people. The money raised to date has not covered the cost of the building, which is already in use."

The vice president said that the college made some classic

mistakes in this campaign. "We did not plan or get advance gifts before announcing the campaign as the experts recommend. We had not done enough analysis to make accurate estimates of the full cost of the building. We did not establish clear understandings with the people promising the funding in the beginning. Some people at Rho still expect that the deficit will be made up, but raising money for a building already in use is a big task."

As a result of that campaign, some of Rho's board members are wary about large-scale fund-raising programs. "They keep talking about that one campaign," the vice president said. "I want them to look forward to something that's going to be successful. We need to walk slowly down this path, which is something we didn't do in our first attempt. We'll announce a campaign with established goals only after careful planning and study. We will hire a consultant and prepare a formal case statement that describes what we want to accomplish and what the costs will be."

This vice president served as the chair of the search committee for the new president. He said, "The search committee has looked very closely at presidential candidates' abilities and desires to be actively involved in fund raising. In state schools not too many years ago, people didn't see fund-raising ability as a qualification the president had to have, but this ability has had a strong influence in our consideration of candidates for a new president."

Board members at Rho are political appointees, and, the vice president said, "Their ability to contribute to fund raising is not considered in their selection. It's happenstance if a board member is able either to give or to influence others to give substantial sums of money. That may change over the years if new members are appointed who have interests and expertise in this area."

The vice president is confident about the future of fund raising at Rho. "With a new president coming and the growing awareness that the state will not provide all the dollars we need," he said, "I think that we can make a significant difference at Rho with a major campaign. And when we have a campaign, we are going to do it right."

Director of Development

The director of development has been in his position for two years, filling a position that was vacant for over a year — a vacancy he believes suggests that administrators at Rho did not think that a central development office was very important. He has worked primarily to set up the office, solicit scholarship funds (which are "mushrooming"), establish a central fund-raising program for unrestricted gifts, and increase overall efforts in annual phonathons. Under his direction, the central office has assumed responsibility for processing and acknowledging all gifts, maintaining donor records, identifying potential gift club members by tracking annual gifts, and sending reminders to alumni who have made pledges — none of which had been done previously by a central staff and some of which had not been done at all. More units on campus are scheduling phonathons because of the central office's aggressive effort to promote calling programs and to assist individual administrators. In the year before the present director arrived, phonathons were held for fourteen nights. In his first year, forty nights were held; sixty nights of phonathons were scheduled for the next year.

The director said, "We were not getting the grass-roots support that we need for long-term stability and for major gifts later on. We need alumni we can count on so our donor base continues to grow. Some alumni have never been asked for a gift because the number of graduates in the early 1970s became overwhelming, and we could not keep up with them. I believe giving to your alma mater becomes habitual. We must let alumni know that we will now ask for a gift every year."

The director explained that in the new program to increase unrestricted funds, schools have exclusive rights to their alumni for five years. Alumni that the schools do not contact or who do not give a gift to the schools are put in the central pool of about 25,000 alumni, whom central development asks for unrestricted funds. The director emphasized, "We don't want to discourage or compete with the schools, but we need unrestricted support. Now the deans realize that they have to get their graduates involved in giving to their schools — with our assistance because we're not trying to work against them — or their graduates become our prospects for unrestricted gifts. We want to make sure we're not missing gifts simply because people have never been asked for gifts."

In 1988, Rho used a telemarketing firm to contact more than 14,000 alumni nondonors for unrestricted support. More than 1,600 alumni pledged $95,330, an increase of 128 percent in unrestricted gifts over the previous year. These donors are now designated as prospects for future unrestricted funds and are asked to donate annually in special phonathons staffed by volunteers from student organizations. The cost for the program for the first year was 69¢ per dollar pledged. In the second year of the program, the cost of renewing this support with an in-house program dropped to 15¢ per dollar.

The director believes that the insistence on autonomy among academic programs has a negative effect on overall fund raising. He said, "Most people here don't think about this institution as a whole. Programs are very autonomous, even within schools. Pharmacy calls pharmacy alumni. Allied health calls allied health alumni." The problem with this, the director said, is that "each program gets small amounts of money that don't do anybody much good. If all the programs pooled their proceeds for the school, the money could be used for projects of significance that might benefit everybody over the long run."

The director also pointed out that individual units only contact previous donors for renewals and do not attempt to enlarge their donor base. He said, "People in some programs don't want our advice about fund raising, but I think as the need for dollars increases, they'll begin to look more and more to us for help. In addition to encouraging other units to get involved in fund raising, we make a special attempt to be helpful to everyone who calls. We make special efforts to accommodate donors, and we never say no when anyone inside the institution asks for help. We are trying to increase our personal contact with everyone, not just donors but with internal people as well."

The director believes that Rho alumni are interested in being involved with the institution and are willing to become donors. "We have some very loyal alumni," he said. "For instance, a long tradition at Rho is a program called the Golden Eagles — people who graduated fifty or more years ago are invited back to campus during graduation week. Some alumni have been coming back to Golden Eagle celebrations for over twenty-five years, meaning they graduated more than seventy years ago, and they still feel connected to the institution. Many of these are people of means who have not been asked for significant gifts. Some deans don't give a hoot about alumni fund raising. They prefer to focus on corporate gifts. But they are overlooking the need to cultivate alumni and develop permanent relationships with them."

Because of the efforts of the new coordinator of alumni affairs, attendance at alumni events is better than it has ever been. The former coordinator was comfortable only with older alumni, the director of development noted, with the result that "no one ever paid any attention to some 20,000 alumni. Our current coordinator makes a special effort to reach newer alumni. Some people on campus are still uncomfortable about alumni relations and fund raising being too closely connected. These people are concerned that alumni will avoid alumni events if they think they're going to be asked for money, but administrators are seeing that we're not chasing people away by asking for their support. We are in the process of creating a development council made up of key alumni to help in fund raising."

The director of development sees opportunity for expansion in almost every area. "We are running a bare-bones operation," he said. "We need people to organize systematic programs for corporate and planned gifts and a proposal writer for foundation gifts." Rho currently has no central program for soliciting gifts from corporations, a task that remains the province of the academic administrators who have established contacts with company managers. The director noted that more faculty members are seeking outside funding. The central office supports these faculty members by facilitating proposal writing, disseminating information about requests for proposals, and holding seminars on writing proposals and seeking funds. "We help with deadlines, proofreading, and word processing," the director said.

Noting that the whole institution is wrestling with strategic planning and beginning to understand the importance of this planning to fund-raising efforts, the director said, "I represent the development area on a number of institutionwide committees and every time I attend a meeting, someone says, 'We need $500,000 for this' and 'We need $500,000 for that.' Only so many $500,000 gifts are out there for an institution of our size. Since we haven't done strategic planning, I realized that I wouldn't know what to say if somebody gave us $500,000 and asked what it would be used for. I took the question of priorities to the executive committee and right away they saw the point, so they developed a list of current priorities, which is a good beginning."

The director was optimistic about the future of fund raising at Rho and said, "Rho has a particular niche. We are not in the higher echelon of the fifteen public institutions in this state, but one of our special contributions is that we are a 'second-chance' institution. Some of our most successful alumni and biggest donors are people who started out at one of the more prestigious universities in the state and didn't make it there. They then came to Rho for a second chance and were successful here. Some of them have not forgotten Rho for giving them that opportunity." Additionally, Rho's excellent reputation in the business world will support broader fund-raising efforts. The director pointed out, "Business people say that graduates from some other institutions know what is in the books, but they've never done it. Rho graduates might not know what it says in the books, but they've done it. Given our strengths as an institution, I think our fund-raising potential is exciting, and that we've only scratched the surface."

Coordinator of Annual Giving

The coordinator of annual giving had been in her position for one year at the time of the site visit. She coordinates phonathons with schools and is responsible for direct mail solicitations, which are sent to faculty, staff, parents, and friends. In 1988, working with volunteers from student government, she raised $18,000 for the library from parents. "Once we identified a specific project, parents were very willing to support it," she said. She is also optimistic about future fund raising at Rho and thinks the development staff has important responsibility for providing leadership in Rho's continued growth. Stating that a major campaign is absolutely necessary for Rho at this time, she added that a campaign "would push us as a staff and as an institution to do the things we need to be doing—adding more central staff, using more formal methods to identify new prospects through donor research, and coordinating fund raising more closely with the schools. Coordination in fund raising should come from our office. I sense throughout the campus a desire to do whatever is necessary to make things better for everyone, but there's no unity. A campaign would provide a focus and set priorities."

Academic Deans

During the time that this book was in final preparation, Grass-muck (1990) wrote that higher education institutions were "beginning to borrow private sector strategies" and to make "an effort to reduce the broad menu of offerings now prevalent at many [institutions]. In the future, many [institutions] will concentrate on excelling in certain programs, while abandoning or closing those that are of lesser quality. . . . [This] is a new idea in higher education" (pp. A1, A30). A full year before this article describing "a new idea in higher education" appeared, a dean at Rho told us that the college had done ten years ago what the article said institutions are now beginning to do.

He said, "It became clear that the state could not afford to fund this school at the level necessary for us to be successful in new technologies. Our alternatives were to be a mediocre school or seek new revenue sources. We decided to focus on what we had to offer that other schools did not have. We closed some programs and expanded and reorganized others. Now we are very targeted and have niches that other people can't occupy."

Noting that the state has a crucial shortage of people at

the midmanagement technical level, the dean said, "The economy of this state is based on productivity, and productivity depends on the quality of management and midmanagement people. That is where we come in. We deliver crucial technical people to a number of industries. The market was clearly there, and nobody else was in it. We began to develop our product line the same way organizations in the private sector do."

This dean focuses on securing in-kind and annual cash gifts from corporations. He pointed out that some corporations have ongoing staff training programs in Rho's facilities. "They are here," he said, "and not at some other university because we have the facilities, which they helped to build. They feel ownership in what we do here. They come see us if we can help them, and if we need their help, we go to see them. We've tried to build vehicles for giving other than the annual gift. For example, several corporations send us a donation every time they get one of our graduates. I recently received a check for $5,000 from a company that had just hired two of our graduates."

This dean wants to see development activities expand: "We need full-time development officers in the schools to develop annual budgets and coordinated approaches for each program area. Rho's future lies in the degree of advocacy we can generate from the private sector." However, he also emphasized that it was important for Rho to be as realistic about its market for private support as it has been about the market for academic programs and students. He said, "The president of a major manufacturing corporation with headquarters near here does a lot for us, and we have provided good people for his company, but we don't get any of his personal wealth. His alma mater gives him fifty-yard-line tickets, and that institution benefits from his personal wealth. We benefit from the corporate resources he controls, and we don't even try to get his personal money. I think that's a more realistic approach for us."

Another dean who thinks that fund raising is a necessary part of his job described Rho as an institution that is "no longer state supported but state assisted" as a result of decreasing state revenues. He emphasized that successful fund raising begins with developing relationships with donors, especially alumni, and involving them in the life of the institution. He said, "Our unit has been raising money longer than almost anyone else on campus. We raise funds by developing credibility and friends. It's much easier to get a dollar from a friend than it is to get one from a person you don't know. But if your friends only see you when you've got your cap in your hand, you won't fill the cap more than once. People give to a cause that they think needs support rather than one that I think needs support, so they must be kept informed about needs and opportunities. Also, in order to make a dollar, you have to put a dollar in initially. Spending money to raise money is a concept that disturbs a lot of people in academia."

Analysis of Fund Raising at Rho

Rho is a good example of an institution at which fund-raising results look good on paper (and even stand out in statistical analyses such as ours) and yet clearly do not represent the institution's full potential or capacity for fund raising. Everyone at Rho is fully confident that the institution must and can increase the scope and outcome of fund raising.

Rho's fund-raising program is in an earlier stage of evolution than the program of any other institution we studied. Because of this, the list of characteristics of fund-raising programs in Chapter One is less appropriate for this institution than for the others.

It is very easy for us as outsiders to say what "should" be done at Rho, and we cautiously offer the following assessment and analysis. Rho is distinctively different from any other institution we studied because it is the only institution in which successful fund-raising results are the by-products of relationships and contacts established for purposes other than raising money. As we see it, this is both good news and bad news for the central development staff. The people at Rho have every reason to be confident about the attractiveness of the college to donors because a substantial group of donors and friends already exists. Additionally, staff members do not have to deal with academic administrators' unrealistic expectations of what the development office should be doing or the administrators' confusion about the need to make time in their busy schedules to be involved in fund raising. However, the central development staff has a perilous path to tread among internal constituents and perhaps among current donors as well, who may believe that everything is working just fine the way it is. At Rho, the challenge is quite different from — and possibly more difficult than — what it would be in an institution that had never sought voluntary support.

Obviously, the critical task at Rho will be to harness the energy and build on the accomplishments already achieved by academic administrators. The outstanding characteristic at Rho is that the institution's image is defined and well known. Even though academic programs at Rho are autonomous, each program supports Rho's central mission to provide well-trained employees and to respond to labor needs in Rho's state.

An emphasis on constituent relations is also an outstanding characteristic in that Rho fulfills its missions by maintaining close relationships with external constituents. The high level of willingness at the college both to involve advisory groups in institutional planning and other affairs and to be flexible in responding to changing demands from the external environment is a real asset that has been and can be further utilized in enhancing fund-raising success. However, Rho has focused almost exclusively on corporate constituencies with only minimal efforts to involve other groups. Not yet characteristic of Rho's fund-raising efforts are presidential leadership, trustees' support and participation, and institutional fund raising priorities and policies. It is very likely that these characteristics will become stronger as the new president takes office and the entire institution moves toward a major campaign.

The new president and the vice president of institutional advancement will be instrumental in leading academic administrators to see that their specific programs will benefit as the institution benefits. One option they might choose to facilitate the process is to implement an assessment and planning process with wide vertical and horizontal participation, taking care to include campus representatives who have been successful in acquiring financial support.

In addition to creating an alumni council to increase participation and outcomes in fund raising, they could create a development council of people in the institution already involved in fund raising and use faculty contacts to recruit volunteers for institutionwide development councils for all donor groups, extending the tradition of using advisory boards that is so familiar to Rho constituencies now.

The president and vice president must also provide direction and support to the central staff members as they continue to strengthen and enhance fund-raising programs that are already effective in many academic areas. The central staff members are fully aware of the sensitive role they play and have wisely cast their role as that of consultants. Their efforts to date have focused on assisting and advising. However, they have a view of the institution that directors of individual academic programs do not have as well as expertise no one else has, in spite of the outstanding fund-raising success others have already achieved. The staff members see the areas in which opportunities have not been taken and in which tactical and strategic errors have been made. They see the areas in which some basic fund-raising know-how can be used to coordinate, expand, and formalize present fund-raising efforts. They will need strong support from the highest levels of the institution to most effectively carry out their work.

In summary, what can others learn from Rho's experiences? The factors we identified as contributing to fund-raising effectiveness at Rho are as follows:

- Strong orientation on the part of the central staff members to provide support, resources, and leadership for fund raising in academic units
- Expanded centralized annual fund program, with an emphasis on securing unrestricted funds without competing with academic units
- A chief development officer with a strong sense of the institution's identity and positive relationships with academic administrators
- Sharp clarity about the institution's niche, mission, direction, and strengths

- Significant participation of college staff members and faculty members in internal campaigns
- Increasing emphasis on major and planned gifts and the development of donor clubs
- Focus on developing a consistent annual fund program designed to provide long-term stability and identify prospects for major gifts
- Efforts to reach alumni who have never given donations
- New emphasis on alumni relations
- Leadership by central development staff members in expressing the need for setting overall institutional priorities for fund raising
- Close relationships with corporate and industry constituents, with an increasing focus on the development of these constituents as donors

10

Close and Personal:

A Private Two-Year College

SIGMA: Close, personal relationships with donors are an outstanding element in Sigma's fund-raising success, along with strong leadership of the chief development officer and president and a well-defined institutional image.

This church-affiliated two-year women's college, with an enrollment of 500 and annual educational and general expenditures of about $3 million, is located in the downtown area of a southern capital city. About 90 percent of the students are natives of the state in which the school is located. More than 90 percent of the students live on campus, and more than 90 percent of the school's graduates transfer to four-year institutions. It is a policy at Sigma to keep commuting enrollment low because residential living is more supportive of the intimate family-type relationships and values the college promotes.

Sigma College has a well-defined identity and a strong personality, arising from such factors as imaginative traditional ceremonies (some playful, some dramatic and dignified), an emphasis on serious education, and friendliness—called "the oldest tradition" at Sigma. The campus is meticulously maintained and has received national and local awards for architecture and landscaping.

Descriptive statistics for institutional characteristics and voluntary support outcomes appear in Table 10.1. Sigma is near the median for all private two-year colleges for educational and general expenditures and tuition; above the median for endowment, expenditures per student, alumni of record, and age of institution; and below the median for enrollment. Endowment

Table 10.1. Descriptive Statistics (1985–1987 Average) for Sigma College (Private Two-Year).

	Range for Type				This Institution		
	High	Median	Low	Actual	Predicted	Difference
Institutional Characteristics:						
Educational/General Expenditures	$7,012,600	$2,960,100	$627,700	$2,800,000	—	—
Endowment	$10,152,800	$1,592,100	$16,400	$9,761,116	—	—
Expenditures per Student	$8,400	$4,400	$1,900	$5,468	—	—
Cost of Tuition	$7,000	$3,800	$1,600	$3,595	—	—
Alumni of Record	17,800	5,700	800	6,440	—	—
Enrollment	2,300	670	200	512	—	—
Age of Institution	200 years	85 years	30 years	130 years	—	—
Fund-Raising Results:						
Total Voluntary Support	$1,249,700	$419,000	$20,200	$809,161	$472,278	+1.71
Alumni Gifts	$592,600	$53,200	$1,500	$182,264	$76,343	+2.39
Nonalumni Gifts	$725,700	$140,100	$0	$316,636	$230,386	+1.37
Corporation Gifts	$144,900	$63,500	$3,300	$144,878	$64,785	+2.24
Foundation Gifts	$560,700	$36,700	$0	$165,383	$153,302	+1.08

at about $8 million more than the median is the most remarkable institutional characteristic of Sigma. Sigma's voluntary support outcomes are all above the median for institutions of this type and above the outcomes predicted for an institution of this type with these institutional resources. Sigma has a higher outcome for corporation gifts than any other college of this type, even though this donor group contributes least to total voluntary support at Sigma. No organizational chart is provided for Sigma because the fund-raising staff includes only the director of development (who reports to the president) and one support staff member.

As recently as the 1960s, Sigma was in serious financial trouble and would have been closed but for the determination of the community to keep the college in operation. The first fund drive occurred in 1962 and led not only to the survival of the college but also to the construction of new dormitories, a recreation center, the cafeteria, and the library. Today, Sigma is free of debt. At the time of the site visit, the college was planning for a major campaign with a projected goal of $15 million. A previous campaign, successfully completed in 1982, raised $5 million. It is likely that trustees will provide as much as half of the goal for the upcoming campaign. In 1989, Sigma received the largest single gift in its history: a trust that will provide in excess of $2.5 million.

President G.

President G. had been at Sigma for six months at the time of the site visit. He had formerly served as an academic dean at two state universities and was experienced in fund raising. He said he particularly enjoyed fund rasing for Sigma because of how much easier it was to raise funds for Sigma than it was to raise funds for his former institutions. He estimated that he spends 25 percent of his time in direct fund-raising activities.

Describing Sigma as "an ornament in the crown of the city," President G. said he was impressed by the commitment and devotion people feel toward the college, the memories former students retain about their days at the college, the ongoing connections graduates maintain with the college, and how those factors have paid off in philanthropic support for Sigma over the years. President G. identified five aspects of life at Sigma that he believes result in a loyal constituency. These are: rich ceremonial traditions that graduates continue to recall for decades; close faculty involvement with students; a family atmosphere promoted by the college's small size and spiritual values; successful student outcomes, which lead Sigma graduates to feel appreciation and affection for the college; and effective efforts on the part of the alumnae association and the development office to maintain contact with former students.

President G.'s agenda for the college includes enlarging the faculty, implementing faculty development initiatives, increasing student financial aid, and upgrading instructional facilities, all of which will require increased revenues from private sources. He believes that numerous factors contribute to successful fund raising at Sigma, including the significant contributions of the thirty members of the board of trustees, the director of development's professional approach to fund raising, Sigma's overall success as an institution that captures and retains people's love and respect, and Sigma's location in a large metropolitan area. Clarity about Sigma's "distinctive niche" has also supported fund-raising efforts. The president remarked, "Although we do not enjoy a reputation for attracting the very best students, we do have a reputation for producing graduates who are enormously successful in completing the last two years in senior colleges."

Because Sigma's endowment is high, some people think of Sigma as "a rich girl's school." President G. says that this image is incorrect, that earnings from the endowment are used to underwrite student costs. In 1989, total costs for tuition, room, board, and books at Sigma were about $6,600 per student. The student body at Sigma is "not a silver spoon crowd," said President G., and some students are "as country as the day is long," he said. He added that Sigma's leadership makes "a continuing decision for Sigma not to be elitist, either financially or academically," but to continue to serve the same middle-class population of the region that has provided students and ample private support in the past.

President G. indicated that the professional advice he gets from the director of development is an important resource for him in his fund-raising work. He supports the director's emphasis on making the fund-raising approach as personal as possible. President G. remembered spending most of his time at other institutions cultivating new prospects. At Sigma, he spends most of his fund-raising time talking to donors about their previous gifts, actual developments on campus as a result of their earlier support, and continuing opportunities for donors to enrich Sigma College.

Fund-Raising Programs

The director of development is assisted by one staff member in a full-time support position. The director creates the annual plan and carries out comprehensive fund-raising activities in which the president, trustees, and volunteers are active participants. Although Sigma receives gifts from all major donor groups, fund-raising efforts include systematic programs directed primarily toward individuals, from whom Sigma receives 62 percent of its total voluntary support each year. The school has systematic programs for solicitation for the annual fund and for endowment, matching, and planned gifts.

The director of development at Sigma has made close, personal contact with donors the signature of fund raising at the school, based on her belief that no gift can be taken for granted. She said, "Our donors don't owe us anything. We have to constantly prove that we're worthy of support. Putting the donor first, rather than what we think may be best for the school, has paid off for us over the long run because donors know that we value them and they continue to feel good about supporting Sigma. Additionally, in our personal contact with donors, we continually emphasize specific accomplishments at Sigma that were made possible by private voluntary support."

Alumnae. Solicitation of alumnae for the annual fund begins in the fall with a general mailing of personalized letters that identify the amount of the donor's last gift. The donor pool is segmented in a number of different ways. One letter is sent to alumnae who have never made a donation. Another is sent to alumnae who gave previously but not last year. And specific letters are sent to other groups, including various donor clubs. All solicitation letters were previously signed by the former president, who added many handwritten notes to the numerous alumnae he knew personally. Because the current president is new to Sigma, the director of development signs the letters, continuing the tradition of writing notes to donors she knows. In addition to receiving solicitations for the annual fund, alumnae graduating in 1959 or earlier receive a newsletter on planned gifts.

Following the annual mailing, student volunteers call approximately 4,000 alumnae during two weeks in November. Either the director, the president, or a volunteer makes personal contact with donors who have given previous gifts of $500 or more. At the time of the site visit, 28 percent of the alumnae donated to the annual fund, a high rate for a two-year college. The director of development said, "Our phonathon is almost as valuable for the interest it generates as for the funds it raises. If we raise $120,000 from a phonathon that costs $20,000 to run, we have a $100,000 profit and have made good contacts with thousands of alumnae."

By December 1, everyone on the donor list has been reached, by either letter, telephone, or a personal visit. Alumnae who make pledges receive a follow-up reminder that is personalized and, to convey how seriously pledges are taken at Sigma, is designed to look like an invoice. Those alumnae who have made pledges but who have not made a gift during the year receive a reminder at the end of the fiscal year.

Through the process of recruiting student callers for the phonathon, the director begins to educate students about what is expected of them as alumnae. In keeping with Sigma's traditions of celebrating meaningful events in students' lives, the school holds a ceremonial luncheon shortly before commencement. At the luncheon, the alumnae director welcomes graduating students as official members of the alumnae association, points out how donations from previous alumnae have enabled the college to flourish, and emphasizes that the financial support of these graduates will be just as important to Sigma's future as the donations of previous alumnae are.

In September, alumnae who graduated earlier in the year are invited back to campus for their first reunion and are asked for their first contribution in December (presumably when they are home from college for Christmas break). Understandably, their gifts are small, but the director believes that early, direct, and continuing contact with alumnae is essential in keeping them closely connected to the college. She pointed out that graduates with associate degrees, particularly those who go on to complete four-year degrees, can easily lose their ties to their first college if the college is not persistent in maintaining that relationship.

Nonalumnae Donors. At Sigma, nonalumnae donors are generally trustees, members of college advisory boards, and parents and grandparents of current and former students. The director of development emphasizes close, personal contact in securing gifts from nonalumnae. She takes a particular interest in not allowing former donors to slip away because of oversight or neglect. She said, "When I came here, the policy was to take parents' names out of the system when their daughters graduated and not to contact them again. I don't remove any names from our mailing list unless someone asks to be removed. At some point in the future, many of these parents are going to have the ability to give, even if they don't now. I was able to go back and find names of parents who had made gifts up to ten years ago when their daughters were here. The other names are lost for good, but we're not losing people anymore."

She now contacts all parents of alumnae annually with a special solicitation letter, includes them in the phonathon in which parents call other parents, and also keeps them on regular mailing lists to keep them informed about current developments at the college. She said, "The first year we didn't get much response to our letter to parents of alumnae, but the second year the response was a little better, and this past year we've done even better. I think we benefit from regular contact with parents and from letting parents know they'll be hearing from us in the future."

Corporations. The corporate development committee of the board of trustees assists the director of development in identifying new corporations to solicit. During the year, the director, often accompanied by the president or a board member, visits each corporation that is a current or recent donor. She may present a proposal or may update the donor on new developments at Sigma. Corporate donors also receive bulletins, magazines, and other materials with news of activities at the college. Corporations on the college's mailing list are almost exclusively local and regional.

The director said, "Most corporations don't think they get much of a return on their investment here. Once in a great while, we will receive a gift from a major corporation, usually less than $10,000. Many local companies with an interest in the welfare of the city give $1,000 to $2,000 to the annual fund each year. I don't think Sigma will ever acquire big corporate gifts, so we concentrate our efforts elsewhere." Nevertheless, with the possibility of having additional staff members in the future and the increased concern and interest of corporations about the quality of general education in the United States, the director foresees the opportunity to develop profitable relationships with a limited number of national corporations that are not donors now.

Foundations. Most foundation support to Sigma is from local or regional foundations. The director of development maintains good relations with foundation donors by making regular annual visits to the foundations to discuss the status of projects funded by the foundations and by making careful decisions about the timing and substance of funding requests. She said, "We don't submit proposals just because it looks like it's time to ask for another gift. Foundation directors have told me that they appreciate my visiting without asking for a gift. If it is appropriate, I talk about projects and may ask when to submit a proposal, but I have also intentionally avoided asking for a gift in some cases, judging that it would be better to wait two to three years before asking again. I'm at a bit of an advantage because Sigma is not in a crisis situation. It helps a great deal that we can afford to wait."

The director believes foundation gifts to Sigma can grow more than corporation gifts. She relies on communicating with other development officers instead of library research to learn about foundations. After identifying a foundation as a prospect, the director asks development staff members at colleges to which the foundation has already contributed gifts about their solicitation approaches. She said, "I do most of my foundation research on the telephone. Talking to someone who has submitted a proposal, visited the foundation, and received a grant gives me a better picture than I can get from library research. Development directors are usually open about sharing information about foundations. I also talk to foundation directors with whom I have good relationships about how to approach other foundations. I do a lot of this kind of research because foundations don't want shot-in-the-dark solicitations." The director estimates that she devotes one day per week to foundation work and less than one day per week to soliciting gifts from corporations.

Analysis of Fund Raising at Sigma

The core outstanding characteristic of the fund raising program at Sigma is its emphasis on personal relationships with donors and other constituencies. This is not only an effective fund-raising technique in its own right but it is also especially appropriate at Sigma because it reflects and is consistent with one of the college's core values — friendliness.

Also outstanding at Sigma is the effective partnership of the president and the director of development. They carry out equally critical roles in fund raising. The president provides leadership in setting the agenda for the college, in providing approval and support for professional fund-raising activities, and in participating actively in maintaining donor relationships and in seeking new gifts. The director of development determines the general and specific fund-raising approaches for each donor group and carries out the majority of solicitations. She also provides critical information and judgments for the president, trustees, and other administrators regarding areas of academic growth most likely to secure funding.

Staff members at Sigma have a long-term commitment to fund raising, as indicated by the president's involvement and the planning for an upcoming major campaign. Intimate understanding of the kind of institution Sigma is and who Sigma's most likely students and donors are is an important characteristic of Sigma's fund-raising program.

The president and the director of development both work to broaden the awareness of and involvement in fund raising of other faculty and staff members. The president often explains to faculty members the roles that they must play in fund raising as representatives of the campus. He has instituted a policy that proposals for funds from external sources are to be coordinated in the development office to prevent multiple solicitations of the same sources. The director of development has worked to broaden her role as consultant and partner to faculty members in their grant-seeking efforts.

Volunteers and trustees play prominent roles in fund raising at Sigma. Sigma is one of the few institutions that we studied in which trustees are major donors, besides providing important information and counsel about new prospects and engaging in actual solicitations. Both the president and the director spoke of the financial contributions and personal investments of board members in Sigma's fund-raising efforts. Under the direction of Sigma's former president, the board evolved from a group that was largely social in nature to an active working group. Experienced board members conduct an informal but effective orientation to ensure that new members understand the importance of board responsibilities and obligations.

In summary, what can others learn from Sigma's experiences? The factors we identified as contributing to fund-raising effectiveness at Sigma are as follows:

- A director of development who reflects the institution's image: bright, female, serious, warm, dignified
- Fund-raising programs that reflect Sigma's institutional strengths, culture, and traditions

- Sharing of leadership, activities, and values by the president and the director of development
- Involvement of trustees and volunteers in high-level fund raising
- A "velvet hammer" approach — persuasive, indefatigable, but gentle
- Clear institutional identity and insightful understanding of how constituents can be motivated to support Sigma
- Comprehensive, systematic professional programs for all important constituencies, all carrying the "signature" — that is, the personal connection — of the overall fund-raising approach and the institution
- Willingness to assume full responsibility for maintaining constituent regard and interest and taking no gift for granted

11

Creating Networks
of Dedicated Friends:

A Public Two-Year College

OMEGA: Committed staff, joined by a new president—and
strongly supported by foundation trustees—make steady progress
in raising money for this college from corporations, foundations,
friends, and alumni.

This community college, with an enrollment of about 6,500 and
annual educational and general expenditures of more than $12
million, is thirty-five miles from a major midwestern city. Descriptive statistics appear in Table 11.1. Omega's institutional
characteristics are all about at the median, except for age of institution. Omega is among the younger community colleges with
which it is compared in Table 11.1. All voluntary support outcomes are above the median for institutions of this type; actual
outcomes are all above or about equal to predicted outcomes.

President R.

President R. had been at Omega almost two years at the time
of the site visit. Describing himself as part of the "new wave"
of community college presidents, he said, "The first wave of
leaders in community colleges is giving way to a whole new
group, including many of us who have been educated in community colleges and who have had professional experience in
community colleges. Previous community college executives
typically received their professional experience in high schools
or universities. This new wave is committed to community col-

Table 11.1. Descriptive Statistics (1985–1987 Average) for Omega College (Public Two-Year).

	Range for Type			This Institution		
	High	Median	Low	Predicted	Actual	Difference
Institutional Characteristics:						
Educational/General Expenditures	$97,272,300	$8,423,500	$1,567,000	—	$12,452,967	—
Endowment	$2,063,200	$58,100	$0	—	$1,346,732	—
Expenditures per Student	$13,300	$1,900	$900	—	$1,917	—
Cost of Tuition	$1,300	$800	$100	—	$1,193	—
Alumni of Record	21,200	9,800	200	—	9,842	—
Enrollment	37,700	7,000	900	—	6,495	—
Age of Institution	100 years	30 years	20 years	—	24 years	—
Fund-Raising Results:						
Total Voluntary Support	$945,400	$96,500	$21,600	$237,715	$321,765	+1.35
Alumni Gifts	$25,400	$900	$0	$6,808	$6,648	0.98
Nonalumni Gifts	$806,300	$18,100	$0	$134,042	$186,852	+1.39
Corporation Gifts	$486,200	$33,200	$0	$71,490	$99,173	+1.39
Foundation Gifts	$106,100	$22,000	$0	$27,284	$29,092	+1.07

leges, and we understand the importance of raising funds from private sources. Over the next decade, systematic fund raising in community colleges will increase dramatically, not only because public resources are tighter but also because of this new wave of energy and optimism about what community colleges can accomplish."

The president discussed the importance of increased private support to Omega. "We cannot remain a premier community college without a better margin of discretionary funds than we have today," he said. "Only 82 percent of our revenue comes from state and local taxes. Students pay only 28 percent of the cost of running the college. We are always going to have to scrape to keep up with the inflationary cost of maintaining what we have, which doesn't leave anything for that creative margin, for leadership, for dabbling in creative opportunities."

To have a dynamic institution, President R. said, "We systematically and continually evaluate the results we're achieving against the real needs of the community. We have to be able to take some risks, and in order to take risks, we need discretionary money. Private support is paramount to the success of our institution and to my role here. We have a very big stake riding on our fund-raising efforts."

Regarding his own role, President R. said, "I spend 10 percent of my time in development. I have always enjoyed establishing relationships and communicating with people. I am fairly gregarious, which is helpful. When they hired me, the board told me they thought this college was the best kept secret in the county, and they wanted me to get the word out. I've spent a good part of my time building bridges and opening doors for the college."

The senior development officer observed, "Our president is probably a better fund raiser than 90 percent of the professionals in the field. He has a special interest in raising money for the college and really enjoys fund raising. Other presidents may do what is necessary, but our new president does it with enthusiasm. He has a very positive image in the college and the county."

President R. identified several fund-raising areas at Omega

that need more formal attention. "We need to cultivate a number of sources that we have not heretofore," he said. "We have not systematically cultivated professional people in the community, which would help us increase funds raised, influence, and contacts. We need systematic programs for planned giving and corporate giving. We have an advanced technology center that provides customized training for corporate leaders, one of the most important ways in which we provide service to the community, but we don't have a program for systematic solicitation of these corporations." One of the first tasks of the new director will be to oversee a feasibility study to guide planning for a major campaign.

President R. indicated that other reservoirs of support for Omega are still untapped. "We opened our library to the community," he said. "Residents pay a dollar for a library card. Seven thousand people in the community used the library last year. We haven't asked them for a donation. About 80,000 people attended events in our theater last year. We've never asked them for a gift. For a program in our new fitness center, we anticipated that about 200 people would enroll, but 550 registered in the fall and 475 registered in the winter. Those are people in the community who pay $30 for use of this wonderful modern facility for a full eleven weeks. What a bargain! We ought to be building on those community ties."

The president said that in addition to pursuing new prospects, Omega needs to initiate more comprehensive fund raising. "My predecessor received over $1.2 million in donated equipment for our technology center for the corporate community. We have another $1 million worth of equipment on consignment. Looking at development in its broadest terms, we ought to be counting those as gifts on our ledger sheets." According to the senior development officer, President R. has already begun an effective in-house marketing program: "I think the most important thing President R. has done for us is to make us more aware of what we have to offer, which has also made the community more aware."

Omega Foundation

All revenues to the college from private sources are channeled through the Omega foundation. The foundation was established in 1973 as a nonprofit corporation to receive gifts for Omega. According to the president of Omega, one college trustee in the early 1970s had "a very entrepreneurial spirit" and attended professional conferences to learn about new developments in community colleges. After learning that some community colleges were developing formal fund-raising programs, he was instrumental in creating the foundation for Omega. By 1988, total assets of the foundation were almost $3 million. The foundation includes the college development office, although salary for the position of executive director of development (vacant at the time of the site visit) is paid by the college. Other development staff members include the senior development officer (who also serves as the assistant secretary/treasurer of the foundation and college alumni relations officer), a secretary, and a bookkeeper. The president expected to fill the position of executive director soon. Since the staff is small, no organizational chart is provided. The executive director of development reports to the president. Other development staff report to the executive director.

Foundation board members are business and civic leaders. The board has thirty members, including five members from the college's board of trustees. The senior development officer said, "We have a waiting list of people who want to serve on the foundation board because they believe in the college's mission. The foundation has a reputation in the county for knowing what it's doing. Being a member of this board is prestigious." Incumbent board members make it clear that newcomers are expected to be actively involved and that the board is a working board. The senior development officer said, "Our board members are directly involved in fund raising, and I'm underlining the word *involved*. Some have built annual gifts to Omega into their corporate budgets. Some don't actually make calls or significant financial contributions, but everyone is involved in making referrals and in opening doors for us. Between 10 and 20 percent of our annual support comes from the board, and we hope to see that increase."

Fund-Raising Programs

Of the twenty-three two-year public colleges in this state's system, only five have foundations, and only these five have organized fund-raising programs. Although there is a prestigious private college in Omega's area, the president noted that it is a college "totally committed to its students and not to the community," which has created the opportunity for Omega to become important to the community as well as to develop a broad base of support.

In President R.'s opinion, Omega has had two "excellent campaigns." The first formal campaign ran from 1977–1980 and successfully raised $1.5 million to supplement $5 million in state funds for a new fine arts center and theater. Following this success, foundation and development officers realized that the community would provide financial support, and they began a campaign in the mid 1980s to increase endowment funds. The goal was $850,000, which was exceeded by almost $150,000 in spite of the fact that unemployment in the area reached an unprecedented high during that period.

The senior development officer said, "The old fund-raising theory that a capital campaign never hurts your annual fund was true in our case. Since the endowment campaign ended, we've raised $300,000 to $600,000 on an annual basis with no active campaign. Most of our support comes from nonalumni individuals, foundations, and corporations. Last year, our best year, we raised about $18,000 from alumni out of the total $613,000 raised. The rest came from 'friends.' We never did anything unique or different, but I think we did the right things right. I spend a lot of time out talking to people. About every six months, I visit all previous and current corporate and foundation donors to tell them what we're doing and to find out if the college is meeting their needs. The answer is not always yes, so I try to bring that information back to the people responsible."

Currently, records of all calls are kept on the computer, but that was not always the case. "I can remember when I ran the donor list out of a shoe box," the senior development officer said. "When we started looking for a computer system, nobody knew what we were talking about — a computer system for fund raising. The foundation wanted a system separate from the college system to ensure that donor records would be confidential. The system is a big plus for us. We key in gifts and generate thank-you letters and receipts. I read all thank-you letters and usually add personal notes. The system logs the gift in the right category and produces monthly, weekly, and daily reports."

Because "the future in fund raising is largely in planned giving," the senior development officer indicated that a more formal program in this area would be developed when the new executive director arrived. This is an appropriate time for Omega to develop such a program because Omega's oldest alumni graduated twenty-five years ago. Although staff members have made no formal solicitations for planned gifts, the senior development officer said, "We have received a number of bequests that we didn't know about until the parties died. Two years ago we got a bequest for $170,000 from a husband and wife. This was 10 percent of their estate. We had no relationship with these people. Imagine what they might have been willing to do for Omega if we had known of their interest and had cultivated them."

Only regional corporations and foundations are solicited for gifts. Although some gifts may come from a corporation's headquarters, they are funneled through local offices. Most grant proposals are prepared in the development office.

Gifts from faculty and staff members contribute to Omega's fund-raising success, both in dollars raised and in influence on other donors, according to the senior development officer. "Before publicly announcing either of our two campaigns, we had in-house campaigns. We solicited all employees and set up a three-year pledge period on a payroll deduction plan. We got 92 percent participation the first time and 90 percent the second time. One of the first things foundation or corporation officers ask when I visit them is 'What are you doing for yourself?' When I say, 'We had 90 percent employee participation in our fund-raising campaigns,' I get their attention right away. Employees donate to Omega because they believe in the college, and it is a good place to work."

Division chairs pick one person in each department to run the campaign and conduct personal solicitations. The senior development officer said, "We suggest that employees pledge 1½ percent of their salaries. We get some pledges for $1 but we also get some for $500, too—more $500 pledges than $1 pledges. Of course, we all signed up here first, and we made sure all the division chairs and solicitors signed up. Everyone feels good about the pride employees have in the college."

Omega has a yearly phonathon to solicit annual gifts from alumni (anyone who has received a degree or certificate). Approximately 80 percent of Omega's alumni live within a two-county area. Alumni who have moved out of this region receive gift solicitations in the mail. Students are paid to call local alumni from the permanent phonathon office of twenty-two phones, located in the foundation office. Consistent with Omega's mission to provide service to the region, the college makes the phonathon facilities available to other community organizations for their fund-raising drives.

Every February, Omega students call prospects four nights a week, using a script prepared by the development office. Callers also update alumni records. Donors may specify how they want their gifts to be used, but in 1989 callers encouraged donors to earmark gifts for a new academic scholars program, a strong priority set by the president. Callers usually reach every local alumnus for whom there is a good phone number. They encourage previous donors to upgrade their gifts and ask previous nondonors to pledge $5 or $10. About 25 percent of alumni who are reached, or 10 percent of all alumni, make gifts to the annual fund. About 90 percent of the pledges result in actual gifts.

The phonathons are spirited events, according to the senior development officer: "Before last year, we had never reached $1,000 in one night, but last year we reached $1,000 every night but one. We take an update every fifteen minutes and announce the total pledged up to that time. The students cheer each other along. When someone gets a $100 pledge, everyone celebrates." A pledge of $200 is about the highest the callers expect; the average phonathon gift is $15. "We don't raise a lot of money from the alumni, but some alumnus might become a major donor in the future because of our phonathon."

Analysis of Fund Raising at Omega

Characteristics that are outstanding at Omega are trustees' participation and support (Omega is one of the few institutions outstanding in this characteristic), presidential leadership, and emphasis on constituent relationships. It was a college trustee who was responsible for the creation of the Omega Foundation and the introduction of fund raising to the college, and foundation trustees have played a strong role in Omega's successful fund raising since then. Membership on the foundation board has come to be associated with status and prestige in the community, which not only speaks well of the foundation's effectiveness but also enhances Omega's fund-raising efforts.

Much of Omega's status as an institution that is effective in fund raising was earned before the arrival of the current president, but the president's vision, entrepreneurial abilities, and leadership have a strong positive impact on current fund raising. Strongly committed to Omega's role as an educational institution and a community resource, President R. sees the need for private support to increase, has a vision about what increased private support will do, and has definite ideas about how to increase that support. He came into an institution that was already proud and effective. His energy and charisma will certainly help Omega to continue to grow. His "gregarious" (as he described it) nature and his abilities to articulate his vision for Omega and generate consensus and enthusiasm among constituents are all assets that are certain to result in both continued progress for the college and increased private support.

Maintaining close relationships with the community is part of Omega's primary mission, and Omega is outstanding in this area, both as a college and as a fund raising organiza tion. Development staff members stress maintaining relationships with corporate and foundation donors as well as continuing contacts with alumni donors. A current priority for the development office is to increase alumni activities, both to enhance fund raising and to keep alumni involved with the college.

Omega's image is well defined and well communicated, in part by the active boards for the college and the foundation. Institutional commitment to fund raising and staff commitment to the institution are also strong at Omega. (Because the chief development officer's position was vacant, we could not evaluate this role. However, given the momentum the college has and the fund-raising priorities of the president, the new chief development officer is likely to play a critical role in institutional affairs.)

The senior development officer has been at Omega almost since the creation of the foundation and was influential in bringing modern fund-raising technology and methods to Omega — skills and know-how he acquired as a development officer in a private research university. He instituted fund-raising ideas at Omega that were novel to community colleges: soliciting alumni for annual gifts and soliciting art and equipment as in-kind gifts. He also brought to Omega the idea that donors are not obligated to an institution but that the institution is obligated to donors.

Aside from the annual phonathon, not much formalized planning underlies fund raising at Omega — with the exception of specific campaigns, which have been highly structured and well planned. As in other institutions, the senior development officer's long tenure at the college, his intimate knowledge of the institution and its constituents, and the relatively small scope of fund raising have been effective substitutes for formal planning at Omega. However, the president's goals for a more comprehensive fund-raising program will require more formal planning processes.

In summary, what can others learn from Omega's experiences? Factors we identified as contributing to fund-raising effectiveness at Omega are as follows:

- Aggressive fund raising, that is, initiating contact, maintaining contact, and asking for gifts on a regular basis
- Realistic assessment of Omega's strengths, opportunities for growth, and likely constituents
- Strong leadership by the board and the president
- A vision for the college and clear priorities that are dependent upon increased voluntary support and increased institutional commitment to fund raising
- Modern technology and systems to maintain records and provide information
- Strong support for and participation in internal campaigns
- Structured, well-planned, and realistic special campaign efforts
- Fund raising based on pride and involvement in the institution
- Clarity about institutional image and donors

12

Reconsidering the Conventional Fund-Raising Wisdom

We have examined the factors related to fund-raising success in ten institutions. None of the institutions were outstanding in all of the characteristics commonly associated with success in fund raising that we listed in Chapter One. Some institutions had strengths in only a few of the characteristics, and no single pattern of factors emerged to fit all institutions. The most common characteristics in these successful fund-raising programs were presidential leadership, institutional commitment to fund raising, chief development officer's leadership and role in setting the institutional mission, and entrepreneurial fund raising. Less common characteristics that we found in these successful fund-raising programs were trustees' participation, volunteers' roles, emphasis on management, staff commitment to the institution, and emphasis on constituent relations.

Our results confirm much of the conventional wisdom about fund-raising effectiveness but also suggest that factors associated with fund-raising success are complex and vary in individual institutions more than conventional wisdom would sometimes indicate. This chapter provides a discussion of our overall findings, based on the characteristics listed in Chapter One. We do not intend to make the case that effective fund raising can be "boiled down" to a few general principles. In fact, we hope our results make the opposite case — that fund-raising effectiveness is multifaceted and complex and has a great deal to do with the context in which the fund raising occurs.

Characteristics of Institutions

The institutional characteristics we consider in this book that are related to fund-raising success are presidential leadership, trustees' participation in fund raising, and institutional commitment to fund raising. This last characteristic includes resource allocation, acceptance of the need for fund raising, definition and communication of institutional niche and image, and institutional fund-raising priorities.

Presidential Leadership

As fund-raising success has become more critical to institutional prosperity, presidents of colleges and universities have been required to assume a greater direct role in fund raising as well as greater responsibility for leadership of the entire fund-raising program. Ideally, the president provides leadership in setting fund-raising priorities. Institutionwide priorities help to ensure that different departments coordinate their funding requests and that the institution's academic, research, and service priorities get funded. The president articulates the institution's mission and its case for support and generates consensus about these among all of the institution's internal and external constituents.

Distinctive presidential leadership in fund raising was a characteristic in nine (one presidency was vacant) of the institutions with successful fund-raising programs. Additionally, the president's interest in fund raising and direct participation in fund raising have increased considerably in each of the institutions over the past ten years.

All nine presidents participated in direct fund-raising activities. Evidence from interviews with the presidents themselves and with other staff members indicates that all of the presidents participated enthusiastically in fund raising. Many of the presidents replaced former presidents who were less than enthusiastic about fund raising. All nine of the presidents were rated by their chief development officers as being either excellent or very good at fund raising. Chief development officers had particular regard for presidents who were willing to ask directly for gifts.

The presidents in these nine institutions have been in office from six months to twelve years. Except for the president who had been in office the longest, each of them had been told during the hiring process that fund raising would have to be a priority in the position. Several presidents were involved in fund raising for the first time in their professional lives. These presidents indicated that they relied heavily for guidance on experienced fund-raising staff members. At Rho, the institution currently without a president, the search committee was very interested, for the first time in the institution's history, in the fund-raising abilities of the presidential candidates.

The amount of time the presidents reported spending on fund raising varied considerably and seemed to be related to several factors, including size and type of institution and maturity of the overall fund-raising program. Presidents in the four largest institutions worked only with major donors, and the time they spent in direct fund raising varied from month to month. The other presidents reported spending from 10 to 90 percent of their time in direct fund raising, and they also all reported wide involvement in fund-raising activities with donors at all gift levels. The two presidents who reported spending 10 percent of their time on fund raising both said this amount of time will increase when their institutions undertake campaigns.

The literature on presidents and fund raising (for example, Fisher and Quehl, 1989) generally emphasizes the influence of presidential participation and interest on donors and overall fund-raising results. The positive effect of presidential leadership on fund-raising staff members is rarely discussed in the literature. In many of the institutions we studied, staff members often spoke of the president when they talked about their own responsibilities and commitments, saying, for example, that they wanted to "help the president achieve his goals." We interpreted such statements to mean that staff members had been personally and directly influenced by the president's ability to generate consensus and confidence. This finding suggests that presidents might do well to attend one or two fewer fund-raising events each year and instead spend this time talking directly with fund-raising staff members about goals and priorities.

Trustees' Participation

Trustees may participate in fund raising in three ways: by making donations, by helping to identify prospects and solicit gifts, and by setting institutional policy that supports and enhances fund raising. These traditional roles evolved in private institutions, where trustees often are selected and appointed primarily for their ability to contribute in these ways. Until recently, trustees in most public institutions were not expected to play much of a role in fund raising, and their capabilities in this area were not a factor in their suitability for appointment to the board. Some presidents and chief development officers in many public institutions have begun to attempt to influence boards to consider candidates' capacities for fund raising.

One of the surprises in our research was that only three of the institutions we studied with effective fund-raising programs had trustee boards that staff members characterized as strong in all three fund-raising roles. Even more surprising, two of the three institutions with strong trustee involvement were public institutions. Overall, trustees' involvement and participation was not a strong characteristic of the successful fund-raising programs we studied, a finding that challenges the conventional wisdom that trustee participation is essential for successful fund-raising programs. However, the remaining seven institutions we studied were working to increase trustees' participation in fund raising, indicating that fund raisers believe that participation of trustees will increase fund-raising effectiveness.

Institutional Commitment to Fund Raising

An institution's commitment to fund raising is evident in the resources allocated for fund raising, the overall acceptance of the need for fund raising on campus, the definition and communication of the institution's niche and image, and the accomplishment of certain institutionwide tasks that facilitate fund raising (such as planning and goal setting for fund-raising priorities and policies). Institutional commitment to fund raising is a strong characteristic of the effective fund-raising programs we studied.

Resource Allocation. The most basic form of institutional commitment is resource allocation — providing money and staff for fund raising. Fund-raising staff members in seven institutions thought that the resources they were allocated were sufficient for effective fund raising. However, staff members almost everywhere said their programs could accomplish more with more staff members, more time, and more resources. New staff positions had been added within the year of our site visits in every institution but three. Two of these three institutions had the smallest fund-raising programs of the schools we studied. In some institutions, staff members thought resource allocations for fund raising were exceptionally generous. Staff in the three institutions (all public) who were not satisfied with the allocation of resources said allocation problems were related to limited funding and understanding at the state level rather than problems on campus.

Acceptance of the Need for Fund Raising. Another form of institutional commitment to fund raising, more complicated and difficult to measure in both amount and impact on fund-raising results, is the degree of acceptance at the institution of the need for fund raising and appreciation of the staff members who raise funds. In seven institutions, we found widespread understanding and acceptance on campus of the need for fund raising. In the three others, this understanding was developing as a result of the direct efforts of the president and chief development officer. Staff members we spoke with were generally more satisfied with resource allocations than they were with the level of campuswide acceptance of fund raising. Nevertheless, most fund raisers were not discouraged by the level of acceptance, indicating that part of their role on campus is to function as

educators about fund raising. Some fund raisers were uncon-
cerned about limited understanding on campus, indicating that
increasing the donors' understanding of the need for private support was what counted, not the understanding on campus.

*Definition and Communication of Institutional Niche and Im-
age. Institutional niche* refers to what the institution actually does.
Institutional image refers to how well, how accurately, and how
extensively information about the institution is conveyed to external constituents. It is not enough for internal constituents to
recognize, support, and be in agreement about the institution's
niche and its value; the institution's "story" must also be per-
suasively and accurately communicated externally. Many managers and presidents in the institutions we studied distinguished
between telling the story and making sure there was a good story
to tell.

Clarity about institutional niche was exceptionally strong
in every one of the institutions with successful fund-raising programs, making this one of the few characteristics that was strong
in every program. Most of the people we interviewed succinctly
articulated the unique contribution of their institution in the
higher education community, and they were knowledgeable
about the particular fund-raising consequences of the institution's being in its specific niche. Also, most people were highly
optimistic about their institution's continued fund-raising success, yet no one appeared to be unrealistic or grandiose about
what their fund-raising programs might achieve. High optimism
and realistic expectations are the result of basic know-how in
fund raising and clarity about the institution.

Clarity about an institution's niche indicates that the niche
has been defined and communicated within the institution. It
also indicates that knowledge of the institution's history and current strengths and aspirations has been disseminated throughout the institution. The image of the institution was well established and well communicated in eight of the institutions we
studied. Staff members recognized the need to improve both
the institution's image and how it was communicated in the remaining two institutions.

Institutional Fund-Raising Priorities and Policies. Institutional priorities for fund raising help focus time and resources on the areas most related to achieving institutional goals. Setting institutional priorities for fund raising has assumed new importance because of several factors, including: the increasingly multidisciplinary character of institutional programs; the increased competition for funds, resulting in policies by funders restricting funding requests; and the substantially increased preference of donors at all levels to give restricted gifts.

The impact of reduced unrestricted gifts was a concern in every institution that we studied. Institution presidents have used unrestricted funds in the past to implement new initiatives and to support projects crucial to the institution overall. As these funds for discretionary use have decreased, the need to establish clear priorities and to focus fund-raising efforts has increased. Without clear direction, fund raisers are overwhelmed by the volume of competing funding needs all institutions have. Fund raisers at all of the institutions we studied agreed that institutional priorities for fund raising were essential to fund-raising success. Institutional priorities for fund raising had been established in eight institutions. In one institution, the process of setting priorities was under way. At the remaining institution, development staff members thought a lack of clear institutional priorities was impeding their work.

How priorities were set varied across institutions. The management style at one institution was particularly autocratic, and it was clear that the president and the chief development officer wielded considerable power in establishing institutional priorities. At the other extreme, in another institution, priorities were set by a two-step process that involved wide participation of internal constituents and participation by over 300 external participants from across the country. The variation in how priorities are set does not seem to have much effect on fund-raising processes or results. What fund raisers consistently said was that it is important that priorities be set, that they be well communicated, and that there be broad acceptance that the priorities are the right ones for the institution at a given time.

Fund-raising policies are needed to support the focus of

these priorities. As fund-raising programs expand and competition for funds continues to increase, many corporations and foundations have tried to control the number of proposals they receive by instituting a policy to review one proposal at a time for any organization. As a result, all but two of the smallest institutions we studied needed policies governing proposal submissions.

Restricting proposal submissions is one of the most emotionally charged fund-raising issues on most campuses. Funding sources with restrictions on proposal submissions are generally among those with the capacity to make the largest gifts, gifts large enough to significantly affect institutional priorities and dramatically alter the future of specific academic units. These funders are also among the best-known funders, which means that they are likely to be the funders that individual departments and faculty members have relied on for small and regular grants.

In seven of the institutions we studied, senior management staff members in the central development office made final decisions regarding proposal submissions, based on institutional priorities and other factors. But only two institutions had formal written policies governing proposal submissions. In one institution, decisions regarding proposal submissions were made in the provost's office.

The necessity to restrict proposal submissions creates problems of conflicting interests on most campuses (between central and decentralized fund-raising staff, between campaign staff and annual fund staff, or between fund-raising staff and faculty). Specific formal policies that spell out how decisions will be made, and that also educate and accommodate faculty members and academic officers as much as possible, seem warranted. Furthermore, negotiations and formal agreements with the funders restricting submissions seem necessary to ensure that funders will express support for institutional policies, assume responsibility for their own policies, and handle nonauthorized submissions in a standard manner.

Characteristics of Fund-Raising Programs

The characteristics of fund-raising programs considered in this book are the chief development officer's leadership, centralized fund-raising programs, successful fund-raising history, volunteers' roles in fund raising, emphasis on management of the fund-raising function (including information and communication; planning, goal setting, and evaluation; and staff development, training, and evaluation), staff commitment to the institution, and emphasis on constituent relations.

Chief Development Officer's Leadership

All of the chief development officers in the institutions we studied provided strong leadership that was cited by others in the institution as a factor in fund-raising success. The chief development officers had diverse backgrounds and varying levels of experience and expertise in direct fund raising. Of the eight officers (two positions were vacant), only half had advanced to their positions from long-term careers in fund raising. One had had a previous career in business. The remaining three were former academic officers in the institutions in which they now serve as chief development officers.

Length of time in position varied for chief development officers as well as for presidents. As a group, chief development officers had slightly more longevity in their positions (an average of slightly more than five years) than the presidents had (an average of slightly more than four years). Half of the chief development officers in the institutions we studied have been in their positions for four or more years. (The "typical" advancement professional has been in his or her current position for four years, according to Turk, 1986, p. 10.)

These chief development officers varied considerably in how they carried out their complex roles, and they did not agree on all aspects of fund raising. For instance, involving volunteers in fund raising and setting dollar goals for fund raisers were two issues about which the officers disagreed. However, the officers were very similar in some areas. All of them demonstrated that they understand and value higher education, are articulate representatives of their institutions and the fund-raising field, have respect for donors, and have high professional standards for themselves and their staff members. Most of them expressed some awe, even after many years' experience, for the process through which Americans voluntarily and generously give from their own pockets to benefit society.

The chief development officers were unanimous in two important convictions about fund raising. First, each of them talked of the importance of fund-raising programs that are designed to provide long-term benefits for the institution. A common belief is that continuity in fund-raising leadership is important to success. Our findings suggest that continuity of commitment to long-term results may be a more essential factor in fund-raising success than long tenure of fund-raising leaders. Second, these chief development officers all had a strong belief in the need for fund-raising decisions and plans to be made within the context of each specific institutional environment. No one was interested in "canned" or "off-the-shelf" programs, and all emphasized how fund-raising decisions reflected overall institutional values and directions. Even when fund-raising programs and activities represented new and sometimes unpopular approaches for the respective institutions, the chief development officers were able to articulate strong cases for how the new approaches were consistent with the basic character of the institution, in spite of the fact that the new direction may have been quite unlike "what we have always done here." When chief development officers hired telemarketing or research firms, their careful selection of the firms was based on the degree to which the firms' approach was consistent with institutional values and needs, not on the firms' claims or accomplishments.

The competition for experienced fund raisers probably will continue to grow, and staff turnover, in a field already characterized by high turnover, will continue to be an issue in many institutions. These chief development officers are protecting their institutions and preparing for staff turnover by making certain that success is less dependent upon the talents of individual fund raisers and more dependent upon systematic fund-raising programs and excellent record-keeping and management information systems.

A chief development officer may fill as many as five different roles in leading the fund-raising process: college or university officer, fund raiser, manager, mentor, and entrepreneur.

(Some chief development officers also have responsibilities for other aspects of institutional advancement. We looked at fund-raising roles only.) In general, the chief development officers at the institutions we studied all carried out responsibilities in each of these roles, but no one model of effective leadership was apparent.

Ideally, the chief development officer, functioning in the role of college or university officer, participates in setting institutionwide priorities and fund-raising goals. Serving as a college or university officer was a primary function for four of the eight chief development officers. All eight functioned to some degree in this capacity. In most of the institutions we studied, the position of the chief development officer had been elevated from middle management to an executive level, confirming the description of the chief development officer by Gilley, Fulmer, and Reithlingshoefer (1986) as one of "the new power brokers" in higher education (p. 84).

Many veteran fund raisers told us that in the not too distant past, when the development officer typically was not part of the executive administrative team, executive staff members and trustees defined the institution's mission and set priorities and then handed the development officer the "shopping list" of projects in need of private funding. In some cases, the development officer knew at once that funding for certain projects would be difficult or impossible to secure. In other cases, the development officer knew the funding climate and market well enough to know that funding sources that might be appropriate and highly beneficial for the institution were left untapped. These mistakes and oversights are less likely to occur when chief development officers participate in overall institutional planning.

Six of the eight chief development officers in these effective programs had direct fund-raising responsibilities. All of those who achieved the position of chief development officer by progressing through fund-raising ranks not only continued to participate directly in the cultivation of donors and solicitation of gifts but particularly relished this part of their job. Two chief development officers who had no fund-raising experience at any other level than that of vice president spent a good portion of their time in direct fund-raising activities and were highly regarded by their experienced staffs for their fund-raising skills.

While all chief development officers had essential management responsibility for planning, monitoring, adjusting, and evaluating staff, budgets, and the content and process of fund-raising programs, they spent varying amounts of time and had widely varying amounts of interest in this facet of the chief development officer's role. In many cases, most internal management functions had been delegated to other senior staff members.

All chief development officers with staff members reporting to them have the option to be mentors. Mentoring provides valuable socialization in most fields. It is especially critical in a field such as fund raising, in which few formal educational programs or processes for gaining credentials exist. Some of the chief development officers were exceptionally well qualified to serve as fund-raising mentors; others were less qualified. Some of those qualified officers took special interest and delight in mentoring, while some paid little attention to this role. In all, four chief development officers functioned in some capacity as mentors.

The entrepreneurial role is the final aspect of the chief development officer's position. An entrepreneur breaks new ground, is willing to take risks, and encourages staff members to move beyond conventional ways of thinking and doing. Although we found entrepreneurial thinkers and actors in almost every institution, they were not always the chief development officers. Four chief development officers were cited by their staffs for entrepreneurial skills.

The results of our research indicate that chief development officers in institutions with effective fund-raising programs vary in how they conceptualize and carry out their multiple roles. Our case studies also indicate that the chief development officer does not have to perform each function of this complex role himself or herself. (See Sorensen, 1986, pp. 42–45, on delegation.)

Examining the variation in the roles of these chief development officers demonstrates that it is important to have a good "fit" between the chief development officer's style and strengths and the needs of the institution. Two particularly interesting examples of "good fit" between the institution and the chief development officer are at Rho and Gamma.

At Rho, of all ten institutions the one in the earliest stages of implementing formal, comprehensive fund-raising programs, previous fund-raising success was the result of the independent actions and efforts of academic officers and faculty members. Executive administrators at Rho saw the need for centralized fund-raising programs to better serve overall institutional needs. The real challenges to the success of fund raising at an institution with this kind of fund-raising history are likely to be internal, and the chief development officer will have to be especially skilled in facilitating internal negotiations and relationships. Rho's chief development officer, while a newcomer to fund raising, has a long history at Rho in various senior roles and also has long-standing positive relationships with key academic leaders of the institution. An administrator with his credentials and experience seems well qualified for the role of smoothing the way toward expanded centralized fund raising, building on the earlier successes of decentralized efforts, and negotiating new fund-raising roles and responsibilities. An outsider, even one with years of professional fund-raising expertise, would likely have a more difficult time in this position than someone who already has a strong network of positive internal relationships.

The president at Gamma thought progress in fund raising should be an urgent priority, and he also had some unconventional ideas about campaigns, donor markets, and volunteers when he hired the incumbent senior vice president for institutional advancement. The president chose as his senior development officer an academic officer noted for his entrepreneurial accomplishments, who also did not need to "unlearn" the conventional wisdom about higher education fund raising. If the president had believed that a classic, traditional program would be best for Gamma at that time, he might have searched for a chief development officer with different credentials.

Centralized Fund-Raising Programs

Each of the effective fund-raising programs had a central fund-raising staff, but further organization of institutionwide fund raising varied across institutions. In general, most fund raisers in these programs believed that a centralized structure is more effective than a decentralized structure. In seven institutions, the fund-raising staff and development activities were completely centralized under the authority of the chief development officer. Of these seven institutions, three had college development officers as well as a central fund-raising staff. Four, with much smaller staffs overall, had only a central staff. College development officers in one institution reported jointly to the chief development officer and their deans. In another institution, college development officers reported only to deans and had functional relationships with the chief development officer and the central development staff. In the remaining institution, where until recently most fund raising was not only totally decentralized but also carried out by academic deans and program directors, a newly created central staff was working to develop and strengthen central fund-raising programs. (For discussions of organizational structure, see Sandberg, 1985; Desmond and Ryan, 1985; Hall, 1990.)

While staff members in the institutions we studied seemed to prefer a centralized structure, we found no proof that one structure is superior to the others. Staff members in completely centralized offices who all report to the same chief development officer face the same problems in communication, coordination, and negotiation that decentralized staff members face. A senior manager at an institution in which the chief development officer's position was vacant indicated that although some people on campus thought that all of their "turf battles" and communication problems would be resolved when a new chief arrived, she believed that such an expectation was unrealistic, and we concur. Neither the "right" leader nor the "right" structure will automatically resolve these problems, which are, in fact, not problems to be solved once and for all but recurrent aspects of the fund-raising process, reflecting the constantly changing status of the institution and its prospects. The mechanisms for dealing with these recurrent issues, rather than organizational structure, will affect fund-raising success.

Successful Fund-Raising History

Almost every person we interviewed discussed current fund-raising programs by describing the history of fund raising at the institution. History is very important to understanding current fund-raising practices because fund-raising success is a developmental process.

All of the institutions that we studied had effective fund-raising programs for the period in which we studied them, but only three institutions had mature (that is, characterized by long years of steady growth) and comprehensive fund-raising programs. One institution, with a history of long success followed by a short period of decline, is making a dramatic "comeback." The other six institutions had histories of successful fund raising in specific areas. In spite of different areas of strength and different histories among these institutions, presidents, managers, and fund raisers on nine campuses talked of the present as a period that would be noted in the institution's history as a period of major changes in fund-raising approaches and breakthroughs to unprecedented annual fund-raising results.

All five of the private institutions we studied had conducted major institutionwide campaigns in the past, and none of the public institutions had had such campaigns. Three institutions were conducting campaigns at the time of the site visit. Staff members at two more were soliciting advance gifts and were within months of formal announcements of campaigns. One institution was between campaigns. In the remaining four institutions, staff members were discussing campaigns and organizing activities designed to move the institution toward its first major campaign.

Fund-raising programs in these institutions reflect current national trends for major campaigns (see Stehle, 1990; Bornstein, 1989). Although raising actual dollars continues to be the immediate purpose for campaigns, the leaders of effective programs design campaigns to do more than raise funds. Campaigns are now designed to develop long-term relationships, educate constituents, and establish higher overall results through such mechanisms as enlarging the number of donors and the size of the average gift to the annual fund, expanding the donor base for major gifts, and changing how the institution is perceived by all constituents. Staff in eight institutions said that a major objective of the current or upcoming campaign was to permanently change the level and scope of the institution's fund raising.

Regardless of the fund-raising area they worked in, most fund-raising managers we interviewed expressed an almost unanimous belief that a strong annual fund was the foundation for ongoing success in every other fund-raising program. Strengthening the annual fund was a priority in all ten programs. Some efforts to raise annual funds were relatively new, which was surprising. Five institutions had annual funds with long histories of progressive success. The remaining five institutions were committed to substantially enhancing their annual funds as the strongest possible foundation for future fund-raising success.

All the institutions used a phone-mail program to solicit gifts for the annual fund, but staffing for annual fund programs varied widely and included paid callers, alumni, student volunteers, faculty and staff volunteers, and fund-raising staff members. Not too long ago, the debate about whether it was acceptable to pay students to make telephone calls soliciting gifts to the annual fund generated considerable heat. The six largest institutions that we studied paid all callers to make telephone solicitations for the annual fund. Five of these institutions hired only students. In three institutions in which callers were paid, alumni, students, faculty members, and administrators also volunteered to make calls.

As the scope of fund raising has increased and technology has become more sophisticated, firms providing support services as well as actual fund-raising activities have increased in number. Only three institutions of the ten we studied had not contracted with commercial firms in the last ten years. Of these three (all public institutions), two will use consultants for planning upcoming campaigns. The commercial services that the institutions were using or had used were for prospect rating, prospect research, consultation for overall fund raising and for campaigns, and telemarketing.

At the time of the site visits, no institution was using extensive outside consulting services. Although four institutions had used consultants for some services in the past five years, six had not. Two institutions' annual fund telemarketing programs were handled by commercial firms, one in an off-site program and one in an on-site program. Three institutions regularly used off-site firms for calling lapsed donors and prospects who had never donated. Five institutions used no outside telemarketing services.

Our research indicates that hiring commercial firms to handle functions that were once carried out by staff members or volunteers is neither uncommon nor prevalent. Fund raisers were very discerning about which firms they used, being careful to select those that, in one manager's words, "represented the institution as well as alumni would."

Entrepreneurial Fund Raising

In their 1986 study, Gilley, Fulmer, and Reithlingshoefer cite "opportunity consciousness" as a condition for excellence in higher education. They define *opportunity consciousness* as leadership's "continuing attention to changes in the environment, in the attitudes of people, and even in the values of society, to any change that can be turned to the advantage of the institution" (p. 61). Although fund raising has always been a creative process, a human exchange, fund raisers have never before been expected to be more innovative and more careful in their use of scarce resources than now. Opportunity consciousness, seasoned with good judgment, is how we define entrepreneurial fund raising.

A number of institutions we studied had fund-raising programs with innovative or unconventional features: the sales orientation at Gamma, the program combining prospect rating and off-site telemarketing at Alpha, the extensive involvement of external constituencies in institutional and fund-raising planning at Zeta. In addition to these approaches, every fund-raising program was breaking new ground by introducing ventures totally new to the particular institution. To the extent that being entrepreneurial means consistently and regularly doing new things, our case studies indicate that entrepreneurial approaches are strongly characteristic of effective fund-raising programs.

Volunteers' Roles in Fund Raising

Some authors (for example, Snelling, 1986) as well as a number of fund raisers quoted in this book believe that fund-raising success is dependent upon the extensive involvement of volunteers. The importance of volunteers in the effective fund-raising programs we studied varied substantially — one of the most provocative and surprising findings of our research. Only four institutions (two private, two public) had strong volunteer programs. In three institutions, staff members had recently begun to emphasize and strengthen volunteer programs. In one institution, staff members purposefully kept volunteer involvement at a minimum. In the remaining two institutions, at which volunteers played little or no role, staff members had no interest in developing volunteers to assist in fund raising.

Involving volunteers in fund raising is not a prerequisite for fund-raising success in all institutions. Whether volunteers are critical for fund-raising success depends upon both the institution's fund-raising history and its tradition of involving volunteers for purposes other than fund raising.

Emphasis on Management of the Fund-Raising Function

In the widely read book *Academic Strategy* (1983), Keller noted that higher education institutions are "among the least business-like and well-managed of all organizations" (p. 5) and "alone among major institutions in the United States . . . have steadfastly refused to appropriate the procedures of modern management" (p. viii). Nevertheless, because fund raising, with its strong focus on bottom-line results, is one of the most business-like endeavors in higher education institutions, we expected to find evidence not only of good management practices but also of strong appreciation for the role of good management in fund-raising programs. In general, this was not what we found, although, as with much else in our research, there were exceptions. Senior staff members in only four institutions emphasized the importance of management. In most institutions, management was generally perceived more as a routine housekeeping chore than as a critical factor affecting overall fund-raising performance. If fund raising is still considered to be a necessary evil on many campuses, management is still considered to be a necessary evil in higher education fund raising on many campuses.

Administrators in academic institutions generally have been judged as failing as managers because of too strong a focus on process and not enough focus on results. Fund-raising managers may have the opposite problem — too strong a focus on results and not enough focus on process. This problem is apparent in the division of labor in most of the fund-raising offices we studied. In most institutions that we visited, the managers also had significant fund-raising responsibilities. In five institutions, the entire management staff all had significant fund-raising responsibilities.

In most instances, staff members who had both significant management responsibilities and significant fund-raising responsibilities felt considerable conflict about remaining on campus "to mind the store" versus "being out there raising money." Sometimes these managers were in conflict because of pressure from senior managers, and sometimes the conflict was more personal and internal, for example, when enthusiasm for fund raising far exceeded interest in managing. While our findings speak well of the energy these development officers have for their essential tasks of raising money, they also suggest that strong management is probably not any more likely to occur in the development office than it does in higher education generally.

Some managers who did not specifically identify management as important to fund-raising success were, perhaps intuitively, good managers. For other managers, a gap existed between the management values they expressed and their management practices. For instance, managers in seven institutions emphasized that teamwork was important to fund-raising success at their institutions, but only in four institutions did managers actually provide structures or processes to facilitate effective teamwork. Without considerable and specific management support and direction, effective teamwork does not occur. It is an organizational fact of life that individual staff members regularly experience conflict between completing their own work assignments successfully and contributing to the overall success of the group.

These kinds of conflicts of interests abound in fund raising and are well understood. However, the criticalness of strong, visible management practices that foster and guide appropriate resolutions of these conflicts as they occur is not well understood. Promoting teamwork is not the only way to resolve these inevitable conflicts of interest, but these conflicts will not usually be effectively resolved without deliberate management practices and policies designed to address them.

In general, strong, deliberate professional management is not particularly characteristic of the successful fund-raising programs at the ten institutions we studied. In the institutions without an emphasis on professional management, other factors and characteristics have substituted for management in the past, such as longevity of staff members in their positions. Although it reflects our bias as well as our educated opinions, we believe all programs will require strong professional management for continuing success as the task of fund raising becomes even more sophisticated, complex, and competitive. We examined in particular three broad areas of management, including information and communication systems; planning, goal setting, and evaluation; and staff development, training, and evaluation.

Information and Communication Systems. Information and communication is the strongest management area across the ten institutions. Most fund raisers we interviewed emphasized that good systems to collect, store, retrieve, and disseminate information were essential for effective fund raising. Fund raisers need information about donors, frequent reports to monitor progress and activity, and clear directives about what is expected of them to function effectively. Additionally, most of the fund raisers emphasized the importance of good communication across organizational levels, with fund-raising colleagues, within the development office, with the rest of the institution, and with external constituencies. How well staff members communicate with each other is strongly influenced by management directives, support, and modeling.

Senior managers in three institutions were especially praised for how well they conveyed performance expectations to staff members. In seven of the ten institutions, fund-raising staff members were generally satisfied with the overall information and communication processes. Three institutions had problems in one or more of the areas related to information and communication and were addressing these problems.

Planning, Goal Setting, and Evaluation. We expected that formal planning, goal setting, and evaluation would be integral to effective fund-raising because of (1) the need to take a more market-oriented view of opportunities and expenditures, circumventing lockstep annual percentage increases in fund-raising goals and budgets; (2) the increased complexity and cost of fund-raising technology and increased competition for philanthropic dollars; (3) the need for long-term investments in fund raising for maximum outcomes; and (4) the increasingly critical role of fund raising for setting and achieving the overall institutional mission. In general, planning, goal setting, and evaluation were not particularly characteristic of the fund-raising programs in our ten institutions.

Although only two institutions had no formal fund-raising plans, only four institutions had comprehensive, extensive plans that were used as working tools. The institution's approaches to fund-raising planning and goal setting varied. One fund-raising program had concrete goals for dollars to be raised and activity levels in all program areas. Fund-raising programs in three institutions were based on plans that set goals for the overall percentage of change in money raised and conceptual goals (examples of conceptual goals are "improve alumni involvement" and "increase personal solicitations"). Fund-raising programs in four institutions were based on conceptual goals only, and two institutions did not set goals.

Regardless of whether planning at an institution was formal or not, development managers, nevertheless, all had a strategic focus, thinking of fund raising as a long-term process and not as a year-to-year or campaign-to-campaign process. Major campaigns promote more intensive and more formal planning. All of the institutions currently or previously engaged in major campaigns had formal plans for their campaigns. Development managers at institutions not engaged in campaigns indicated that formal planning would precede upcoming campaigns.

In spite of our thinking that formal planning would help eliminate lockstep annual percentage increases in goals, for the most part, staff members in well-established programs essentially set goals by looking at past years' results and adding a certain percentage of increase. The amount of increase usually was more intuitively than scientifically derived, reflecting the optimism that regular annual increases in overall giving to higher education have generated. If and when the trend reverses and giving to higher education stabilizes or begins to drop, managers in all institutions will have to become more methodological and strategic in their planning and goal setting. In new programs, when staff members set specific goals, they were often guided by results achieved in what they considered to be peer institutions. Some fund raisers thought it was better to set high goals and fall somewhat short if necessary. Some thought it was better, particularly for donors and volunteers, to set more reasonable goals and be certain of achieving them.

No institution conducted formal, comprehensive evaluation of its fund-raising programs, but Gamma's formal monitoring procedures came closest to systematic program evaluation. In other institutions, most notably Zeta, staff members conducted informal evaluations.

Staff Development, Training, and Evaluation. Of particular note in a field in which most practitioners do not have formal training for their jobs was our finding that fund-raising managers in only three institutions strongly emphasized staff training and staff development. Three institutions held yearly staff retreats for staff development, program planning, and team building. Staff members in the six largest institutions we studied received merit raises based on performance evaluations.

Many fund-raising managers indicated that competition for experienced staff members was currently a more serious problem to them than direct competition for funds. As competition for staff members continues to grow, more and more institutions will be forced to hire staff members with limited or no direct fund-raising experience. On-the-job training and systematic staff development programs in development offices are likely to increase as this trend continues.

Staff Commitment to the Institution

Although we do not underestimate the importance of the fund-raising staff to fund-raising success, we were not able to devote much time to studying characteristics of fund-raising staffs. We did, however, assess staff commitment to the institution, for two reasons. Our first reason was that Gilley, Fulmer, and Reithlingshoefer (1986) identified this factor as one of the "ten fundamentals" of excellent institutions (p. 12). The second reason was because of the widespread belief, best described (and refuted) in this study by President M. at Zeta, that staff commitment to institutions is not particularly characteristic of the fund-raising field.

We encountered strongly committed staff members in every institution we studied — without exception — but we did not always judge this strong commitment to be to the institution. Almost every one of the more than 100 people we interviewed left us with a lasting and distinct impression of competence, knowledge, and earnestness; yet in seven institutions, most staff members did not appear to have strong commitment to the institution.

Staff members who were not committed to their institutions were committed to professional excellence, to improvement in their personal work skills, and to the success of their programs. People in the institutions in which staff members were more strongly committed to professional goals than to the institution itself were more formal with us and with each other than staff members in the other institutions, and the atmosphere was more "corporate" than "collegiate" in these institutions. People in the institutions in which staff members were strongly committed to the institution, though clearly not lacking in professionalism, were much more informal with us and with each other, and the atmosphere was more "collegiate" than "corporate." Although it is difficult to define precisely a corporate or collegiate atmosphere, we found, on the basis of our small sample, that in a collegiate atmosphere the energy was more exuberant, and staff members spoke often of how much fun they had working. In more corporate atmospheres, the energy was more subdued, and staff members spoke often of how much personal satisfaction they got from their work.

Staffs characterized by commitment to institutions created very different workplace climates than staffs characterized by commitment to professional goals, but our research results indicate that either orientation can provide the basis for fund-raising success. Our results suggest further that strong staff commitment to the institution is related to personal ties with the institution. In the three institutions with strong staff commitment to the institution, most staff members had strong personal ties to the institution. In one of the institutions, about half of the staff members had strong ties to the institution, and in the other six, most staff members did not have strong personal ties to the institution. We also found that whether staff members feel or do not feel a deep commitment to the institution may be more an aspect of the institution's culture than a personal characteristic of individual staff members. Some institutions simply evoke more passion in their constituents than others; some institutions evoke more restrained respect.

Indeed, Gilley, Fulmer, and Reithlingshoefer (1986) list staff commitment to the institution as an institutional quality rather than as a quality of the staff. They wrote that the institution is responsible for "capturing allegiance" and found at the twenty schools they studied that the effort to build commitment to the institution was "an integral part of the overall college mission" (p. 36). At Alpha, we found a concerted effort, beginning at the presidential level, to strengthen institutional commitment throughout the university.

Emphasis on Constituent Relations

Many fund raisers use the tin cup as a metaphor for an earlier time in fund-raising history, when demonstrating need was the most powerful case for support. Over time, fund raising has evolved to the point at which it is still necessary for institutions to demonstrate need (to avoid appearing greedy), but it is also essential for institutions to demonstrate that they are worthy of support. Demonstrating worth means demonstrating the capacity to provide products and services that donors view as important. For-profit companies have long understood that success is dependent upon supplying something that consumers want and that the only way to know what consumers want is to become very knowledgeable about the consumers. Peters and Waterman, in their book on excellence in business corporations (1982), call this approach staying "close to the customer" (p. 14). Gilley, Fulmer, and Reithlingshoefer (1986), writing about higher education institutions, call it "keeping an eye on the community" (p. 13).

We expected to find exceptional strengths in constituent (donor, alumni, faculty, community) relations in institutions with successful fund-raising programs. Although every institution we studied had strong relationships with one or more of its constituencies, only two institutions (both public) were outstanding in all constituent relationships.

We did find presidents, managers, and fund raisers in every institution who emphasized that future fund-raising success would depend more and more on constituent relationships and that the institutions were responsible for initiating and maintaining these relationships. Although every institution acknowledged gifts in a systematic way and some institutions had long histories of donor recognition programs, staff members in almost every institution referred to the need for improved recognition of donors.

Only four of the institutions had long-standing, comprehensive alumni relations programs; three of these four were public institutions. Three institutions (all private) had recent but strong commitments to improve alumni relations. In the remaining three institutions, development staff members were aware of the need for stronger alumni relationships and better alumni programming.

Eight institutions (five public and three private) had strong regional or community identities. Each of these institutions used its regional position as an asset in fund raising. Staff members in five institutions identified faculty members as an important constituency that the staff serves and displayed their commitment to work closely with faculty members and academic administrators. Overall, our results indicate a growing awareness in each institution of the need to develop constituency-based approaches in all fund raising efforts.

Table 12.1. Characteristics Outstanding in Specific Institutions.

Characteristic	Institution
Presidential Leadership	All but Rho (Chapter Nine)
Trustees' Participation	Zeta (Chapter Six) Sigma (Chapter Ten) Omega (Chapter Eleven)
Institutional Commitment to Fund Raising	Alpha (Chapter Two) Gamma (Chapter Four) Zeta (Chapter Six) Kappa (Chapter Eight) Sigma (Chapter Ten) Omega (Chapter Eleven)
Resource Allocation	Alpha (Chapter Two) Gamma (Chapter Four) Zeta (Chapter Six) Omega (Chapter Eleven)
Acceptance of the Need for Fund Raising	Alpha (Chapter Two) Beta (Chapter Three) Gamma (Chapter Four) Zeta (Chapter Six) Kappa (Chapter Eight) Sigma (Chapter Ten) Omega (Chapter Eleven)
Definition and Communication of Institutional Niche and Image	All
Institutional Fund-Raising Priorities and Policies	Alpha (Chapter Two) Beta (Chapter Three) Gamma (Chapter Four) Zeta (Chapter Six) Kappa (Chapter Eight) Sigma (Chapter Ten) Omega (Chapter Eleven)
Chief Development Officer's Leadership	All but Delta (Chapter Five), Kappa (Chapter Eight), and Omega (Chapter Eleven)
Entrepreneurial Fund Raising	Alpha (Chapter Two) Gamma (Chapter Four) Zeta (Chapter Six) Kappa (Chapter Eight) Rho (Chapter Nine)

Table 12.1. Characteristics Outstanding in Specific Institutions, Cont'd.

Characteristic	Institution
Volunteers' Roles in Fund Raising	Alpha (Chapter Two) Beta (Chapter Three) Zeta (Chapter Six) Theta (Chapter Seven)
Emphasis on Management of the Fund-Raising Function	Alpha (Chapter Two) Gamma (Chapter Four) Zeta (Chapter Six) Theta (Chapter Seven)
Information and Communication Systems	Alpha (Chapter Two) Gamma (Chapter Four) Zeta (Chapter Six) Kappa (Chapter Eight) Omega (Chapter Eleven)
Planning, Goal Setting, and Evaluation	Alpha (Chapter Two) Gamma (Chapter Four) Delta (Chapter Five) Zeta (Chapter Six)
Staff Development, Training, and Evaluation	Gamma (Chapter Four) Delta (Chapter Five) Zeta (Chapter Six)
Staff commitment to Institution	Delta (Chapter Five) Theta (Chapter Seven) Kappa (Chapter Eight)
Emphasis on Constituent Relations	Beta (Chapter Three) Theta (Chapter Seven

Note: Centralized Fund Raising Programs and Successful Fund Raising History have been excluded from this table because all institutions had a centralized fund-raising office and some history of past success in fund raising.

Summary and Conclusions

Table 12.1 lists the characteristics we examined in our research and the institutions in which each characteristic was outstanding. Each characteristic was outstanding in at least two institutions. Presidential leadership, chief development officer's leadership, and definition and communication of niche and image were outstanding in most institutions. Each institution was outstanding in from three to fourteen characteristics. The average number of outstanding characteristics per institution was eight. These results indicate that the characteristics listed are related to fund-raising success, but institutions do not need to be outstanding in all characteristics to be successful in fund raising.

From our research, it appears that few rules apply to effective fund raising. Although not actually a prerequisite for fund-raising success, leadership in fund raising at all institutional levels and significant institutional commitment to fund raising are definite factors that can make a difference in fund-raising success. If these factors are not present in an institution seeking to improve fund-raising performance, our research strongly indicates that these areas should receive primary attention. The importance of strength in other areas seems more related to the nature of the institution rather than to a concrete formula for fund-raising success. For example, fund-raising programs in some institutions may not require strong volunteer or trustee support but may fail without such support in other institutions.

One of the few general rules to be gleaned from our research is that fund raising must capitalize on the strengths and untapped potential of institutions. Since our results do not point to "recipes" for fund raising and we believe the institutions we studied are good examples, the most important factor in making decisions about fund-raising programs may be insight into one's own institution. Furthermore, these case studies illustrate that fund-raising success is, in the end, the result of deliberate, sustained efforts to raise money. Although many of these institutions enjoyed fortuitous circumstances or benefited from fortunate events at some time or another, in each case, the fund-raising results that led to the identification of the institution as successful were the consequences of sustained and active efforts. Not one of these institutions was fortunate enough to be able to raise significant amounts of private support by virtue or worth alone.

These are, of course, not new ideas in fund raising, but we hope this book will help these old ideas to achieve renewed prominence in discussions of fund-raising effectiveness in the 1990s, particularly as the technology of fund raising becomes more and more sophisticated. To be sure, we do not mean to oversimplify fund-raising success, but it seems apparent that leadership, sustained effort, and a genuine institutional commitment — all of which are anything but simple — are the basics upon which successful fund-raising programs are built. The final chapter contains assessment guidelines for analyzing and improving fund-raising programs.

13

Assessing Fund-Raising Effectiveness:

Questions to Start With

Assessment of a fund-raising program is the first step in improving fund-raising effectiveness. In many cases, a good assessment will provide specific direction for how a program can be improved. In other cases, how to improve a program may not be so obvious. Since a full-scale program assessment and improvement model is beyond the limits of this book, we have provided references for further reading on most topics.

The following lists of questions are designed to facilitate and stimulate reflection about the qualitative aspects of a fund-raising program. The lists do not include questions regarding critical financial and technical aspects of a program.

The President

1. Does the president provide strong leadership for fund-raising efforts?
2. Does the president see fund raising as a major responsibility of his or her position?
3. Does the president encourage and facilitate the setting of institutionwide priorities for fund raising?
4. Does he or she effectively articulate the institution's mission and case for support to all constituents, internal and external?
5. Is the president enthusiastic about fund raising?
6. How extensive is the president's actual fund-raising experience?

7. Does he or she effectively rely on the fund-raising expertise of the chief development officer and staff members?
8. How much time does the president spend on fund-raising
activities? Is this amount of time sufficient?
9. How does the president's participation in fund raising affect
the fund-raising staff?
10. Are the president's goals for the institution clear to the
fund-raising staff?
11. Is the president an effective fund raiser? Does he or she
ask for gifts directly?

(For information about the president and fund raising, see
Adams, 1989; Association of American Colleges, 1975; Davenport, 1989; Fisher and Quehl, 1989; Rowland, 1986a, 1986b.)

Trustees

1. Are trustees donors?
2. Do trustees participate in the identification and solicitation of donors?
3. Do trustees demonstrate a clear understanding of the importance of fund raising in their policy making?
4. Are the president and chief development officer trying to
nurture and expand trustees' involvement in fund raising?

(For information about trustees, see Pocock, 1989.)

Resource Allocation and Acceptance of Fund Raising

1. Are the resources allocated for fund raising sufficient for
meeting fund-raising goals?
2. Is the need for fund raising widely understood and accepted
on campus?
3. Who are the people on campus who have a clear understanding of the need for fund raising? Who are the people lacking in this understanding?
4. Are efforts under way to develop and enhance understanding of fund-raising goals, efforts, and costs across
campus?

5. How will increased understanding among internal constituents facilitate fund-raising efforts at this institution?

Niche and Image

1. What are the unique contributions of this institution to the higher education community?
2. How widespread, internally and externally, is the shared understanding of what this institution stands for?
3. What are the implications and consequences for fund raising of the institution's being in this particular niche? What obvious but overlooked donor constituencies emerge? What particular fund-raising approaches are especially indicated? Should any specific fund-raising approaches definitely be avoided?
4. Are fund-raising efforts and resources focused and differentiated to reflect the institution's particular character and needs?
5. Are efforts under way at the institutional level to enhance and communicate an attractive image?
6. How well defined and well communicated is the institution's image?
7. Are fund raisers articulate and accurate in communicating the institution's niche and image?

(For information on institutional niche and image, see Kotler and Fox, 1975.)

Fund-Raising Priorities and Policies

1. Have institutional priorities for fund raising been set and widely communicated?
2. Is there broad consensus that these priorities are the right ones for the institution at this time?
3. Do fund-raising priorities reflect the overall institutional mission and goals?
4. Are expectations for fund-raising results neither overly grand nor too limited? Do these expectations accurately reflect the institution's potential for fund raising?

5. How do institutional fund-raising priorities provide direction and focus for fund-raising planning and efforts?
6. How are competing interests regarding proposal submissions handled?
7. Are proposal submission policies well defined and well understood by units with potentially competing interests?
8. Have formal agreements and understandings been negotiated with funding organizations that restrict proposal submissions?
9. Have proposal submission policies been clarified with outside funding organizations?
10. How are proposal submission policies and guidelines communicated to faculty members and all other people with fund-raising interests?

(For information on institutional priorities, see Whetten and Cameron, 1985.)

Chief Development Officer

1. Does the chief development officer understand and value higher education?
2. Is the chief development officer an articulate representative of his or her institution and the fund-raising field?
3. Does the chief development officer convey not only understanding of but also respect for the philanthropic process?
4. Does the chief development officer have high professional standards for himself or herself and the staff?
5. Is the chief development officer committed to fund-raising programs designed for the long-term benefit of the institution?
6. To what extent does the chief development officer emphasize fund-raising programs that reflect the distinct character and needs of the institution?
7. Does the chief development officer function at an executive level as a college/university officer?
8. Does the chief development officer have fund-raising expertise and direct fund-raising responsibilities?

9. Does the chief development officer effectively control or delegate internal management duties?
10. Does the chief development officer function as a mentor to new staff members?
11. Does the chief development officer function as an entrepreneur?
12. Are the chief development officer's abilities and skills the right "fit" for the institution? In what areas does he or she excel? What areas does he or she need to strengthen?
13. Is the chief development officer's overall fund-raising philosophy consistent with the institution's current needs and character?
14. Is the chief development officer an effective leader?

Centralized Fund-Raising Programs

1. Are there a central office and staff to reflect the institution's commitment to institutionwide fund-raising priorities? How does the central office support college or unit fund-raising efforts?
2. What is the organizational structure of fund raising at the institution, and how does the structure reflect institutional character and fund-raising needs?
3. Is the present organizational structure the appropriate one for this institution?
4. Who supports the structure? Who wants to see the structure changed?
5. What problems could be resolved with a change in organizational structure? What new problems would result? What case can be made for a change in the organizational structure?
6. Regardless of organizational structure, how are problems involving communication, coordination, and negotiation of competing interests handled?

(For information on organizational structure, see Desmond and Ryan, 1985; Hall, 1990; Sandberg, 1985.)

Successful Fund-Raising History

1. What is the history of fund raising in this institution? How does this history affect today's program decisions and program character?
2. What is the institution's level of maturity in fund raising? How will current fund-raising efforts increase the level of maturity?
3. What fund-raising programs already under way are serving the institution well? What programs need to be improved? What new programs need to be developed?
4. Are formal programs or efforts under way to solicit gifts from all major donor groups (alumni, nonalumni, corporations, and foundations) and to solicit all major types of gifts (annual, capital, major, and planned)?
5. How well does the mix of programs at this institution reflect institutional priorities and assets? What program areas need to be improved or abandoned?
6. Have there been previous major campaigns? At present, is the institution planning a campaign, actually involved in one, or between campaigns?
7. What external and internal indicators are used to determine when the institution is ready to undertake a major campaign?
8. Is there an understanding on campus of the difference between a campaign to meet specific needs and purposes and a campaign to change the level and scope of fund raising?
9. What is the history of major campaigns at this institution? What have these prior campaigns, successful or unsuccessful, taught the institutional community about fund raising for this institution?
10. What outside professional services are being used or being considered? What is the rationale for using outside services?
11. How are outside services selected?
12. Are these services meeting institutional needs?
13. How are results and costs associated with purchased services evaluated?

14. How do services provided by outside firms reflect the institution's character and values?

(For information on campaigns, see Bornstein, 1989; Davis, 1986; Dove, 1988; Dunn and Adam, 1989; Gurin, 1986; McIntosh, 1986; and Stehle, 1990.)

Entrepreneurial Fund Raising

1. In what ways are fund-raising programs entrepreneurial for this institution?
2. Who takes risks in fund raising? Who supports risk taking?
3. What fund-raising efforts that do not conform to conventional wisdom about fund-raising success are effective in this institution?
4. What entrepreneurial fund-raising approaches can be developed for this institution?

(For information on entrepreneurial fund raising, see Taylor, 1986.)

Volunteers

1. Do volunteers play a large part in the fund-raising program?
2. Does this institution use volunteers extensively in capacities other than fund raising?
3. Are there volunteers already active on behalf of the institution in other areas who can be recruited for fund raising?
4. Is developing or enhancing a strong volunteer cadre for fund raising feasible for this institution? Would developing such a cadre be worth the effort?

(For more on the role of volunteers, see Goodale, 1987.)

Emphasis on Management

1. Do the people in charge of fund-raising have professional management skills and abilities?
2. Is management of the fund-raising process taken seriously, or is management considered a "necessary evil," something that "gets in the way" of raising money?

3. How are the fund-raising and management responsibilities balanced?
4. What are the management strengths in this fund-raising effort? How can they be enhanced?
5. What are the management shortcomings in this fund-raising effort? How can they be improved?
6. What is the management style in the development office? How does this style reflect management style throughout the institution?
7. Is teamwork valued and supported in this institution or is the emphasis on individual performance?

(For information on management of fund raising, see Bennett, 1987; Soiffer, 1989; Sorensen, 1986; Tuckman and Johnson, 1987; Young, 1987.)

Information and Communication Systems

1. How effective are the systems to collect, store, retrieve, and disseminate information?
2. Is information about donors and prospects, activities under way, and progress toward goals readily available and widely shared?
3. Are clear expectations and directives available to all fund-raising staff members? Do all fund-raising staff members have sufficient information about expectations and progress of other staff members?
4. What procedures or policies support and enhance communication between all fund-raising staff members, between the fund-raising staff and other institutional units, and between the fund-raising staff and external constituents?

Planning, Goal Setting, and Evaluation

1. What is the strategic mission of the development office? Does this mission fully reflect the institution's fund-raising potential?
2. Are fund-raising program plans oriented toward a market approach rather than an approach based on the institution's needs?

3. Are goals set for fund raising? How specific and concrete are these goals? How measurable are these goals?
4. Are fund-raising goals concrete and specific with respect to activities and dollars raised, based on percentage increases, or are the goals conceptual?
5. Is the planning done appropriate for this institution?
6. Is fund-raising planning formal or informal? deliberate or intuitive? autocratic or participative? Should the way planning is now done be changed to better support fund-raising goals and expectations?
7. Who participates in fund-raising planning? How much input do institutional leaders, external constituents, and fund-raising staff members have in planning and goal setting?
8. How is fund raising evaluated?
9. How are goals determined? How are percentage increases determined?
10. How are economic conditions, past fund-raising history, and overall fund-raising potential considered in fund-raising goals?
11. Which other higher education institutions are appropriate fund-raising peers for this institution? What can be learned from the experiences of these other institutions?

(For information on planning, goal setting, and evaluation see Dunn, Terkla, and Adam, 1986; Frantzreb, 1986; Loessin and Duronio, 1990; Loessin, Duronio, and Borton, 1988; Nahm, 1986; Whaley, 1986.)

Staff Development, Training, and Evaluation

1. Is staff turnover a problem? If so, why? How can problems leading to high turnover be resolved?
2. How well do the values and attitudes of staff members reflect the institution's character and needs?
3. Do staff members attend either in-house or outside training and professional development programs?
4. How is staff communication facilitated?
5. How is staff performance evaluated and rewarded?

Staff Commitment to Institution

1. Do staff members have strong personal ties to the institution? How do these personal ties enhance fund raising?
2. What are fund-raising staff committed to: the institution? the fund-raising field? fund-raising ideals and values? personal success and achievement? How do these commitments enhance fund raising?
3. How can staff commitment more supportive of institutional goals and values be developed?

(For more information on issues concerning fund-raising staff members, see Boardman, 1989; Carbone, 1987; Carter, 1989; Clewis and Panting, 1989; Levine, 1989; Moran and Volkwein, 1988; Turk, 1986.)

Constituent Relations

1. Are fund-raising efforts designed to respond to the needs and interests of donors?
2. How are donors cultivated, solicited, acknowledged, and recognized?
3. What efforts are under way to keep donors informed and involved in the life of the institution?
4. How do alumni relations programs facilitate fund raising?
5. Does the institution have a distinctive role in or relationship with the community or region that is fully utilized for fund raising?
6. Is there an internal campaign to solicit faculty and staff members?
7. How does the fund-raising staff develop and maintain close relationships with deans and faculty members and educate internal constituents about fund raising?

(For information on constituent relations, see Leed, 1987; Melchiori, 1988; Trachtman, 1987.)

Reviewing these questions should not only provide an overall view of the fund-raising program under consideration but should also clearly identify major strengths and weaknesses in the program, as well as the more obvious and feasible areas for improvement. The results of the research reported in this book indicate strongly that successful fund-raising programs do not have outstanding characteristics in all areas. Instead, successful fund-raising programs have been designed to fully utilize and build on current institutional strengths. No institution that continues to survive is excluded from the possibility of improving its performance in fund raising, provided that human, financial, and material resources are used wisely. Sustained growth and good performance in fund raising are neither a matter of luck nor even a matter of past history. Success in fund raising is, more than anything else, the end result of people asking other people for gifts. The assessment questions should give some indicators about how that basic process of people asking other people for gifts can be strengthened and improved. Good luck!

References

Adams, M. F. "Teamwork at the Top: The Development Officer's View." *Currents,* 1989, *15* (7), 16–18.

Allbright, T. "A Capital Campaign Sampler: Status of 219 Drives." *Chronicle of Philanthropy,* Mar. 6, 1990, pp. 8–9.

Association of American Colleges. *The President's Role in Development.* Washington, D.C.: Association of American Colleges, 1975.

Bennett, R. L. "Ten Management Maxims: Guidelines to Help You Get More from Your Development Dollar." *Currents,* 1987, *13* (4), 29–32.

Boardman, R. B. "Bringing Staff Around: To Coax the Best from Tomorrow's Fund Raisers, Harvard Spends Time on Training Today." *Currents,* 1989, *15* (7), 32–35.

Bornstein, R. "Adding It Up." *Currents,* 1989, *15* (1), 12–17.

Brittingham, B. E., and Pezzullo, T. R. *The Campus Green: Fund Raising in Higher Education.* ASHE-ERIC Higher Education Report, no. 1. Washington, D.C.: George Washington University, 1990.

Bush, B. H. "What Fund Raisers Should Know About the Law." Paper presented at 3rd annual symposium, Indiana University Center on Philanthropy, Indianapolis, June 1990.

Carbone, R. F. *Fund Raisers of Academe.* College Park, Md.: Clearinghouse for Research on Fund Raising, 1987.

Carter, L. K. "Basic Training: Point New Employees in the Right Direction with a Thorough Orientation." *Currents,* 1989, *15* (7), 26–29.

"Challenges for the 1990's." *Chronicle of Philanthropy,* Jan. 9, 1990, pp. 1, 12–14, 16–20.

Clewis, J. E., and Panting, J. I. "Off to a Good Start: Give New Staff a Boost with Formal Performance Evaluations." *Currents,* 1989, *15* (7), 38–44.

Council for Aid to Education. *Voluntary Support of Education 1982-1983*. New York: Council for Aid to Education, 1984.

Council for Aid to Education. *Voluntary Support of Education 1983-1984*. New York: Council for Aid to Education, 1985.

Council for Aid to Education. *Voluntary Support of Education 1984-1985*. New York: Council for Aid to Education, 1986.

Council for Aid to Education. *Voluntary Support of Education 1985-1986*. New York: Council for Aid to Education, 1987.

Council for Aid to Education. *Voluntary Support of Education 1986-1987*. New York: Council for Aid to Education, 1988.

Council for Aid to Education. *Voluntary Support of Education 1987-1988*. New York: Council for Aid to Education, 1989.

Davenport, D. "Teamwork at the Top: The President's View." *Currents,* 1989, *15* (7), 12-15.

Davis, B. C. "The Possible Dream: Base Your Campaign Formula on a Feasibility Study." *Currents,* 1986, *12* (10), 20-26.

Desmond, R. L., and Ryan, J. S. "Serving People Needs." *Currents,* 1985, *11* (3), 42-44.

Dove, K. E. *Conducting a Successful Capital Campaign: A Comprehensive Fundraising Guide for Nonprofit Organizations.* San Francisco: Jossey-Bass, 1988.

Dunn, J. A., Jr., and Adam, A. "Patterns of Fund-Raising Proceeds and Costs, 1982-83 Through 1986-87." Paper presented at Council for Advancement and Support of Education Assembly, Washington, D.C., July 1989.

Dunn, J. A., Jr., Terkla, D. G., and Adam, A. "Comparative Studies of Fund Raising Performance." In J. A. Dunn, Jr. (ed.), *Enhancing the Management of Fund Raising.* New Directions for Institutional Research, no. 51. San Francisco: Jossey-Bass, 1986.

Duronio, M. A., and Loessin, B. A. "Fund Raising Outcomes and Institutional Characteristics in Ten Types of Higher Education Institutions." *Review of Higher Education,* 1990, *13,* 539-556.

Duronio, M. A., Loessin, B. A., and Borton, G. L. "A Survey of Fund Raising Methods: Implications for Management." Paper presented at annual meeting of the American Educational Research Association, New Orleans, Apr. 1988. (ED 296 651)

Duronio, M. A., Loessin, B. A., and Nirschel, R. J., Jr. "The Price of Participation." *Currents,* 1989, *15* (4), 39–44.

Fisher, J. L. "Establishing a Successful Fund Raising Program." In J. L. Fisher and G. H. Quehl (eds.), *The President and Fund Raising.* New York: American Council on Education and Macmillan, 1989.

Fisher, J. L., and Quehl, G. H. *The President and Fund Raising.* New York: American Council on Education and Macmillan, 1989.

Frantzreb, A. C. "Enough Already: Planning on Its Own Won't Bring in the Money." *Currents,* 1986, *12* (10), 36–37.

Gilley, J. W., Fulmer, K. A., and Reithlingshoefer, S. J. *Searching for Academic Excellence: Twenty Colleges and Universities on the Move and Their Leaders.* New York: American Council on Education and Macmillan, 1986.

Glennon, M. "Fund Raising in Small Colleges: Strategies for Success." *Planning for Higher Education,* 1986, *14,* 16–19.

Goodale, T. K. "Teaching Volunters the Art of Asking." *Fund Raising Management,* 1987, *17* (11), 32–38.

Grassmuck, K. "Clouded Economy Prompts Colleges to Weigh Changes." *Chronicle of Higher Education,* Jan. 31, 1990, pp. A1, A28, A30.

Gurin, M. G. "The Changing Campaign: A Veteran Counselor Shares Lessons Learned over Three Decades." *Currents,* 1986, *12* (10), 6–12.

Hall, M. R. "The Division of Responsibilities for Advancement Activities Between the Central Development Office and the Academic Units at Research Universities." Paper presented at 3rd annual symposium, Center on Philanthropy, Indiana University, Indianapolis, June 1990.

Jaschik, S. "States Spending $40.8-Billion on Colleges This Year: Growth Rate at a 30-Year Low." *Chronicle of Higher Education,* Oct. 24, 1990, pp. A1, A26-A28.

Keller, G. *Academic Strategy: The Management Revolution in American Higher Education.* Baltimore: Md.: Johns Hopkins University Press, 1983.

Kotler, P., and Fox, K. A. *Strategic Marketing for Educational Institutions.* Englewood Cliffs, N.J.: Prentice-Hall, 1975.

Leed, J. "Beyond the Ask: Ten Other Ways to Involve Faculty in Fund Raising." *Currents,* 1987, *13* (8), 14–18.

Leslie, J. W. *Focus on Understanding and Support: A Study in College Management.* Washington, D.C.: American College Relations Association, 1969.

Levine, S. H. "Continuing Education: Training Resources for Your Rookies." *Currents,* 1989, *15* (7), 30–31.

Loessin, B. A., and Duronio, M. A. "The Role of Planning in Successful Fund Raising in Ten Higher Education Institutions." *Planning in Higher Education,* 1990, *18,* 45–56.

Loessin, B. A., Duronio, M. A., and Borton, G. L. "Questioning the Conventional Wisdom." *Currents,* 1988, *14* (8), 33–40.

McIntosh, P. B. "Big Business: Even a $450-Million Campaign Must Follow Fund-Raising Fundamentals." *Currents,* 1986, *12* (10), 28–30.

McMillen, L. "Americans Gave More to Charity Again in 1989; Total Topped $100-Billion for 2nd Straight Year." *Chronicle of Higher Education,* June 13, 1990a, pp. A1, A23.

McMillen, L. "Gifts to Colleges Rise 8.8% in Year; Reach Record $8.9 Billion." *Chronicle of Higher Education,* May 30, 1990b, pp. A1, A26, A27.

Melchiori, G. S. (ed.). *Alumni Research: Methods and Applications.* New Directions for Institutional Research, no. 60. San Francisco: Jossey-Bass, 1988.

Millar, B. "Baby Boomers Give Generously to Charities, Survey Finds, but Their Willingness to Do Volunteer Work Is Questioned." *Chronicle of Philanthropy,* July 24, 1990, pp. 1, 12–13.

Moran, E. T., and Volkwein, J. F. "Examining Organizational Climate in Institutions of Higher Education." *Research in Higher Education,* 1988, *28,* 367–383.

Nahm, F. C. "There Is a Method to This Management: How to Set up Strategic Planning and Keep It Going." *Currents,* 1986, *12* (10), 44–48.

Peters, T. J., and Waterman, R. H., Jr. *In Search of Excellence: Lessons from America's Best Run Companies.* New York: Harper & Row, 1982.

Pickett, W. L. "An Assessment of the Effectiveness of Fund Raising Policies on Private Undergraduate Colleges." Unpublished doctoral dissertation, School of Education, University of Denver, 1977.

Pocock, J. W. *Fund-Raising Leadership: A Guide for College and University Boards.* Washington, D.C.: Association of Governing Boards of Universities and Colleges, 1989.

"President's Proposal Would Cut Aid to Students, Boost Science Spending." *Chronicle of Higher Education,* Feb. 7, 1990, p. A1.

Rowland, A. W. (ed.). *Handbook of Institutional Advancement: A Modern Guide to Executive Management, Institutional Relations, Fund Raising, Alumni Administration, Government Relations, Publications, Periodicals, and Enrollment Management.* (2nd ed.) San Francisco: Jossey-Bass, 1986a.

Rowland, A. W. *Key Resources on Institutional Advancement: A Guide to the Field and Its Literature.* San Francisco: Jossey-Bass, 1986b.

Sandberg, J. R. "Organizing Your Operation: Which Model Should You Use?" *Currents,* 1985, *11* (3), 45–49.

Snelling, B. W. "Recruiting, Training, and Managing Volunteers." In A. W. Rowland (ed.), *Handbook of Institutional Advancement: A Modern Guide to Executive Management, Institutional Relations, Fund Raising, Alumni Administration, Government Relations, Publications, Periodicals, and Enrollment Management.* San Francisco: Jossey-Bass, 1986.

Soiffer, S. M. "Data for Development: A Listing of Dos, Don'ts and Dammits." Paper presented at 1989 Symposium for the Marketing of Higher Education, Cincinnati, Nov. 1989.

Sorensen, R. S. "Take This Job and Love It." *Currents,* 1986, *12* (2), 42–45.

Stehle, V. "Capital Campaigns: Bigger, Broader, Bolder." *Chronicle of Philanthropy,* Mar. 6, 1990, pp. 1, 10–12.

Taylor, K. "Why We Need Better Marketing: Philip Kotler Says a Sales Job Isn't Good Enough." *Currents,* 1986, *12* (7), 44–50.

Trachtman, L. E. "Where Advancement Fails: A Dean Tells Why Faculty Give Advancement an F — and How You Can Improve Your Grade." *Currents,* 1987, *13* (8), 10–13.

Tuckman, B. W., and Johnson, F. C. *Effective College Management: The Outcome Approach.* New York: Praeger, 1987.

Turk, J. V. "The Changing Face of CASE." *Currents,* 1986, *7* (6), 8–13.

Vigeland, C. A. *Great Good Fortune: How Harvard Makes Its Money.* Boston: Houghton Mifflin, 1986.

Weber, N. (ed.). *Giving USA, 1989.* New York: AAFRC Trust for Philanthropy, 1989.

Whaley, J. C. "Start Right: Build a Solid Foundation with Thorough Institutional and Campaign Planning." *Currents,* 1986, *12* (10), 14–18.

Whetten, D. A., and Cameron, K. S. "Administrative Effectiveness in Higher Education." *Review of Higher Education,* 1985, *9* (1), 35–49.

Willmer, W. K. *The Small College Advancement Program: Managing for Results.* Washington, D.C.: Council for Advancement and Support of Education, 1981.

Young, D. R. "Executive Leadership in Nonprofit Organizations." In W. W. Powell (ed.), *The Nonprofit Sector: A Research Handbook.* New Haven, Conn.: Yale University Press, 1987.

Index

A

Academic deans, at public baccalaureate college, 170–172
Academic planning, and fund raising, 22
Adam, A., 5, 232, 234
Adams, M. F., 227
Advance gifts: at private baccalaureate college, 152; at public research university, 40
Advisory boards: for planning, 111–113; at public baccalaureate college, 173, 174; at public research university, 50–52, 57
Allbright, T., 2
Alpha University: annual fund at, 17, 18, 23 26; aspects of fund raising at, 13–33; background on, 13–17; central development office at, 16, 18, 31; characteristics of, 222, 223; communication at, 26, 27, 31; constituent relations at, 19, 27, 29, 32; descriptive statistics on, 14; effectiveness at, 33; entrepreneurial style at, 213; foundation gifts at, 26–28; fundraising activities at, 26–30; fundraising history at, 17–20; fundraising program at, 30–33; institutional commitment at, 16, 30, 31–32; management at, 22–23, 30, 31; organizational chart for, 15; planned and major gifts at, 28; presidential leadership at, 20–21, 27, 30–31; research and development services at, 29–30; staff members at, 19–20, 22, 31, 32, 220; vice president of univer-

sity development and alumni affairs at, 21–23, 30–31; volunteers at, 19, 26, 32
Alumni, with multiple degrees, 25. *See also* Constituent relations
American Broadcasting Company, 47
Annual fund: at private baccalaureate college, 153–154; at private comprehensive university, 117, 119; at private doctoral university, 73; at private research university, 17, 18, 23–26; at private two-year college, 181, 183; at public baccalaureate college, 162, 169–170; at public doctoral university, 97–100; at public research university, 52–53; at public two-year college, 192, 194, 196; success of, 212
Association of American Colleges, 227
Association of American Universities, 6

B

Baccalaureate colleges: private (Kappa), 144–158; public (Rho), 159–175
Bennett, R. L., 233
Beta University: advisory boards at, 50–52, 57; alumni relations at, 45–48, 56–57; annual fund at, 52–53; aspects of fund raising at, 34–59; background on, 34–36; characteristics of, 222, 223; corporate gifts to, 53–54; descriptive statistics on, 35; director of

243

Index

university, 56, 57; and resource allocation, 201, 227–228

Institutions: characteristics of, 6–7, 10, 198–204; private baccalaureate (Kappa), 144–158; private comprehensive (Zeta), 107–123; private doctoral (Gamma), 60–79; private research (Alpha), 13–33; private two-year (Sigma), 176–186; public baccalaureate (Rho), 159–175; public comprehensive (Theta), 124–143; public doctoral (Delta), 80–106; public research (Beta), 34–59; public two-year (Omega), 187–196; qualitative characteristics of, 10, 222–223; range and median for characteristics of, 10; selection of, 8–9; strengths of, 224, 236

Internal campaign: at public research university, 48–49; at public two-year college, 193–194

J

Jaschik, S., 4
Johnson, F. C., 233
Juvenile Diabetes Foundation, 3

K

Kappa College: annual fund at, 153–154; aspects of fund raising at, 144–158; background on, 144–147; campaigns at, 151–153, characteristics of, 223, 224; constituent relations at, 156–157; descriptive statistics for, 145; effectiveness at, 157–158; entrepreneurial style at, 153, 156; fund-raising activities at, 150–154; fund-raising program at, 154–158; institutional commitment at, 154–155; management information system at, 154, 156; organizational chart for, 146; planned giving at, 153; presidential leadership at, 147–150, 154; staff members at, 146–147, 154, 155–156; trustee role at, 149–150

Keller, G., 214
Kotler, P., 228

L

Leadership. *See* Chief development office leadership; Entrepreneurial fund raising; Presidential leadership
Leed, J., 235
Leslie, J. W., 10
Levine, S. H., 235
Loessin, B. A., 6, 234

M

McIntosh, P. B., 232
McMillen, L., 2, 3, 4
Major campaigns: at private baccalaureate college, 151–153; at public baccalaureate college, 164–165, 170; at public comprehensive university, 130–131; at public doctoral university, 86–89; at public research university, 39–42; at public two-year college, 192, 196
Major gifts: at private research university, 28; at public comprehensive university, 134; at public doctoral university, 96–97; at public research university, 39–42
Management: of advanced prospects system (MAPS), 120, assessing, 232–234, benefits of emphasis on, 214–218, 223; communication in, 26, 27, 31, 64–65, 69, 216–217, 233; planning and goal setting in, 217–218; at private baccalaureate college, 154, 156; at private comprehensive university, 118, 120, 122; at private doctoral university, 71–72, 76, 77; at private research university, 22–23, 30, 31; at public comprehensive university, 131, 136, 142–143; at public doctoral university, 103, 105; at public research university, 57–58; and staff development and training, 218

Marketing: at private comprehensive university, 122; at private doctoral university, 65–66

Media coverage: for private doctoral university, 70, 71; for public research university, 41, 47

Melchiori, G. S., 235

Michigan, University of, success of, 9

Millar, B., 4

Moran, E. T., 235

N

Nahn, F. C., 234

Nirschel, R. J., Jr., 6

O

Ohio State University, campaign by, 2

Omega College: annual fund at, 192, 194, 196; aspects of fund raising at, 187–196; characteristics of, 223, 224; community ties of, 190, 194, 195; constituent relations at, 192–193, 195; corporate in-kind gifts to, 190, 196; and corporations, 131; descriptive statistics for, 188; effectiveness at, 196; entrepreneurial spirit at, 191; faculty gifts at, 193–194; foundation at, 190–191, 192, 194, 195; and foundations, 193; fund-raising activities at, 191–194; fund-raising program at, 194–196; major campaigns at, 192, 196; phonathons at, 194; planned giving at, 193; planning at, 196; presidential leadership at, 187, 189–190, 195; staff members at, 191, 193–194, 195; trustees at, 191, 194–195

P

Panting, J. I., 235

Parent relations: at private research university, 29; at private two-year college, 182–183; at public

baccalaureate college, 170; at public comprehensive university, 138; at public doctoral university, 97–98

Peters, T. J., 221

Pezzullo, T. R., 4, 5

Pickett, W. L., 10

Planned giving: at private baccalaureate college, 153; at private research university, 28; at public comprehensive university, 135; at public two-year college, 193

Planning: assessing, 233–234; benefits of, 217–218; at private comprehensive university, 111–113, 118, 120–121; at private doctoral university, 73–75; at private research university, 31; at public baccalaureate college, 169; at public comprehensive university, 135–136; at public doctoral university, 104–105; at public two-year college, 196

Pocock, J. W., 227

Presbyterian church campaign, 3

Presidential leadership: assessing, 226–227; benefits of, 198–200, 222, 224; at private baccalaureate college, 147–150, 154; at private comprehensive university, 110, 111–115, 121; at private doctoral university, 60, 63, 67, 71, 76–77; at private research university, 20–21, 27, 30–31; at private two-year college, 178–180, 184–185; at public comprehensive university, 127–129, 140, 141; at public doctoral university, 85, 86, 89–91, 103–104; at public research university, 38, 56, 57; at public two-year college, 187, 189–190, 195

Private institutions: baccalaureate (Kappa), 144–158; comprehensive (Zeta), 107–123; doctoral (Gamma), 60–79; research (Alpha), 13–33; two-year (Sigma), 176–186

Prospect ratings: by private comprehensive university, 119–120; by

at, 107–123; background on,
107–110; characteristics of, 222,
223; constituent relations at, 116,
120; descriptive statistics for,
108; development director at,
118–121; effectiveness at,
122–123; entrepreneurial style at,
213; fund-raising activities at,
113–115; fund-raising program
at, 121–123; informal evaluation
at, 218; institutional commitment
at, 121–122; management at,
118, 120, 122; marketing at, 122;
organizational chart for, 109;
planning at, 111–113, 118,
120–121; presidential leadership
at, 110, 111–115, 121; staff members at, 122, 219; trustee participation at, 110, 112, 113, 115,
116–117, 121; vice president for
institutional advancement at,
115–118, 121; volunteers at, 122